COMPUTER APPLICATIONS

Code 165

X

With Practical Material

[Prepared according to the latest syllabus and guidelines issued by the CBSE, New Delhi]

Including APPENDIX containing:

- Chapter-wise Assertion and Reasoning Type Questions
- Chapter-wise Case Study Questions

by

RANJU SOOD

M.Sc. Computer Science (Gold Medallist) M.Ed.

AVICHAL PUBLISHING COMPANY

Industrial Area, Trilokpur Road, Kala Amb 173030, Distt. Sirmour (HP)

Delhi Office: 1002 Faiz Road (opp. Hanumanji Murti), Karol Bagh, New Delhi 110005

Published by:
Avichal Publishing Company
Industrial Area, Trilokpur Road
Kala Amb 173 030, Distt. Sirmour (HP)

Delhi Office:
1002 Faiz Road (opp. Hanumanji Murti)
Karol Bagh, New Delhi 110 005 (India)
Ph.: 011-41525819, 35543752
Email: info@apcbooks.co.in
Website: www.apcbooks.co.in

ISBN–978–93–6333–622–3

First Edition: 2003
Reprint: 2004
Second Edition: 2008
Third Edition: 2010
Fourth Edition: 2011
Reprint: 2012
Fifth Edition: 2013
Sixth Edition: 2014
Reprint: 2015, 16
Seventh Edition: 2017
Reprint: 2018, 19
Eighth Edition: 2020
Reprint: 2021, 22, 23
Reprint: 2025

The earlier editions of this book were published under the name **Foundation of Information Technology**.

Price : ₹ 495.00

Laser Typeset by:
Laser Tech Prints (P)

Printed at:
Capital Offset
Bawana Industrial Area, Delhi

Preface

This book titled **Computer Applications** has been written for class X strictly according to the latest syllabus prescribed by CBSE. However, it can be used by anyone interested in learning about the internet, web designing (HTML) and programming techniques of Python and Scratch. The book starts with giving a basic know how of internet and the commonly used web terminology. It then familiarises the readers with the various services available on the internet and how to use them optimally and securely. An elementary knowledge of various generations of mobile technologies is also imparted. Since internet has become the need of the day, so it is very essential for its users to follow an ethical behavior while using it. Keeping this in mind, a complete chapter has been dedicated to various netiquettes. The focus of the book is also given extensively on developing the skills to design web pages and websites using HTML. The later part of the book deals with Scratch and Python programming for which a colorful, easy and interesting approach has been used.

Salient features of the book are:

- This book is based on Windows 10 platform.
- The elements and tags for web page and website designing have been explained by using HTML4.
- Scratch 3.0 and Python 3.3 have been used to demonstrate their programming skills.
- Screenshots of successfully executed programming codes and their outputs have been used in the book for error-free learning.
- Effort has been made to include examples for each programming concept to show its practical implementation.
- Each chapter is followed by a set of solved questions and exercises comprising of objective type, short answer and long answer type questions.
- Questions from previous years CBSE question papers have also been included with solutions at the end of the relevant chapters.
- A separate chapter has been prepared exclusively to provide practical material for lab exercises mentioned in the syllabus.
- Latest CBSE Sample Question Paper with solutions has been included in the book for the reference of the students followed by two Practice Papers with solutions as per the pattern of the Sample Paper.

Immense efforts have been put to keep the book error-free and updated according to the latest software available. I must acknowledge the whole-hearted support rendered by the Editorial team of Arya Publications, especially Ms. Kavita Bhatia.

There is always a scope of improvement. Any suggestions for the same will be gratefully acknowledged. Kindly feel free to contact at the following e-mail addresses.

All the best and Happy reading!

soodranju@hotmail.com
editorial@apcbooks.co.in

Ranju Sood

Syllabus

Computer Applications

CLASS X (Code 165)

Learning Outcomes

1. Ability to create a simple website
2. Ability to embed images, audio and video in an HTML page
3. Ability to use style sheets to beautify the web pages.
4. Ability to write iterative programs with Scratch/Python.
5. Ability to Interface a web site with a web server and record the details of a user's request.
6. Ability to follow basic cyber ethics
7. Ability to familiarize with network concepts.

Distribution of Marks and Periods

Unit No.	Unit Name	Marks	Periods	
			Theory	Practical
1.	Networking	5	05	05
2.	HTML	12	30	50
3.	Cyber ethics	5	05	10
4.	Scratch/Python Theory	8	15	60
5.	Practicals	70	-	-
	Total	100	55	125

Unit 1: Networking

- Internet: World Wide Web, web servers, web clients, web sites, web pages, web browsers, blogs, news groups, HTML, web address, e-mail address, downloading and uploading files from a remote site. Internet protocols: TCP/IP, SMTP, POP3, HTTP, HTTPS. Remote login and file transfer protocols: SSH, SFTP, FTP, SCP, TELNET, SMTP, TCP/IP.
- Services available on the internet: information retrieval, locating sites using search engines and finding people on the net;
- Web services: chat, email, video conferencing, e-Learning, e-Banking, e-Shopping, e-Reservation, e-Governance, e-Groups, social networking.
- Mobile technologies: SMS, MMS, 3G, 4G.

Unit 2: HTML

- Introduction to web page designing using HTML: create and save an HTML document, access a web page using a web browser.

- HTML tags: html, head, title, body, (attributes: text, background, bgcolor, link, vlink, alink), *br (break), hr (horizontal rule), inserting comments, h1..h6 (heading), p (paragraph), b (bold), i (italics), u (underline), ul (unordered list), ol (ordered list), and li (list item). Description lists: dl, dt and dd. Attributes of ol (start, type), ul (type).*
- Font tags (attributes: face, size, color).
- Insert images: img (attributes: src, width, height, alt), sup (superscript), sub (subscript).
- HTML Forms: Textbox, radio buttons, checkbox, password, list, combobox.
- Embed audio and video in a HTML page.
- Create a table using the tags: table, tr, th, td, rowspan, colspan
- Links: significance of linking, anchor element (attributes: href, mailto), targets.
- Cascading style sheets: colour, background-colour, border-style, margin, height, width, outline, font (family, style, size), align, float.

Unit 3: Cyber Ethics

- Netiquettes.
- Software licenses and the open source software movement.
- Intellectual property rights, plagiarism and digital property rights.
- Freedom of information and the digital divide.
- E-commerce: Privacy, fraud, secure data transmission.

Unit 4: Scratch or Python (Theory and Practical)

Alternative 1: Scratch

- Revision of the basics of Scratch
- Sprite, tempo, variables, and events
- Coordinates and conditionals
- Drawing with iteration
- Update variables repeatedly, iterative development, ask and answer blocks
- Create games, animated images, stories and songs

Alternative 2: Python (only for children with special needs)

- Revision of Python basics
- Conditionals: if, if-else statements
- Loops: for, while (e.g., sum of first 10 natural numbers)
- Practice simple programs

5. Lab Exercises

- Create static web pages.
- Use style sheets to enforce a format in an HTML page (CSS).
- Embed pictures, audio and videos in an HTML page.
- Add tables and frames in an HTML page.
- Decorate web pages using graphical elements.
- Create a website using several webpages. Students may use any open source or proprietary tool.

- Work with HTML forms: text box, radio buttons, checkbox, password, list, combo box.
- Write a blog using HTML pages discussing viruses, malware, spam and antiviruses.
- Create a web page discussing plagiarism. List some reported cases of plagiarism and the consequent punishment meted out. Explain the nature of the punishment in different countries as per their IP laws.
- Create simple stories with Scratch (involving at least two objects/characters) and iteration OR write programs for finding the sum/product of first *n* natural numbers using Python.

Breakup of marks for the practicals:

Unit No.	Unit Name	Marks
1.	**Lab Test (30 marks)**	
	HTML (design one web page based on a diagram)	15
	Scratch or Python (write one program)	15
2.	**Report File + viva (25 marks)**	
	Report file: At least 10 HTML pages, and at least 5 Scratch/Python programs.	20
	Viva voce (based on the report file)	5
3.	Project (that uses most of the concepts that have been learnt)	15

Contents

NETWORKING

1. Internet 1
2. Services Available on the Internet 16
3. Web Services 23
4. Mobile Technologies 41

HTML

5. Hypertext Markup Language and Its Elements 47
6. HTML Continued 83

CYBER ETHICS

7. Cyber Ethics 150

SCRATCH/PYTHON

8. Scratch 162
9. Python 182

PRACTICALS

10. Lab Exercises 202

- Latest CBSE Sample Question Paper (with solutions) 219
- Practice Paper I (with solutions) 226
- Practice Paper II (with solutions) 234

Internet

1

- Network, Internet, Working of the Internet
- World Wide Web, Web servers, Web clients, Websites, Web pages, Web browsers, Blogs, News groups, HTML, Web address, E-mail address
- Downloading and uploading files from a remote site
- Internet Protocols: TCP/IP, SMTP, POP3, HTTP, HTTPS
- Remote login and file transfer protocols: SSH, SFTP, FTP, SCP, TELNET

1.1 INTRODUCTION TO INTERNET

Until the last few decades, the computer was considered to be the ultimate technological invention. However, unlike earlier, the usage of computer is not confined to any organisation, or to any specific function like the retrieval and processing of data. In fact, there is no area of our life where the computer has not stepped in, to make our work easy and fast.

The areas which have been revolutionised the most are the Information and Communication. In fact, the present age is being called the age of the ICT (Information and Communication Technology). The credit for all of this, goes to the Internet, which has advanced communication greatly and there is no end to it. The internet has connected the whole world with its network such that, now no information is location bound and no individual is inaccessible. We have become so dependent on its services that it is difficult to imagine a life without the internet. So, in this unit we will first learn about the working of the internet and some of the terms related to it. After that, we will learn about the various set of rules or protocols that are followed on the internet, while transferring data.

Network: When two or more autonomous computers are linked together, such that they are able to communicate with each other, they are said to be in a network. Here being autonomous means that none of the computers control the working of other computers, on the network.

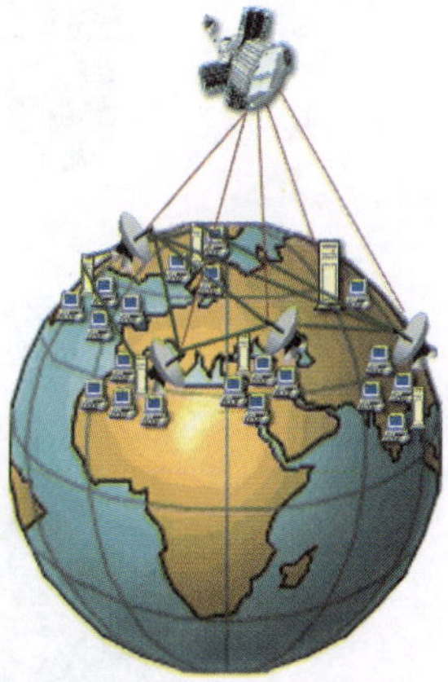

Fig. 1.1: Network

Internet: The internet is a worldwide network of various computer networks. Various similar and dissimilar smaller computer networks are joined together to form a large global network. Internet contains millions and millions of computers of different configurations and using different operating systems, yet they are able to communicate with each other.

1.2 WORKING OF THE INTERNET

All the computers participating in a network are linked either physically with Ethernet cables or wirelessly using the WiFi or the Bluetooth technology. It is not just the computers that form a network; there are several other devices also, such as the web servers, ISP servers, routers, etc., which help in the working of the internet. The Fig. 1.2 shows how the computers are connected over the network.

A **client/web client** is a computer or software which interacts with another computer (called the server) over the network, to obtain the information required by the user. Each client is connected to the internet through the Internet Service Provider **(ISP)**. The ISP is an organisation which provides internet access to its customers. Some of the popular ISP's in India are Airtel, BSNL, MTNL and Reliance Communications.

A **server** is a computer or a device which provides the service requested by the client, over the network. There are different types of servers in use, like the Web server, Mail server or the File server, each one being different, based on the specific services they provide. For example, Mail server deals with sending and receiving e-mails and a Web server finds the requested web pages on the internet.

So, basically when a person works from his/her computer and accesses information on the internet, using the Google or any other website, then the computer used by him/her is the client. When the Google searches for the information required by the client and accesses it from any specific computer where the required information is stored, the specific computer which provides the required information to Google is called the server. Each device on the network has a unique address allotted to it, which is called its Internet protocol address or **IP address.**

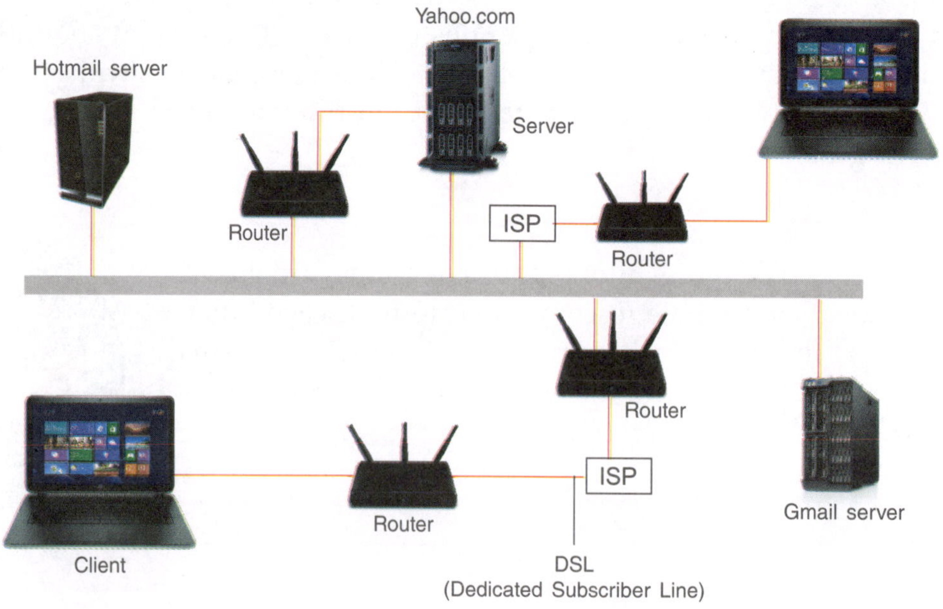

Fig. 1.2: Working of the Internet

Let us now learn how the data travels on the internet, using the example of an e-mail. Suppose, a client wants to send an e-mail from his Gmail account to a receiver, with a Hotmail account. Then, firstly, the e-mail is sent to the Gmail server by the ISP server. The Gmail server then forwards it to the Hotmail server where the e-mail rests, till the receiver logs in to his Hotmail account to access the mail.

The data sent on the internet, is broken down into small units called **packets**. Each packet has its address of origin and the destination address. These packets are directed to their destination by a networking device called the **router**. The router reads the destination address of the packet and sends it on the desired route. When the packets reach their ultimate destination, they are reassembled again. The router also controls the traffic on the network.

1.3 WEB TERMINOLOGY

Let us now understand some of the terms, we come across, while using the Internet.

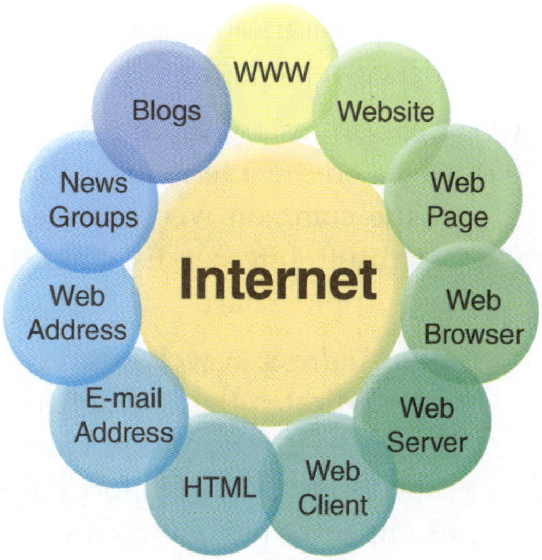

(i) ***WWW:*** **The World Wide Web** (WWW), commonly known as the Web, is a pool of information in the form of documents and other web resources, which are accessible over the internet. These web resources may be interlinked and can be located, using the **Uniform Resource Locator** or the **URL** (such as: https://www.anything.com/).

(ii) ***Web Server:*** A web server is a computer or software which provides the service requested by the web client. The server machine has software servers to provide specific services, e.g., an e-mail server deals with sending and receiving e-mails and a web server finds your requested page on the internet. AOL server, Microsoft's Internet Information Services are some examples of web servers.

(iii) ***Web Client:*** A web client is a computer or software that sends some service requests to some other hardware or software over the internet. The web browser at the user's end is an example of a web client.

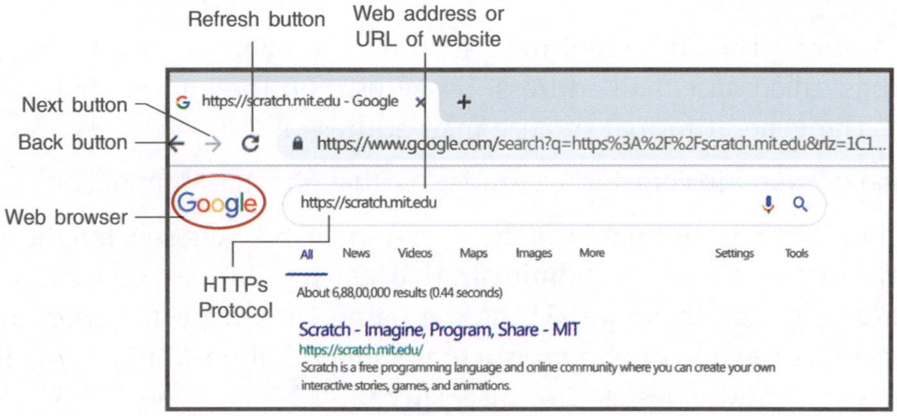

Fig. 1.3: Searching for a website

(*iv*) ***Website:*** A website is a single web page or a collection of interrelated web pages, containing information and is linked to a common URL. A website is designed using a language called the **Hypertext Markup Language (HTML)**. This is a relatively simple language with additional features for formatting of text, inserting graphics, images and **hyperlinks** (links to other documents). A website generally has links to other texts, which may be a part of the same website or any other website. The first page of a website is called its **home page** and is the introductory page. It generally has some basic information about the website and a table of contents, which are hyperlinks leading to further information.

(*v*) ***Web Page:*** A document on WWW containing a combination of text, graphics and links to other web pages is called a web page. It is designed using HTML (Hypertext Markup Language) and is accessible using its URL. When a web page is displayed, the back button on the brower's window (Fig. 1.3) opens the previously visited web page and the Next button opens the next web page. The Refresh button when clicked reloads the currently opened web page again.

(*vi*) ***Web Browser:*** An application used to view web pages on the internet is called a web browser. Some of the common web browsers are Google Chrome, Microsoft Internet Explorer/Edge, Mozilla Firefox and Apple Safari.

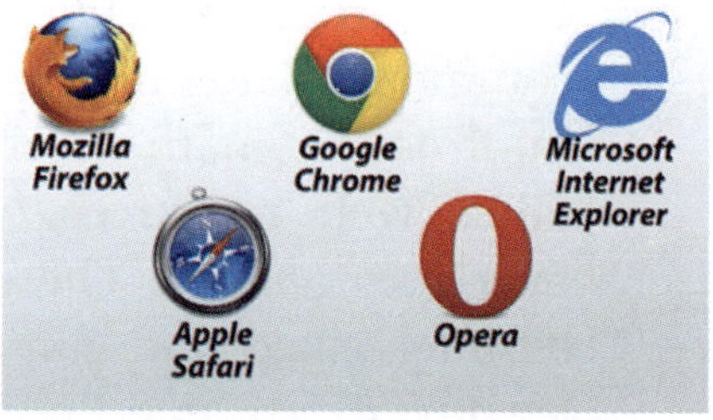

Fig. 1.4: Various Web Browsers

(*vii*) ***Web Address:*** A web address is an Internet address that indicates the location of a specific web page, file or document on the **World Wide Web**. It is also called the URL (Uniform Resource Locator). For example, https://www.indianexpress.com/

ADDITIONAL INFO

Some applications are browser dependent and so might not be accessible from a particular browser. It is, therefore, recommended to have two or more browsers downloaded on the machine.

(*viii*) ***HTML (Hypertext Markup Language):*** It is the most widely used markup language for designing web pages and other web applications. It allows the use of text, graphics, audio, video and even hyperlinks in the document. Hyperlinks are the links that allow the user to jump to another document or to another section of the current document. The web browser receives the HTML code of the document from the web server and converts it into a web page which we can understand and interact with.

(*ix*) ***E-mail Address:*** The address of the e-mail box, to or from which e-mails are sent or received, is called an e-mail address. Every user on the internet has a unique e-mail address. The general format of an e-mail address is:

<local part>@domain.com For example, parthavghosh34@gmail.com

where, local part is the name of his/her e-mail box chosen by the user and the domain is the name of the administrative agency or the service provider. In the above example, "parthavghosh34" is the name chosen by the user and "gmail" is the domain. All major providers, such as Gmail, Yahoo Mail, Hotmail and others, treat the e-mail addresses as case insensitive.

(*x*) *Blog:* A blog is an online diary or journal, located on a website. It is an electronic platform where the owner of the blog can write his views and thoughts about anything and also receive the ideas and thoughts of the readers of the blog. A blog includes text, pictures, videos, animations, etc. Since a blog exists merely for personal use; to make it public, the owner would have to set his/her blog "Public", for public access. All posts or links to posts on a blog are displayed in reverse chronological order, with the most recent ones appearing on the top. The person writing the blog is called a **blogger**.

(*xi*) *Newsgroups:* A newsgroup is an internet based electronic platform used for discussions about any particular topic. These topics range from politics, sports, movies to any event in particular, etc. A user can join a newsgroup by registering on it. Messages posted by the users of the newsgroup are forwarded to a news server, which then sends them to other participating servers. Then, the other users can read the posts by accessing the newsgroup.

(*xii*) *Downloading and Uploading:* Downloading files means transferring files from a web server to an external device like your computer, tablet or phone. Receiving an e-mail is an example of downloading a file.

Files are considered to be uploaded when they are transferred from a computer or any other electronic device to a central server on the internet. For example, when sending an e-mail.

1.4 PROTOCOLS

Protocols refer to the set of rules which have to be followed for communication on the internet. Hence, all the devices using the internet will have to follow the protocols for successful communication. Some of the protocols are discussed below:

(*i*) *IP (Internet Protocol):* It is the protocol for sending data over the internet. Since data is transmitted in the form of small packets, with each having the destination address, it is the duty of the IP to make sure that the packets reach their destination.

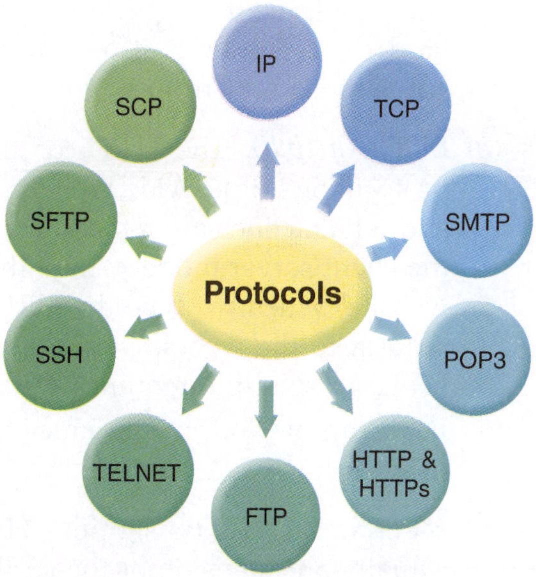

(*ii*) *TCP (Transmission Control Protocol):* It is the protocol which ensures that the data packets received at the destination are arranged in the correct order or sequence. It is also responsible for providing a transmission channel between the two ends, for the data transfer. The TCP and IP protocols work together and are hence referred to as the TCP/IP protocol which is the basis of data transfer on the internet.

(*iii*) *SMTP (Simple Mail Transfer Protocol):* It is the protocol that checks the authenticity of the e-mail and then directs its transfer, over the internet to the receiver's end. The process of sending an e-mail, using the SMTP protocol is as follows:

- The sender's e-mail client like the Outlook, Gmail or Yahoo uses the SMTP to send a message to the mail server.

- The mail server again uses the SMTP to forward the e-mail to the correct mail server at the receiver's or recipient's end.
- The client and the server then exchange information regarding the sender, receiver and their domain.
- If the domain of receiver's address is directly connected to the server, then the e-mail is immediately delivered, otherwise it is forwarded to another server which is in the range of receiver's domain.
- If the receiver's server is down or busy, the server stores the mail and retries to send it, periodically. If still after several attempts, the sending fails, then the sender's server is informed about the unsuccessful delivery, which then sends the "Undelivered" alert to the sender. In case, there are no issues with the receiver's server, the e-mail is delivered to the receiver.

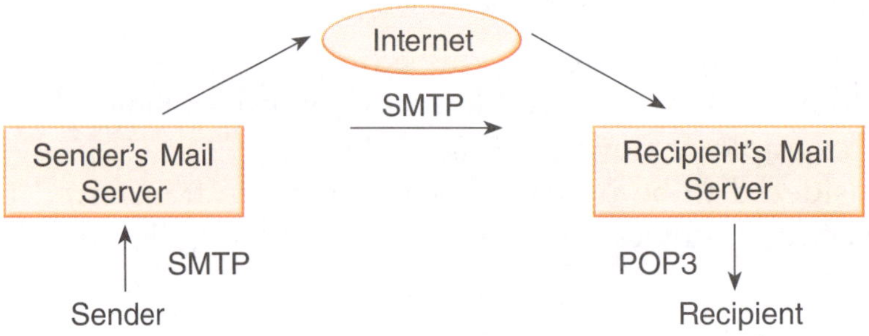

Fig. 1.5: SMTP Protocol

(*iv*) ***POP3:*** The POP stands for **Post Office Protocol** and 3 is its latest version. POP3 is the simplest method of delivering e-mails. It receives and holds the e-mail until the recipient picks it up. When the recipient connects to the mail server to retrieve his e-mail, the messages are downloaded from the mail server and stored on user's hard disk. The POP also allows the user to open his/her e-mail account to check any e-mails sent from any computer at any other location.

(*v*) ***HTTP (http://):*** The HTTP or the Hyper Text Transfer Protocol is the underlying protocol on World Wide Web. It defines how messages are transmitted on the internet and what actions are to be taken by the browsers and the servers. The HTTP follows the client-server model where the browser is the client and the web server hosts the website. When we type the URL of a website, the browser uses the HTTP to send a request to the web server. The web server then processes the request and uses the HTTP to send the required web contents to the browser.

For example, http://cbse.nic.in indicates that cbse.nic.in is the website accessed using http.

(*vi*) ***HTTPS:*** The HTTPS signifies Hyper Text Transfer Protocol Secure. This protocol is actually an extension of the earlier protocol, the **HTTP**. Since the internet can be an unsafe place for certain kinds of information, using just HTTP was not sufficient. Hence, the **Secure HTTP** was developed as a step towards more secure internet usage. The HTTPS is a protocol used to ensure safe and secure communication between the user and the website, by encrypting the data. Encryption means that the two parties communicating with each other agree upon a code. This code is then used to translate their communication in an arbitrary combination of characters which is not understood by the third party. Only the sender and the recipient are able to decode the communication. Hence, the data remains secure.

For example, when the user requests the browser to connect to a website using https, it contacts the server which hosts the website. Next, when the browser is allowed by the server to connect to the website, the session is encrypted using the **Secure Sockets Layer** or **SSL protocol**. The browser and the server send each other unique codes which are used for encryption, for rest of the talk. So, if a hacker tries to intercept, he/she will not be able to use the information as he/she wouldn't know how to decode it, e.g., *https://www.india.gov.in/* uses the Secure HTTP.

Therefore, it is always advisable to check whether the website uses HTTP or HTTPS, before entering any confidential information like credit card details.

1.5 REMOTE LOGIN AND FILE TRANSFER PROTOCOLS

A login that allows a user to connect his/her computer to another remote computer through a network, as if the computers were directly connected to each other, is called the **remote login**. After logging in remotely, both the computers are also able to communicate and transfer files and data to each other.

There are several file transfer protocols that ensure safe and secure, file transfer. Some of them are discussed below:

(*i*) ***TELNET:*** TELNET is a command line protocol which allows the user to connect his/her computer which is the client, in this case, to a remote computer which is the host, over the internet using the TCP/IP protocol. The client needs to have an account with the host in order to access the data on the host. Once the connection is established, the client becomes a virtual terminal to the host after which two-way communication is permitted between the client and the host. Telnet also allows a user to interact with a program that is running on the host. The host can also respond to input from the client. From the security viewpoint, the main drawback of telnet is that all the information is sent in clear text, which may lead to capturing and misuse of passwords by any hackers on an unprotected network.

(*ii*) ***File Transfer Protocol (FTP):*** The file transfer protocol or FTP is a protocol which is widely used to transport and receive large files over the internet. It can also be used to send configuration files and software updates, for network switches and routers. The FTP does not encrypt the information being received and sent between the host and the client, so it can be captured by hackers.

(*iii*) ***Secure Shell (SSH):*** The Secure Shell or SSH is a protocol that provides secure remote login from one computer to another. It also provides authentication, encryption and data integrity to secure the network communications.

It is a secure alternative to the non-protected login protocols (such as telnet), and the insecure file transfer methods (such as FTP).

The Secure Shell or SSH is capable of providing:

- a secure command-shell to edit files and access customer databases from remote login.

- a secure file transfer, and remote access to a variety of TCP/IP applications via a secure tunnel.
- port forwarding which allows data from normally unsecured TCP/IP applications to be sent, through an encrypted tunnel to the destination.
- authentication of username and passwords to the server.

(*iv*) ***Secure File Transfer Protocol (SFTP):*** The Secure File Transfer Protocol or SFTP is a subsystem of the Secure Shell protocol. It is a separate protocol layered over the Secure Shell protocol to handle file transfers.

- SFTP encrypts both the username/password and the data being transferred.
- It uses the same port as the Secure Shell server, eliminating the need to open another port on the firewall or the router.
- Using SFTP also avoids the network address translation issues that can often be a problem with the regular FTP.

(*v*) ***Secure Copy (SCP):*** The Secure Copy or SCP allows copying of files between the user's computer and a remote computer or between remote networks. It uses the SSH protocol for data transfer, and uses the same authentication method as SSH. It also provides the same security as the SSH.

KEY TERMS

Network When two or more autonomous computers are linked together, so that they are able to communicate with each other, they are said to be in a network.

Internet A worldwide network of computer networks.

URL (Uniform Resource Locator) An internet address that indicates the location of a specific web page, file or document on the World Wide Web.

Encryption Translating the contents of a data package into an arbitrary combination of characters, so that it is not understood by any unauthorised person.

ISP (Internet Service Provider) The organisation that provides internet access to its customers.

Data Packets The data broken down into small units called **packets** for transmission on the internet.

IP Address A unique address allotted t°o each device on the network.

Router A networking device that directs the traffic on the Internet.

World Wide Web (WWW) Also called Web, it is a pool of information in the form of documents and other web resources which are accessible over the internet.

Web server A computer or software which provides the service requested by the web client.

Web client A computer or software that sends service requests to some other hardware or software over the internet.

Hyperlinks The links or references on a web page that allow the user to jump to another document or to another section of the current document.

Home Page The first page of a website.

Website A collection of web pages.

Web page A document on Internet that contains text, graphics and links.

Web browser Software that enables us to view web pages on Internet.

Web address An Internet address that indicates the location of a specific web page, file or document on the World Wide Web.

HTML A language used to design web pages.

Blog An online diary or journal located on a website. It is an electronic platform where the owner of the blog can write his views and thoughts about anything and then receive the ideas and thoughts of others.

Newsgroup An Internet based electronic platform used for the discussion about a particular topic.

Downloading Transferring files from a web server to an external device like a computer, tablet or phone.

Uploading Files are considered to be uploaded when they are transferred from a computer or any other electronic device to a central server on the internet.

IP or Internet Protocol A method or set of rules of sending data over the internet.

Protocols The set of rules followed by computers which form a part of Internet.

TCP The protocol which ensures that the data packets received at the destination are put in correct order or sequence.

HTTP The underlying protocol on World Wide Web. It defines how messages are transmitted on the internet and what actions are taken by the browsers and the servers.

HTTPS A protocol used to ensure safe and secure communication between the user and the website by encrypting the data.

SMTP A set of commands that check the authenticity of the e-mail and then direct its transfer over the internet to the receiver's end.

POP3 The simple method of delivering emails. It receives and holds the emails until the recipient picks it up.

Remote Login A login that allows a user to connect his computer to another remote computer through a network as if the computers were directly connected to each other is called remote login.

Telnet A command line protocol that allows you to connect your computer which is the client in this case, to remote computer which is the host, over the internet using TCP/IP.

FTP A protocol that is widely used to transport and receive large files.

Secure Shell A protocol that provides secure remote login from one computer to another. It also provides authentication, encryption and data integrity to secure network communications.

SFTP A subsystem of the Secure Shell protocol. It is a separate protocol layered over the Secure Shell protocol to handle file transfers.

SCP or Secure copy Allows copying of files between user's computer and a remote computer or between remote networks.

POINTS TO REMEMBER

- In a network, all the computers are autonomous but are able to exchange information with each other.
- Data is transmitted over the network in the form of small packets having addresses of sender's node and destination's node.
- Airtel, MTNL, Reliance Communications, etc. are some of a few ISPs in India.
- Mail server sends/receives e-mails and web server finds the requested page on the internet.
- The general format of an e-mail address is
  <local port>@domain.com

SOLVED QUESTIONS

Q1. How are computers and other devices on the network connected?

Ans. The devices on the network are physically connected mostly using Ethernet cables and wirelessly connected using Bluetooth or WiFi technology.

Q2. Name some other devices besides computers that form a part of internet.

Ans. Various other devices like web servers, dedicated servers like ISPs, routers, etc., also form a part of internet.

Q3. How can a device be located on a network?

Ans. Every device on the network is allotted an IP address by which it can be identified and hence located.

Q4. How do the data packets on the internet reach their destination address?

Ans. Each packet has its address of origin and the destination address. The router reads the destination address of the packet and sends it on the desired route. Once they reach their ultimate destination, they are reassembled again.

Q5. Mala is given the following text and instructed to speak some sentences about what the text indicates. Provide her with some information that you think would help her.
https://www.pixel.com/

Ans. The above text is a web address or a Uniform Resource Locator (URL) of a website named pixel.com on the world wide web and it is a secure site, since it is using Hypertext Transfer Protocol Secure (HTTPS).

Q6. When we visit a website, what is the first page that is opened called? What does this page generally display?

Ans. The first page is the introductory page of a website and is called the home page. It generally has some basic information about the website and has a table of contents which are hyperlinks that lead to the related contents on either the same page or on a different web page of the same website, or on a web page of some other website.

Q7. Asha's gmail address is ashamittal23@gmail.com. Her friend Jyoti sent her an e-mail but typed Asha's e-mail address as ASHAMITTAL@GMAIL.COM. Will the e-mail reach Asha's Inbox?

Ans. Yes, the e-mail will reach her inbox as most of the commonly used e-mail service providers treat e-mail addresses as case insensitive. Gmail is one such service so it does not matter if the e-mail address is written in uppercase or lowercase, Asha will be able to receive the mail in her Gmail account.

Q8. Which protocol is used to transfer the e-mail from recipient's server to recipient's computer?

Ans. POP3 is used to transfer the e-mail from recipient's server to recipient's computer.

Q9. If there is some problem in recipient's server or it is not able to forward the e-mail due to some issue, which protocol sends an "undelivered" message to the sender?

Ans. It is the work of Simple Mail Transfer Protocol to send an "undelivered" message to the sender.

Q10. Bhoomi has to buy a scientific calculator online from a shopping site. How would she make sure that the site on which she is making the payment, is secure?

Ans. Bhoomi should do the transactions only on the websites which use the https protocol.

Q11. Amit has a hairline fracture and cannot move out of his house, so he has taken permission from his superior to work from home. He logs into the office network and starts sending and receiving data. What is this method of logging into a distant computer called? Name a secure protocol used for sending files in this case.

Ans. The facility of logging into a distant computer and accessing its data is called remote login. SFTP (Secure File Transfer Protocol) is used for secure file transfers.

EXERCISES

I. Very Short Answer Type Questions

Multiple Choice Questions:

1. A device can be located on the internet by its
   (a) configuration (b) brand (c) IP address (d) Owner's name
2. Internet connects computers
   (a) having same configuration. (b) having cable connection with each other.
   (c) following same set of rules. (d) all of the above.
3. Protocol used by computers on Internet is
   (a) TCP/IP (b) ARPANET (c) NSFnet (d) URL
4. TCP stands for .... protocol.
   (a) travel and communicate (b) transmission configure
   (c) transmission control (d) transport chip

5. A computer or software that makes resources available to clients on a network is called
(a) browser (b) node (c) server (d) router

6. A web page consists of
(a) text (b) graphics (c) links (d) all of the above

7. Software used to view resources like web pages, on Internet is called
(a) server (b) WWW (c) URL (d) web browser

8. Internet explorer is a
(a) website (b) web page (c) web browser (d) web server

9. HTTP stands for
(a) Hyper Text Translation Process (b) Hyper Text Transport Process
(c) Hyper Text Transfer Protocol (d) Hyper Text Transport Protocol

10. A set of rules that supervises the flow of information on the Internet is
(a) HTTP (b) HTML (c) URL (d) TCP/IP

11. The Internet facility is provided by an organisation called
(a) web browser (b) search engine (c) ISP (d) Microsoft

12. The language used for designing web pages is
(a) C++ (b) HTML
(c) HTTP (d) any programming language

13. Each computer connected to the Internet should
(a) have a unique IP address.
(b) have a WiFi connection.
(c) be physically connected to other computers.
(d) have a special configuration.

14. The URL contains
(a) protocol name (b) browser name (c) computer type (d) location of user

15. The Blog is a
(a) hardware (b) software
(c) social networking service (d) browser

16. The protocol used for delivering e-mail from the mail server to the user's computer is
(a) SMTP (b) POP3 (c) HTTPS (d) SSH

17. The protocol that provides secure remote login is the ....
(a) SMTP (b) POP3 (c) HTTPS (d) SSH

18. The protocol that allows copying of files between two remote computers is the
(a) HTTPS (b) POP3 (c) SCP (d) SMTP

19. Web clients are
(a) the people who do transactions on internet.
(b) the people who request to visit a website.
(c) software that is used to design web pages.
(d) software that acts as an interface between the user and the server.

20. Which of the following protocols direct the transfer of e-mail from sender to receiver?
(a) TELNET (b) FTP (c) SCP (d) SMTP

Fill in the blanks:

1. A worldwide network of computer networks is called ....

2. A standard set of rules/protocols by which we can retrieve information on Internet is called ....

3. The most commonly used protocol on the Internet is ....
4. ISP stands for ....
5. An address used to locate web page on www is called ....
6. A web page is designed using the .... language.
7. Links to other web pages are called ....
8. In the e-mail address, shristi@ymail.com, ymail.com represents ....
9. .... allows copying of files between the user's computer and a remote computer.
10. .... is a subsystem of secure shell protocol to handle secure file transfers.
11. For secure financial transactions, sites using .... protocol should be used.
12. .... allows users to open his/her email account from any computer, and at any location.
13. The Outlook and Gmail use .... protocol to send a message to the mail servers.
14. The process of coding the data before transmitting it is called ....
15. While sharing any confidential information on a website, we should ensure that the website is using .... protocol.

II. Short Answer Type Questions

1. What is the Internet?
2. Define protocol.
3. Can two computers of different configurations become a part of same network?
4. How does the information on Internet reach its destination?
5. Which is the most commonly used network protocol?
6. What is an IP address?
7. From where can one get Internet Access Account in India?
8. Write short notes on:
   (i) WWW (ii) Web browser (iii) Web server (iv) Website
   (v) Web page (vi) HTML (vii) URL (viii) HTTP
   (ix) Newsgroup
9. Name any two web servers and web browsers.
10. Which service is primarily served by the web server?
11. What is an ISP? Name two ISPs operating in India.
12. Expand:
    (i) HTML (ii) HTTPS (iii) TCP/IP (iv) URL
    (v) SMTP (vi) SFTP (vii) SSH (viii) SCP
    (ix) FTP
13. What are the different parts of an e-mail address?
14. Differentiate between web address and e-mail address.
15. What is a blog? What is it used for?
16. What is meant by SMTP?
17. What steps should the mail server take, if the recipient's server is down?
18. What is meant by POP3?

19. How is HTTP different from HTTPS? Which of the two should be used, while making online payments?
20. Which technology is used by HTTPS for secure data transfer?
21. What is the SSH?
22. How does the SFTP enhance the security while transferring data as compared to FTP?
23. What is TELNET? What is its weak point?
24. What is meant by remote login?
25. State the difference between uploading and downloading of a file.

III. Long Answer Type Questions

1. Explain the working of Internet.
2. How can a web page be created and viewed?
3. Explain the process of sending email using SMTP.
4. How is the HTTPS made secure? Explain.
5. Which protocols are used for remote login and for transferring large files? State their key features.

Previous Years' Solved Examination Questions

I. Very Short Answer Type Questions

Multiple Choice Questions:

1. Which of the following is a web browser? (2019)
   (a) Java Script (b) HTML (c) Facebook (d) Google Chrome
2. T in FTP stands for (2019)
   (a) TABLE (b) TRANSACTION (c) TRANSFER (d) TOTAL
3. Full form of FTP is: (2018, 2014)
   (a) File Transfer Protocol (b) Fast Transfer Protocol
   (c) Full Transfer protocol (d) File Transit Protocol
4. Which of the following is/are popular web browser(s)? (2019)
   (a) Firefox (b) Safari (c) Navigator (d) All of the above
5. The Protocol used to transfer file from client to server and vice versa is (2018C)
   (a) HTTP (b) FTP (c) STP (d) FTTP
6. A link used to navigate or open other web pages on a website on internet is called (2019, 2014)
   (a) Higher link (b) Hyperlink (c) Hetero link (d) None of the above
7. What does TCP Stand for? (2014)
   (a) Transmission Central Protocol (b) Transmission Control Protocol
   (c) Transparent Central Protocol (d) Transparent Control Protocol
8. Which of the following is not an essential requirement for internet to work? (2014)
   (a) TCP/IP (b) Web browser (c) Computer (d) Web Camera
9. The following refers to transfer of files from internet to computer. (2014)
   (a) uploading (b) downloading (c) Send (d) Receive

Answers: **1.** (d) **2.** (c) **3.** (a) **4.** (d) **5.** (b) **6.** (b) **7.** (b) **8.** (d) **9.** (b)

II. Short Answer Type Questions

1. What is a Blog? (2018C, 2019)
2. Define search engine. Give example also. (2018C, 2017)
3. Discuss the purpose of HTTP. (2019)
4. Name the protocol used for uploading and downloading data from remote sites. (2019, 2017)
5. What is the full form of URL? (2019)
6. What is the purpose of a web browser? (2019)
7. Give the names of any two web browsers. (2019)
8. Write the full forms of
   (i) WWW (ii) FTP (iii) ISP (iv) HTTP (2019,2016)
9. Differentiate between website and web page with suitable examples. (2019)
10. What is a web address? (2019)

Answers:

1. A blog is a discussion or website giving information published on WWW and consists of informal text entries.
2. Search engine is software which carries out search on the World Wide Web for the information that we want to retrieve, e.g. Google, Yahoo.
3. HyperText Transfer Protocol is a system by which computers communicate to each other across the World Wide Web.
4. FTP – File Transfer Protocol
5. URL – Uniform Resource Locator
6. A web browser is an application used to access and view websites, e.g. Google Chrome, Mozilla Firefox, Apple Safari.
7. Google Chrome, Apple Safari (or any other).
8. i) World Wide Web
   ii) File Transfer Protocol
   iii) Internet Service Provider
   iv) Hypertext Transfer Protocol
9. Website is a collection of web pages with different types of information on a subject, e.g. www.cbse.in; www.amazon.in.
   Web page is a part of the website, e.g. www.cbse.nic.in/index.html, homepage of any website.
10. An internet address of a website is called a web address.

2 Services Available on the Internet

Information Retrieval, Locating sites using search engines and finding people on the net

2.1 INTRODUCTION

The Internet is now an integral part of our lives. It is not only a ready source of information but also hosts a variety of social networking websites that have transformed the way we socialise and interact. Instant communication with anyone, anywhere in the world is now possible with the Internet. The ocean of information is also further deepening with the immense amount of content that is shared on social networking sites. In this chapter, the various services which help in information retrieval, locating sites and finding people on the Internet have been discussed. The chapter also discusses ways by which we can quickly and concisely search for information and people.

2.2 INFORMATION RETRIEVAL (IR)

Information retrieval is the task of obtaining information from a vast collection of content available on www, by making a query on the internet. Information on the internet is present in the form of text or even multimedia content on the web pages. Search engines help in finding information on the internet.

A **search engine** is a software tool that helps to find the desired information on the web, in response to any query made by the user. Google, Yahoo, Bing, etc., are some of the popular search engines. Search engines allow the user to input a phrase or a keyword as a query, in case the user does not know the exact URL of the website.

Many search engines provide specific services also, which help the user to speed up his/her search. For example, Google Maps is a service for locating places. News, Videos, Images are directories which can be searched for the specific multimedia or text content contained in them.

2.3 LOCATING SITES USING SEARCH ENGINES

The main role of a search engine is to find the websites, having the requested information. For this, the query has to be typed in the search bar of the search engine. Some of the features allowed by search engines to help locate a website, to retrieve information from the www are:

(i) *Boolean features:* The use of **"AND"** between the keywords retrieves links to all the websites, that contain all the keywords mentioned by the user. Using **"OR"** retrieves links of sites which have any of the mentioned keywords and using **"NOT"** gives links to those sites, which do not have the mentioned keywords.

For example, Searching for **"food AND beverages"** will display links to all the websites which have contents about both **food** and **beverages**.

Whereas, searching for **"food OR beverages"** will display websites that have content related to either only food or only beverages or both.

(ii) *Operators:* A '+' sign between two keywords indicates that both words have to be searched together for their occurrence in the content. For example, Searching for **"food + beverages"** will search all the websites which have the two words food and beverages in its title.

Using '-' sign represents OR so the sites with either food or beverages or both will be displayed.

Enclosing the keyword in double quotes minimises the search to only the specific keyword and no other form. For example, if the keywords are Himalayan rivers then links to all the websites containing the keywords are displayed including the River system of India, Himalayan and peninsular rivers of India, etc. But if the keywords are enclosed in double quotes then links to only the websites related to Himalayan rivers will be displayed.

(iii) *Proximity feature:* The proximity feature searches for phrases or consecutive words that occur within a certain number of words from each other. The proximity operators are composed of a letter (N or W) and a number (to specify the number of words). The number cannot exceed 255.

For example, Internet N5 services will look for web pages with phrases like Internet and its services, services provided by internet, etc.

Typing in - "Internet W5 services" - will look for the words **internet** and **services** within the proximity of 5 words provided that these two words should be in the same order in the search results. Therefore, for web pages with the phrase - "**services on the internet"** will not be considered as the order of words is changed here.

(iv) *Using URLs:* The fastest way of retrieving a website is by typing its web address or URL.

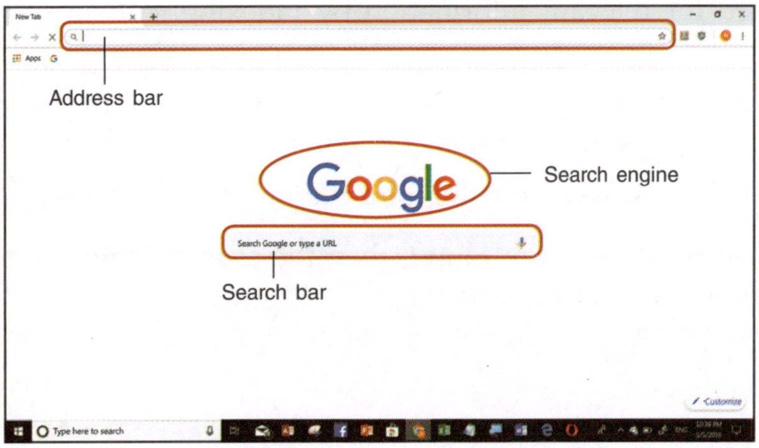

Fig. 2.1: Home page of Google Search Engine

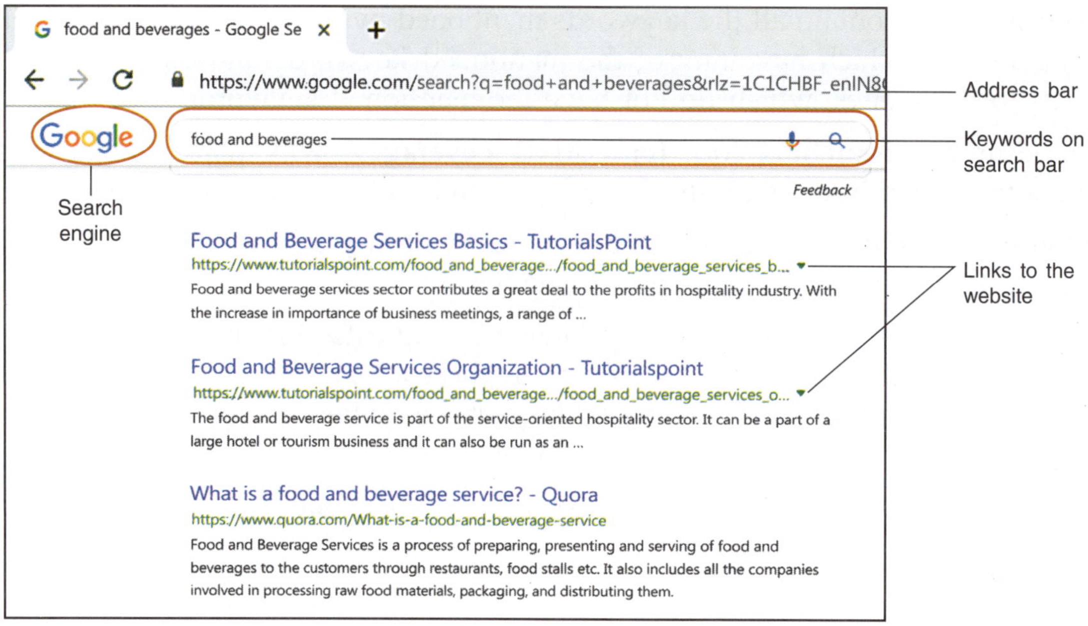

Fig. 2.2: Using keywords to search

(v) ***Limit:*** Limits can be enforced on the type of the retrieved pages like mentioning the date, language, file types, etc.

Many search engines provide specific services also, which help the user to limit his/her search. *For example*, Google Maps is a service for locating places. News, Videos, Images are directories, which can be searched for the specific multimedia or text content contained in them.

Working of search engine

A search engine does not go directly to the web to search for the given keyword. Instead, it looks for the keyword in the index of the predefined database. The following components of the search engine begin to work as soon as the query is typed in the search bar:

- **Web crawlers**, also known as **web spiders** or **web robots** (BOT) are software components which undertake the task to search and collect web pages for the Information Retrieval (IR) system.
- **Indexing Software and Database:** The information collected by web crawlers from the web is filtered for relevant information by indexing software and is stored in the database.
- **Search Interface:** The search interface is an interface between the user and the database and it helps the user to search through the database.

  The web crawler then searches for the information in the database.

When the relevant web pages are found, then the search engine shows the web pages as a result in the order of their importance.

2.4 CHALLENGES FACED DURING INFORMATION RETRIEVAL

- Information is present on a large scale in the form of numerous web pages on several websites. So searching for a webpage quickly, is a very tedious task.
- Owing to the ambiguity in the language used (languages like English, Hindi, or other languages), it is very difficult to find a perfect match for the user's query. Keywords which are homonyms should be carefully used, since the same word might have several meanings. So, it might happen that we are looking for information on 'BAT', which is used in cricket to hit the ball, and we might get information related to the animal 'BAT' also.

2.5 FINDING PEOPLE ON THE NET

With the arrival of internet in our lives, the world seems to have shrunk smaller. We are able to communicate with people sitting in any part of the world. There are many social networking sites that provide the facility of sending instant messages or video calling and searching for our friends, with whom we have lost contact over time.

So, before we start our search for someone on the internet, we should collect all the pieces of information that we have about him/her, as these would help in our search. Then we should try searching on various websites which are specifically meant for finding people on the internet. Some of such websites are mentioned below:

- **Facebook** is one of the largest **social networking** sites on the web, where people post their messages, photos and videos. These days almost everyone has an account on Facebook, so the probability of finding a person on facebook is extremely good. The search can be done by typing the person's name or his/her e-mail address. To narrow down the search, the place where that person is from, or the school or college he/she has studied at, or the organisation he/she is in or has worked for, or even date of birth if known, can also be typed.
- **Twitter** and **Instagram** are the other two very popular microblogging social networking sites. Chances of finding a person on these websites are also very high.
- **LinkedIn** is another website which gives professional information related to a person, provided his/her name is known.
- In order to find someone on the web, we can also take the help of **Google search engine**. By typing the name of the person in the search bar, a list of favourable results is displayed. Google brings us results from several websites, news sources, blog platforms, etc., which might be related to the person's social media accounts, web profiles, e-mail addresses, contact details, and other public records.
- **Truecaller** is an application which helps in finding the phone number of a person from his/her name and vice-versa.
- There are several other websites that help in finding people, but some of them are specific to the country or have some security conditions, because of which they are restricted to a particular location.

KEY TERMS

Information retrieval The task of obtaining information from a vast collection of content on www by making a query on the internet.

Search engine A software tool that helps find the desired information on the web in response to a query made by the user.

POINTS TO REMEMBER

- Search engines help in finding the information on the internet.
- The components of a search engine are web crawlers, database and indexing software and search interfaces.
- Some of the features allowed by search engines for locating a website to retrieve information from the www are Boolean features, Operators, Proximity features, URLs and limits.
- Web crawlers, or web spiders or web robots are software components which collect web pages for the IR system.
- Some basic challenges are faced during Information retrieval due to large scale information existing on the web and ambiguity in the language used.
- Facebook, twitter, Instagram, LinkedIn, Truecaller are some of the websites and apps that can be used for finding people on the internet, apart from searching on the Google.
- Google search can also be used to find the profile or a link to a person's activities if he has ever used any of the above sites or has been in any newsgroup.
- The proximity feature of the Search engine searches for phrases or consecutive words that occur within a certain number of words from each other.

SOLVED QUESTIONS

Q1. State two services available on internet.

Ans. Internet provides the service of retrieving information on any topic, by locating the appropriate website. Internet also helps us in finding people on the www.

Q2. What is the text typed in the search bar called?

Ans. The words typed in the search bar are called the keywords and help in filtering the information from the web.

Q3. Mamta wants to find information related to rivers originating in Himalayas. She has typed 'Rivers' in the search bar. Which links will be displayed in response to her search and will they serve the purpose?

Ans. Since, Mamta has typed 'Rivers', the websites having information about rivers in general, rivers in different parts of the world, any story or song related to rivers, in fact all the websites which have the keyword River, will be displayed. So, she will have to search for the required information in these websites, which is not what is actually desired. So she should be more precise in writing the keywords.

Q4. Recently, there has been a cyclone, in a part of the world and Rajat wants to see the latest news, updates related to it. Where on the internet will he find these updates directly?

Ans. Rajat should type 'cyclone' in the search bar and then choose the News directory of the search engine. He can further limit his search by using the options like sort by date or sort by relevance under the Tools button.

Q5. In what order are the website links displayed in response to a query?

Ans. The links to the websites are arranged in the order of relevance.

EXERCISES

I. Very Short Answer Type Questions

Multiple Choice Questions:

1. Google is a
   (a) search engine (b) social networking site
   (c) URL (d) protocol
2. Finding people on the Internet can be done by
   (a) e-mail (b) Facebook (c) Telnet (d) FTP
3. Which of the following is an online network of professionals?
   (a) Facebook (b) LinkedIn (c) Instagram (d) Twitter
4. A software tool that helps to find information from the web, in response to a query is
   (a) Operating system (b) Website
   (c) Search engine (d) Web server
5. Which of the following applications helps in locating a place?
   (a) Facebook (b) Twitter (c) Google Maps (d) LinkedIn
6. The components of search engine that help in collecting webpages for IR system are
   (a) Web crawlers (b) Robots (c) Spiders (d) All of the above
7. Which of the following apps helps in identifying the owner of a phone number
   (a) Truecaller (b) LinkedIn (c) Translator (d) Google Maps

Fill in the blanks:

1. We can limit our search for information by giving .... or ....
2. Words typed in the search bar are called ....
3. .... and .... can be used for finding people on the Internet.
4. Web crawlers are also called .... or ....
5. Links to the retrieved documents against a query are listed according to their score of ....
6. .... is the social networking site where people upload their photos, videos and messages.
7. .... sites allow people to socially interact with each other.
8. The fastest way of accessing a website is by typing its .... in the address bar.

II. Short Answer Type Questions

1. What is the purpose of the search engine?
2. State three features that can limit your search while looking for information on the web.
3. What are keywords?

4. Mr. Sharma is working in a multinational company. He has lost contact with his colleagues who used to work with him in his previous company. How can he locate them?
5. Arti wants to search for information about Hindi novels written by Premchand? What should she type as keywords?
6. Name a few popular social networking sites.
7. Sonam has got a project work on non-renewable sources of energy. Anita promised her to get information on the topic from the Internet. Which service of internet will she use?
8. What do you understand by Information Retrieval?
9. What are the components of a search engine?
10. What are web crawlers?
11. What is meant by proximity feature? How does it help in locating a website?
12. What are the two basic challenges faced by a search engine while retrieving information in response to a query?

III. Long Answer Type Questions

1. How does a search engine work when a query is typed in its search or address bar?
2. How do the Boolean features help the search engine to locate a website?
3. Is social networking a boon or a bane? Give two arguments in favour of each.

Web Services

3

Chat, E-mail, Video Conferencing, E-learning, E-banking, E-shopping, E-reservation, E-group, E-governance, Social Networking

3.1 INTRODUCTION

The Internet has become widely popular mainly because of the services it provides. It has virtually touched each and every field of our lives. Besides being used as a tool for information retrieval, the other major uses of the Internet are fast communication (text and multimedia), advertising, as education resource and the most important of all e-commerce, i.e., electronic commerce. This feature mainly deals with online transactions and has made online shopping and online reservations possible. The uses of the Internet are unlimited. Let us explore some of the important services of Internet.

3.2 E-MAIL

E-mail means electronic mail. The e-mail service of the internet allows sending and receiving mails between the computers and smart phones on the internet. For sending an e-mail, we need to have an e-mail account and the receiver's e-mail address.

There are various **search engines** on the web like Google, Yahoo, Bing, Ask.com, etc. Some of these, like the Google and Yahoo, also provide us the facility of creating an e-mail account. Such accounts are called web-based e-mail accounts. In such e-mail accounts, an e-mail address would appear as xyz123@hotmail.com or xyz123@gmail.com. Some ISPs also provide the user with e-mail accounts. The message to be mailed can be designed online (while you are connected to the Internet) or offline (while you are not connected to the Internet) using any word processor like MS Word. The recipient receives the e-mail as soon as he/she accesses his/her e-mail account.

Advantages of e-mail

- The cost to send an e-mail is negligible.
- The time taken to send an e-mail is only a few seconds.
- An e-mail can reach even the non-accessible and remote areas of the world within few seconds.
- E-mails sent and received can be stored on a memory device forever.

- The e-mail can be sent or forwarded to as many people as we want at the same time itself.
- Various kinds of attachments can also be sent along with an e-mail.

Disadvantages of e-mail

- The receiver should have access to a computer or a smart phone to receive the e-mail.
- The internet facility should be available at both the sender and the receiver ends.
- We might receive a lot of junk mails called spams.
- E-mails lack the humane touch as the emotional bonding that develops between people on talking to each other directly or over phone is missing.

But inspite of all these factors in today's world, having an Internet connection and an e-mail account is a must. The following figure shows the contents of a Gmail account window.

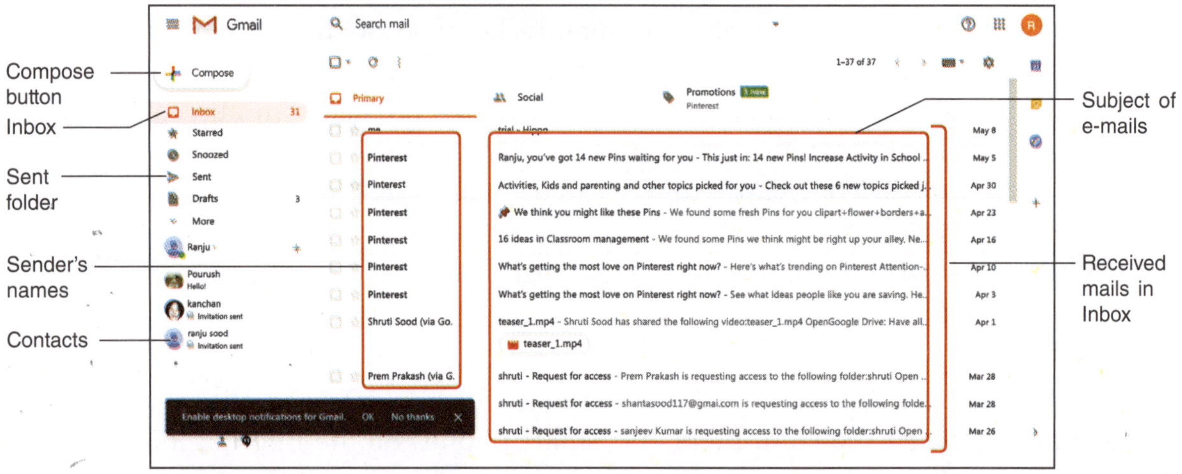

Fig 3.1: Gmail account window

The frequently used options of the above window are:

(i) *Inbox:* It is just like your letter box which contains all the incoming e-mails. The Gmail window displays some of the recently received e-mails from the inbox.

(ii) *Sent:* This folder contains all the e-mails sent by you.

(iii) *Compose:* This option helps in composing an e-mail, which means writing an e-mail and then sending it.

Clicking on the **Compose** button will display a new message box (Fig. 3.2).

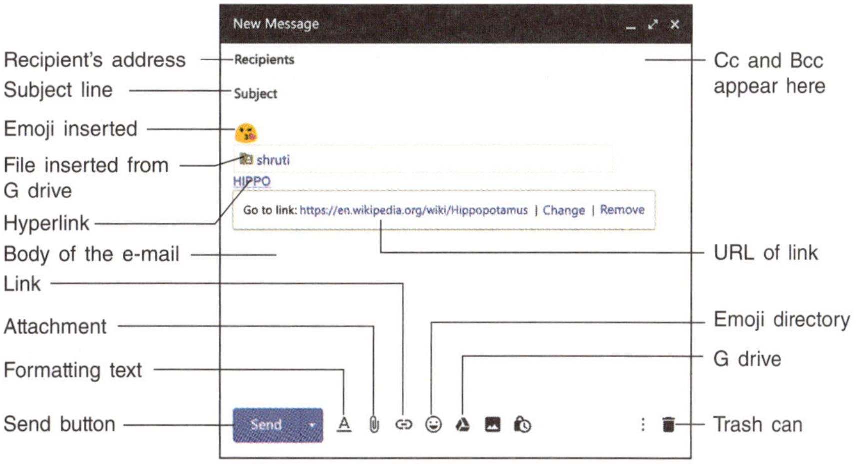

Fig 3.2: E-mail message box

Components of the New Message box:

(a) **To Recipients:** The recipient's e-mail address is entered here. You can also send the e-mail to more than one recipient. Use comma to separate the e-mail addresses.

(b) **Cc:** It stands for Carbon Copy. All the addresses that you enter here will receive a copy of the e-mail. Each receiver will also get to know to whom else, the same e-mail has been sent.

(c) **Bcc:** It stands for Blind Carbon Copy. It means that the person receiving the e-mail will not get to know to whom a copy of the e-mail has been sent. Once you leave the Recipient's box and move to subject box, Cc and Bcc options disappear from the message box.

(d) **Subject:** The subject of the e-mail should be precise and indicate about the content of the e-mail.

(e) **Body:** The actual message is typed in the body section of the e-mail.

(f) **Attachment:** Sometimes, we may have to send a file along with the e-mail. We can send it as an attachment. Clicking on the symbol helps us browse for the file on our computer and then attach it with the e-mail.

(g) **Formatting:** The formatting of the message can be done by clicking on A, which will display a formatting toolbar.

(h) **Hyperlink:** Hyperlinks can also be included in the e-mail by highlighting a word or a picture (that will act as the hyperlink) in the message. The word HIPPO has been used as the hyperlink in Fig. 3.2. Clicking on the link icon at the bottom of New Message window, opens the **Edit Link** dialog box displaying your hyperlink. In

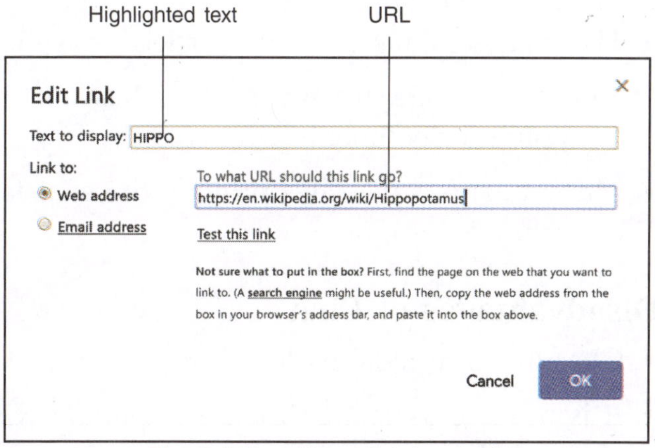

Fig. 3.3: Inserting a link in e-mail

the **web address** tab, the URL of the website should be typed and then **OK** button should be pressed. Now when the receiver clicks on the word HIPPO in the e-mail, the recipient will be directed to the website of the URL linked to the word HIPPO. In short, the website of the given URL will open.

(i) **G Drive:** Files stored on Google drive can also be included in the e-mail by clicking on the G drive icon.

(j) **Emojis:** Emojis are the visual representation of an emotion, object or symbol. They are used to make the message interesting.

(k) **Trash can:** To delete/discard an e-mail, one should click on the Trash can icon.

(l) **Send:** Once the message is ready to be sent, clicking the **Send** button will send it to the recipient.

3.3 CHAT

Chatting is a real time service offered by the Internet. Using this service, we can type messages in a chat box which is also instantly received by the person, we are chatting with. We can also receive their responses instantly. The messages may be in the form of plain text or it may include multimedia objects like images, audio and video. Chatting can also be done with a group of people, who share the same field of interest. These people might not know each other and can be from any part of the world. For such form of chatting, one has to join a chat room.

A chat room is an online platform where a group of people get together and chat about a particular subject of interest.

Chat rooms can focus on any aspect of human interest like a sport, politics, movies, mythology, etc. Various sites, such as Yahoo, provide a directory of chat sites. One has to register with a chat site to become its member. On some websites, there is no need for registration. For example, if you are logged into your Gmail account, you can chat with your contacts. Facebook, Snapchat and WhatsApp are the most common chat applications used these days.

Advantages of Chat

- It is an easy way to be in contact with the near and dear ones.
- It is an inexpensive method as compared to telephonic calls.
- The chat sessions can be recorded as well.
- One can engage in various other tasks while chatting, like reading through the e-mails or typing a document.
- Many business websites provide the chat facility to their customers for instant feedback or technical support.

Disadvantages of Chat

- Chatting can make us lose track of time as we get engrossed in it.
- It is not necessary that the other person with whom one is chatting, would understand correctly the intent of any remarks made.

- One must be careful to not hurt the sentiments of the other people involved in the chat.
- While chatting with strangers we should be very careful, as the stranger might trick us into sharing some confidential information which he/she might use to harm us later.

3.4 VIDEO CONFERENCING

A video conference is a method of live, visual communication between two or more people residing in separate locations. It provides high-quality audio and video transmission, which enables successful communication between the two ends.

Fig. 3.4: Video conferencing session

Video conferencing has become very popular with **business organisations**, where business associates can work on a project in joint collaboration. In **educational institutes**, the students in one country can attend lectures of a subject expert from another country using video conferencing. In the field of **news reporting,** a reporter can easily show live videos of an incident which might have occurred several miles away from the newsroom, this being very commonly seen on television nowadays.

Another area, where video conferencing is used extensively is the **recruitment** in foreign companies, or **admission** to foreign universities. For this purpose, the people are interviewed using video conferencing by the organisation heads sitting abroad. It almost appears as if a face-to-face interviewing session was going on. This saves the expenses of the interview board members from having to fly down to the person to be interviewed and vice-versa.

Skype for Business (Microsoft) and G suite (Google) are the most commonly used software for video conferencing.

Advantages of Video Conferencing

- Video conferencing saves time and money as the participants are not required to travel to meet each other.
- The participants at different locations and in different time zones can work on the same project simultaneously, thus minimising the delay which generally occurs due to communication gap.
- Video conferencing is very useful while interviewing a person as his/her visual expressions can also be used to judge his/her personality.
- It acts as a helpful tool in customer care services as the customer can show the actual problem live. This helps the technicians to solve the problem either by telling the customer what steps to take to resolve the problem, or visit the site with the problem specific tools.

Disadvantages of Video Conferencing

- For successful video conferencing, dedicated hardware and software are required at both the ends during a video conference.

- Technical problems like hardware failure, network connection issues, software issues, etc., cause the call to be interrupted.
- A slight delay between responses due to longer distances disrupts the flow of conversation.

3.5 E-LEARNING

One of the major boons of Internet which has brought revolution in the field of education, is the electronic learning or e-learning.

E-learning is the use of electronic devices (computers, tablets or phones) to deliver educational/training content to learners. E-learning allows one to learn anywhere and usually at any time, as long as one has a properly configured computer. E-learning can be in any of the following forms:

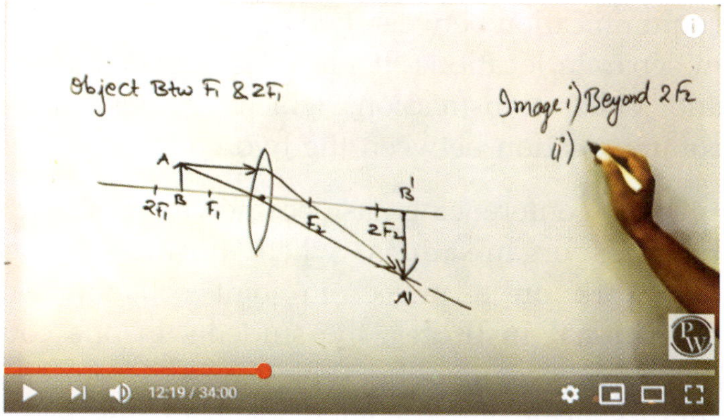

Fig. 3.5: E-learning

(i) Accessing information from the world wide web which can be considered as a knowledge database. One can find answer to any query, on any topic, by just typing the keywords.

(ii) Many educational sites provide online support also, to the learners by means of chatting or instant messaging. This helps the learners pass on their queries and get them resolved quickly. Such facilities are available 24X7.

(iii) Many educational software are available on CDs or on the internet which help in self-paced learning. Educational sites like meritnation.com and khanacademy.org are very popular among students these days.

(iv) Learning can also take place in real time with a live instructor, imparting the training. In such a setup, everyone logs in at a set time and can communicate directly with the instructor and with each other. This type of training usually takes place via internet websites or audio and video conferencing.

Advantages of E-learning

- The experts from other countries can share their views and knowledge without the barrier of language, location and time.
- A learner can learn at his/her own pace and also learn at a time and place convenient to him/her.
- No time is lost in travelling to distant college/campus for learning.

Disadvantages of E-learning

- E-learning gives the facility of self-paced learning which sometimes becomes a disadvantage. Since, there is no real time check on how much one has learned in a time duration, one tends to be lethargic at some point and switch on to some other task.

- Most of the online assessments are objective which do not let the student explains his/her own view point.
- The student's work, whether it is a project report or an assignment, is done and submitted online in this method. Hence, authencity of the student's work cannot be judged and is a matter of great concern.
- E-learning does not provide hands-on practical experience.

3.6 E-BANKING

E-banking or Electronic banking is simply the use of electronic and telecommunications network for delivering various banking products and services. Electronic banking is also called virtual banking, online banking, or internet banking or simply net banking. Through e-banking, a customer can access his account and conduct several transactions using his computer or mobile phone (mobile banking). The ATM is also an e-banking device, which helps us withdraw cash without having to go to the bank. Funds can also be transferred using the EFT or Electronic Fund Transfer method from one bank account to another, or to e-wallets provided by apps like Paytm or Mobikwik etc. These funds or e-wallets can then be used for making cashless payments.

Some of the banks are Virtual banks or Internet banks which exist only on the web and do not own any physical location.

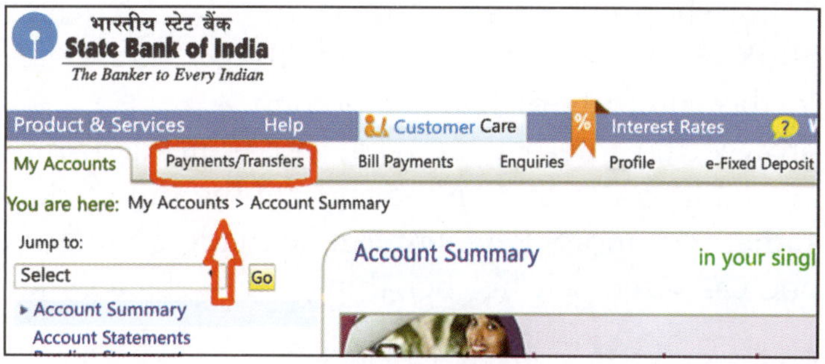

Fig. 3.6: Net banking

In the present scenario, maintaining the online security of the bank accounts is very essential as anyone knowing our password could login to our bank account and get away with all our cash. So, banks are taking various security measures to combat online money frauds. More about these methods will be discussed later in Chapter 7.

Advantages of E-banking

- Online banking is convenient and comfortable as one does not have to visit the bank for making transactions.
- Transactions can also be made from anywhere and anytime.
- E-banking increases the efficiency of the banking staff as they have to deal with lesser number of manual transactions.
- It is also cost effective as the postage expenditure is reduced, since online transactions are paperless.
- In e-banking, the service requests and transactions are dealt with electronically, so there is less probability of human error and the transactions are also done faster and more efficiently.
- Linking the billing accounts like electricity, water, telephone, etc. with the bank account relieves a person of deadlines, as the bill amount gets directly deducted from the bank account.

Disadvantages of E-banking

- In E-banking, there is no personal interaction between the customers and the bank staff as such. Hence, the bank cannot advice its customers on how to manage their finances.
- Security is a major issue regarding online banking, as there are fraudsters who are constantly devising new ways to hack accounts or steal confidential information.
- Netbanking facility is being enjoyed only by a very small fraction of the population due to illiteracy and lack of infrastructure.

3.7 E-SHOPPING

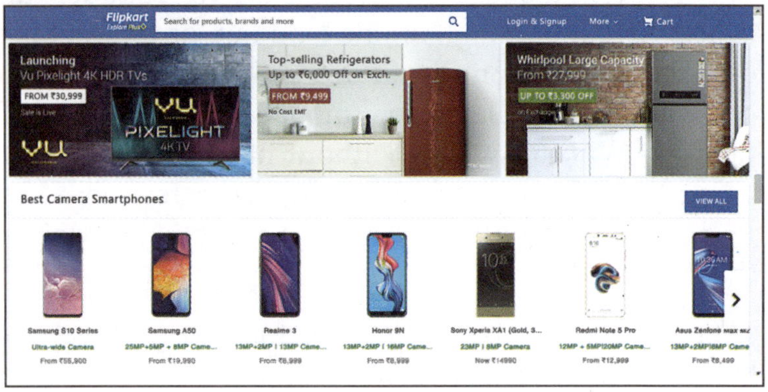

Fig. 3.7: E-shopping website

With the world getting wider, traffic on roads getting out of control and people becoming busier than ever, the facility of E-shopping (electronic shopping) is a blessing. Electronic shopping means buying goods or services from a seller over the internet. There are various online shopping sites like Amazon, FlipKart, Myntra, etc. One can sit in the comforts of his/her home, browse the Internet for whatever is needed, make a selection from the various options available, order that online and get the things delivered at the doorstep within 2-3 days or sometimes more. Payment can be made online or at the time of delivery. Not only buying, one can even sell his/her things on websites like eBay, OLX, etc.

Advantages of E-shopping

- Online stores are available 24X7 and the customer can shop at any convenient time from any location.
- Convenience is the most valuable virtue of e-shopping. The customers can save on gas, avoid heavy traffic and parking snarls.
- Online stores offer goods and services at very competitive prices and hence, the customer can compare the prices on many available price comparison websites and make the best choice.
- Many online stores post the reviews of customers who have already purchased the product, which help the future customers to judge and buy, based on their experiences.
- There is also the facility of easy returns without questions being asked. The customer can either opt for refund or even replacement of the product, if not satisfied.

Disadvantages of E-shopping

- Shipping charges are often levied on goods purchased so the discount offered is of no particular benefit.
- Sometimes a wrong product or damaged product is delivered and has to be replaced which results in delays.

- Many a times, the customer is not sure if the site he is interacting with, is a secure and authentic site or not.

3.8 E-RESERVATION

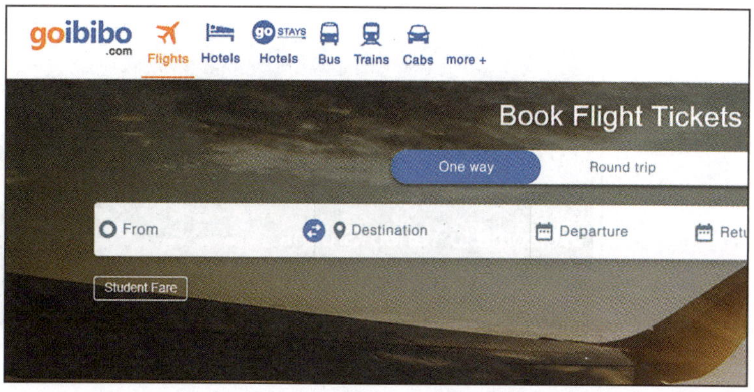

Fig. 3.8: Example of E-reservation site

E-reservation or Electronic reservation is a facility offered on the internet for real-time reservations and online enquiry about the availability of air tickets, train tickets, hotels, motels, etc. The e-reservation facility is interactive. If there is no availability, one can try for other options or another date. The confirmation of the booking is also received online. Customer makes the payments using options like cards, payment apps or netbanking. Nowadays, reservation can be made on mobile phones also. Cleartrip, MakeMyTrip and Goibibo are some of the e-reservation websites.

Advantages of E-reservation

- Any reservation, be it train, air, hotels, bus, taxi or any other possible service, it can be done from anywhere, to anywhere and at any time.
- One can compare the ticket prices offered by various sites.
- There is also no need to hop from site to site for different types of reservations for different services. There are sites that make reservations for the trip right from the transportation services to hotel bookings and restaurants, and sight seeing.
- From the business perspective, since the payments are received in advance, chances of getting duped by customers who enjoy the facilities on credit, is minimised.

Disadvantages of E-reservation

- Since the payments are made online in advance, some sites do not make full refund in case of cancellations.
- In case of any help or query, one has to depend on the customer care service which generally is not very satisfying.
- Sometimes, it may also happen that the customer is not satisfied with the facility for which he/she has paid.

3.9 E-GROUP

An e-group or electronic group is a community on many social networking sites. It allows the users to create, post, read and comment on a topic being discussed in the group.

Being a member of a particular e-group puts one on the mailing list of that group. It ensures that one receives timely information regarding events, meetings, etc. related to the group. Interaction with the other group members is also possible and this helps one to remain in the loop, and be aware of what is happening in the group.

Fig. 3.9: Yahoo Groups site

E-group initially started as a facility provided by a small IT company to facilitate making mailing lists. However, this facility became so popular that after a few years the company was taken over by Yahoo and came to be known as Yahoo! Groups. Presently Yahoo! Groups and the groups on Facebook and WhatsApp are famous and in fact every organisation, be it a school or a company or a housing society, or college pass-outs of a year, all of them have formed their own groups. It is in fact a great way of keeping in touch with the people of our choice and the people who share similar interests.

One can also find a group of any particular interest and become its member by sending an online request. In fact, anybody can start a group of its own and request his/her friends to join it.

Advantages of E-group

- A message can be shared with a number of people (group members) at the same time.
- E-groups are available on the internet 24X7.
- People who are shy of speaking, can share their views, as much as they want.
- One can save a group chat and go back to it.
- One can learn from the experiences of other group members and share one's own experiences too.
- Sometimes, the members of the group prove to be a great moral support for others.

Disadvantages of E-group

- People who are not very good at writing or typing, find communication on e-groups very inconvenient.
- In textual exchange, as there is no physical clue of the other person, sometimes their views are misinterpreted.

3.10 E-GOVERNANCE

E-governance or Electronic governance is the application of Information and Communication Technology by the government agencies and departments, to communicate with the citizens, other government departments and business organisations. E-governance helps in delivering government services and improving the functionality of the administrative system. It aims at bringing transparency in the system and delivering prompt service to the citizens.

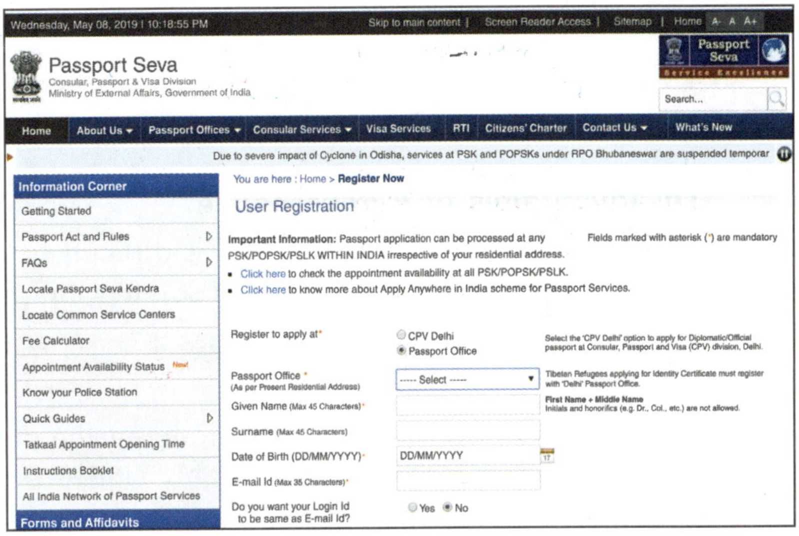

Fig. 3.10: Passport service sites

Fast communication between the various government departments, has helped them to work in co-ordination with each other, which in turn, has also increased the pace of policy and decision making.

Various government departments offer online facilities like the registration of birth/death, application for passport/ Aadhar card/PAN card, online payment of property tax, income tax, etc. This convenience helps citizens, pay their dues without delays and also access various facilities, faster. It also increases their confidence in the government, since they get the feel that the government is indeed taking steps to make the life of its people easy.

> **ADDITIONAL INFO**
>
> Digi locker is a one of the facilities provided by the government of India under the Digital India Scheme where an Indian citizen is allotted 1GB of secure space for a Digi locker account to store the digital copy of important documents like Aadhar card, driving license, certificates, etc., and access them anywhere anytime.

Furthermore, certain agencies help the government in collecting data related to various fields like census, air traffic, traffic on various roads and highways, pollution in different cities and tourism to name a few. The data collected across the various digital platforms is analysed and used to improve the services, upgrade the facilities and make new policies.

Advantages of E-governance

- The use of technology has improved the speed of communication which has resulted in quick interaction between various sectors of government. Thus, the process of policy making and implementation has gained speed.
- Cost of stationery has decreased as the communication and documentation is done using computers.

- Transparency in the work of government has increased as it allows the public to be informed about what the government is working on as well as the policies they are trying to implement.
- With transparency comes accountability. The citizens can also question the government, if they find any discrepancy in its working.

Disadvantages of E-governance

- Computer-illiterate citizens find it difficult to avail the services of e-governance, once the previous alternative ways of solving the problem have been withdrawn.
- E-governance may lead to privacy issues, as it is a gigantic task to keep the data of such a large population secure.
- There is also the added cost of training the government employees on the working of e-governance and also hiring highly skilled professionals for the same.
- Indirectly, e-governance also results in job losses, as many manual jobs are now replaced by technology.

3.11 SOCIAL NETWORKING

Social networking refers to the use of social media websites for interaction, where individuals are linked together by a common interest or relationship like friends, family, etc. It is a way of letting others know what one is doing and also to know what the others are doing. Many social networking websites like Facebook, Instagram, Snapchat, Twitter, etc., have become so popular that it is quite rare to find a person who is not registered on at least one of them.

Fig. 3.11: Social Networking sites

A user on a social networking website can create his/her profile mentioning his/her date of birth, address, fields of interest, and even upload his/her photograph. The user can create an album of his/her own and can make it either public or private. The user can send a friend-request to any other user or vice-versa. Accepting or rejecting a friend request is also the discretion of the user. So, being on a social networking site, is like communicating with the people one already knows and also, making new friends. The user can choose his/her own privacy settings and decide who can access which part of his/her profile. So, in case of having a long-lost friend one need not look too far. One would just have to browse through any of these social networking websites and be back in touch again.

Advantages of Social Networking

- Social networking provides worldwide connectivity, so searching for an individual or interacting socially is easier and faster.
- One is never lonely if one is registered on a social networking site. This is due to the fact that one can find various social groups and individuals, who share the same interest on social media.

- Information can be shared instantaneously. Teachers can also make their teacher-student group, where the students can get their queries solved and teachers can share their resources. Similarly, manager-staff groups can also be formed where the manager and the staff can keep each other informed about the recent developments in the organisation.
- The social media is a powerful advertising tool. One can reach a vast number of potential customers by advertising on the social media.
- Social media websites like Twitter and Instagram are the best places to know about the current happenings in the world.

Disadvantages of Social Networking

- An innocent comment may sometimes be misunderstood by the people on social media and hence, one might have to suffer backlashes.
- Sharing too much of personal information can prove harmful. It is like inviting others to invade your privacy.
- Cyber stalking and cyber bullying are very common cyber-crimes on the social media.
- Sometime one ends up spending much more time on social media than one should, thus, loosing precious time, ignoring several other tasks, which would be requiring more priority.
- Many social networking sites sell our private information to business houses and we unknowingly become their advertising targets.

KEY TERMS

E-mail A service of internet that allows sending and receiving mails between the computers on the internet.

Chatting A real time service of the internet which helps people connect with other individuals or with a group of people in chat rooms.

Chat rooms The platforms where a group of people get together and chat about a particular topic or just chat.

Video conferencing A method of live, visual communication between two or more people residing in separate locations, which helps in saving time and money.

E-learning The use of the internet to deliver educational or training content to the learner.

E-banking The use of electronic and tele-communication network for the purpose of delivering various banking products and services.

Internet banking The use of internet for delivering various banking products and services. It is called also virtual banking, online banking or net banking.

Virtual Banks The banks that exist only on the web and do not own any physical location.

E-shopping A facility available on Internet wherein one can shop/sell online and even pay online.

E-reservation The most convenient facility available on Internet for online real time reservation of hotels, tickets, etc.

E-group The online groups maintained for a group of people with similar interests and anybody wanting to join such groups need to register themselves with the group.

E-governance The application of ICT by the government in governing the country and providing services to its citizens, in a faster and easier way.

Social networking One of the facilities of internet which helps its members to connect with more and more people of common interests, on the social media platforms.

Emojis The visual representation of an emotion, object or symbol.

POINTS TO REMEMBER

- All the incoming mails get stored in the folder named Inbox.
- A person receiving Bcc marked e-mail does not get to know to whom a copy of the same e-mail has been sent.
- A person receiving Cc marked e-mail gets to know the list of all other recipients of the same e-mail.
- Files can be sent as attachments with an e-mail.
- Video conferencing is beneficial when the participants are placed at distant geographical locations.
- Money is transferred online using Electronic Fund Transfer methods. Sites like Paytm, Mobikwik allow making electronic payments instead of cash payment.
- Data collected across various digital platforms is analysed and used to improve public services and governance.
- Social networking sites have brought the world closer but if one is not careful, one can become a victim of cyber frauds.

SOLVED QUESTIONS

Q1. Anjana's dad has been posted in a remote area which has access to internet but there are no computer training institutions. She wants to persue a course in Python. How can she achieve her aim?

Ans. Anjana can use the e-learning service of the internet to enrol herself in any online course in Python. Most online training courses provide certificates also on the competition of the course. In case she does not require a certificate, there are also several tutorials available for free on YouTube that she can watch and learn.

Q2. Meeta has bought a hair dryer from a site on the internet. Which web service has she used and how can she pay for the article?

Ans. Meeta has made use of the e-shopping service of the internet. She can either make the payment online using net banking or payment apps like Paytm and PayPal. She can also pay offline, to the delivery person using her debit/credit card.

Q3. Mukul has applied for a job in a multinational company and the company's HR head wants to interview him. The problem is that Mukul stays in India and the HR head works from abroad. How can the interview be conducted with minimum cost?

Ans. Video conferencing can be done between Mukul and the HR head so that they can visually communicate with each other in real time, from their respective locations with minimum cost.

Q4. What do you understand by privacy settings on social networking sites?

Ans. Privacy settings allow the account holder to decide who can access his/her posts. The posts can be made public so that everyone can view or can be made private so that only the account holder can view.

Q5. How has ICT helped the government in increasing its pace of work?

Ans. Faster communication between the various government departments has helped them to work in co-ordination with each other which in turn has also increased the pace of policy and decision making.

Q6. Radha has bought a product online but is not satisfied with its quality. What method of communication can she use to inform the supplier about her complain?

Ans. The websites providing services to customers usually provide the facility of complaint registeration, using e-mail or chat. Some sites also allow the customer to directly call and verbally speak to the supplier.

Q7. Shruti wants to send a large file which contains videos and cannot attach it to an e-mail. How can she send the file to her company's manager from her Gmail account?

Ans. Shruti can save the file in G Drive and then insert the file using the G Drive icon, in her e-mail.

Exercises

I. Very Short Answer Type Questions

Multiple Choice Questions:

1. An e-mail can be sent to
   (a) a receiver even if he/she is offline
   (b) a person who has an e-mail account on some other search engine
   (c) many people at a time
   (d) all of the above
2. Cc option is used to
   (a) send a copy of an e-mail to another e-mail address
   (b) attach another file with your message
   (c) copy a message to your account
   (d) all of the above
3. Bcc option is used to send a copy of e-mail to
   (a) a visually impaired person
   (b) several people without letting them know sender's address
   (c) several people without letting the other recipients know
   (d) all of the above

4. An e-mail received by you can remain on your computer
   (a) forever until you delete it
   (b) only for a limited period of time
   (c) only till it is unread
   (d) can be deleted by the sender
5. E-mail stands for
   (a) easy mail
   (b) electronic mail
   (c) enriched text mail
   (d) none
6. Virtual banks are the banks that
   (a) physically exist
   (b) exist only on the internet
   (c) exist in video games
   (d) are very reliable
7. Online banking allows:
   (a) transferring of funds
   (b) checking account details
   (c) online payments
   (d) all of the above
8. Which of the following is not required during e-learning ?
   (a) Internet
   (b) Computer or tablet or smartphone
   (c) Learning software
   (d) Blackboard and chalk
9. Which of the following can be a part of an e-mail message?
   (a) emojis
   (b) hyperlinks
   (c) files
   (d) all of the above
10. Skype is not used for
   (a) video conferencing
   (b) e-mailing
   (c) chatting
   (d) social networking
11. E-governance refers to
   (a) governing the electronic media.
   (b) use of ICT by the government to do its work.
   (c) governing a process with ease.
   (d) laws made by the government to keep a check on the internet.
12. Which folder contains the received mails?
   (a) Inbox (b) Draft (c) Label (d) Flagged
13. Which folder has a copy of all the sent mails?
   (a) Draft (b) Inbox (c) Sent (d) Groups

Fill in the blanks:

1. E-shopping stands for ....
2. Facebook is an example of ....
3. .... is required besides the e-mail address to log on to your account.
4. .... button is used to send a file along with your e-mail message.
5. WWW can also be called a .... database.
6. Flights and hotels can be booked online using .... sites.
7. Buying products online is called ....
8. The facility of registering birth/death online with the Municipal Corporation falls under e-...................... .
9. For conducting off-shore interviews .... is used.
10. Making payment from the bank account using the internet, is an activity of e-............., while providing the facility to pay Income tax online comes under e-................ .
11. A bank that exists only on the web and does not have any physical location is called ....

II. Short Answer Type Questions

1. Differentiate between Chatting and Video Conferencing.
2. Name any two objects that can be inserted in an e-mail message.
3. Give two advantages of internet for schools.
4. Name some popular social networking sites.
5. How is e-learning beneficial in the present scenario?
6. How does e-learning help a student?
7. How does e-learning help a teacher?
8. What facilities are provided by e-reservation?
9. Rekha has joined an NGO which looks after people in an old age home. She visits them every alternate day and talks to them. Some days when she is not able to visit them, she talks to them face-to-face using a computer and the Internet.
   (i) Which service of the internet does she use to watch and talk to them?
   (ii) Since, the old people are not able to go out to banks and for shopping, which facility can they use on Internet for the same?
10. Name any two facilities on the internet that have been provided to the citizens by the government of India.
11. How has e-governance helped in increasing people's faith in the government?
12. What is mobile banking?

III. Long Answer Type Questions

1. Explain the various services provided by Internet.
2. How has e-shopping made our lives simpler?
3. How is the payment made against e-shopping and e-reservation?
4. How is e-group different from social networking?
5. State five areas where the use of ICT has helped the government in increasing the efficiency of its work.
6. Write two advantages and two disadvantages of the following:
   (i) e-mail (ii) e-banking
   (iii) e-groups (iv) e-shopping
   (v) e-reservation (vi) social networking (vii) e-learning

Previous Years' Solved Examination Questions

I. Very Short Answer Type Questions

Multiple Choice Questions:

1. Which of the following is an e-shopping website? (2019)
   (a) Flipkart (b) Amazon (c) Snapdeal (d) All of the above
2. Some of the services available on internet are: (2013)
   (i) E-mail (ii) HTML
   (iii) Video conferencing (iv) XML
   (a) (i) & (iv) (b) (i) & (ii) (c) (i) & (iii) (d) (ii) & (iv)

Answers: 1. (d) 2. (c)

II. Short Answer Type Questions

1. Write down one main advantage of e-banking. (2018C)
2. Match web service/URL of Column A with corresponding web service/URL in Column B. (2018C)

Column A	Column B
(i) e-learning	(a) http://www.india.gov.in
(ii) http://www.irctc.co.in	(b) e-banking
(iii) e-governance	(c) e-reservation
(iv) http://www.onlinesbi.com	(d) http://www.w3schools.com
(v) social networking site	(e) video conferencing
(vi) https://webskype.com	(f) https://www.facebook.com

3. Name any two services offered by internet. (2017)
4. Name any one ISP. (2017)
5. Write the URL of any e-banking website. (2019)
6. Briefly explain the significance of Social networking through Internet in our day to day life. (2013)
7. What is e-learning? Mention any two main benefits with the use of information technology. (2014)

Answers:

1. Very convenient to customers as they are not required to visit the bank.
2.

(i) e-learning	(d) https://www.w3schools..com
(ii) http://www.irctc.co.in	(c) e-reservation
(iii) e-governance	(a) http://www.india.gov.in
(iv) http://www.onlinesbi.com	(b) e-banking
(v) social networking site	(f) https://www.facebook.com
(vi) https://web.skype.com	(e) video conferencing

3. E-banking, E-learning
4. Airtel, BSNL (*any one*)
5. https://www.icicibank.com (*any other suitable*)
6. Social networking sites help us to connect to people and get updated. They reduce geographical distances. They also make aware of the social happenings and events.
7. Learning with the help of electronic resources like computers, smart phones, internet etc. is called e-learning.

   Advantages:

   (i) It is time saving as well as removes the distance barrier between the learner and the teacher.

   (ii) It has quicker delivery cycle as compared to class room based teaching.

   (ii) It is less expensive to setup an e-learning environment. (*any two*)

Mobile Technologies 4

SMS, MMS, 3G, 4G

Every now and then new models of mobile phones, tablets, smart watches and televisions are being launched. Each one of them comes with newer and more advanced features taking the quality and quantity of the communication to a higher level. The continuously evolving technology is the force behind this progression. This chapter explains how the short text messaging expanded to the multimedia messaging and the various generations of mobile communication technology that made it possible.

4.1 SMS

The **SMS** or **Short Message Service** also known as text messaging, is the exchange of short alphanumeric text messages between mobile devices like mobile phones. It is the most basic communications technology available for instant mobile data transfer at a very minimal cost. One SMS can hold up to 160 alphanumeric characters.

A SMS message follows the below mentioned path:

- The SMS goes from a mobile device to a Short Message Service Centre (SMSC).
- The SMSC then contacts the mobile networks to get the recipient's subscriber's location.
- The message is then sent in the form of a small data packet, to the destination device.

> The first SMS message was sent in 1992 via Vodafone's GSM network.

The above process is known as the **store and forward** method.

Apart from one-to-one personal text messaging there are companies also, which provide personalised communications channel to send the following types of SMS:

Transactional SMS: E-commerce companies and banks send SMS for every transaction. For example, if one places an order online to buy something, he/she will get a message immediately on their mobile from the shopping site regarding the order placed and also an alert SMS from the bank, through which the online payment was made. Such SMS are called the **Transactional SMS.**

Promotional SMS: SMS is also used by companies to promote their business. They use this facility to keep the customers informed about their new offers, new products and other benefits. These types of SMS are termed as **Promotional SMS.**

Bulk SMS: Government departments like Income Tax, Election Commission, Health Department also send alerts through SMS to the citizens to keep them informed about important events and dates. Since such SMS are sent in bulk, they are called **Bulk SMS**. Schools also use bulk SMS to inform the parents about any important circular sent through their children, or to inform regarding a sudden holiday or an event.

4.2 MMS

The **MMS** or **Multimedia Messaging Service** is a wireless communication technology that allows exchange of messages with multimedia content between mobile phones and other devices. Multimedia messages may include text messages along with audio, video clips and still images. There is no limit to the size of the MMS. The messages are sent to the message centre from where they are then sent to the recipient via internet. If the receiver handset is not capable of receiving MMS, the MMS can be viewed using a web browser.

The videos and pictures that we send on Facebook or WhatsApp fall under the category of MMS.

4.3 GENERATIONS OF MOBILE TECHNOLOGY

With every passing decade, the mobile technology is advancing by one generation. It started in the 1980's with the launch of the first generation called 1G, then came 2G in 1990's. With this trend continuing, we are ready to welcome 5G in 2020's. Let us now study how the mobile technology has evolved over the generations:

First Generation (1G)

The first generation (1G) was launched in the early 80's. It used the Advanced Mobile Phone Service (AMPS) cellular networks, which were based on Frequency Division Multiplexing Access (FDMA) technology. In FDMA, the available frequency band is divided into channels of equal bandwidth. A specific frequency band is then given to one signal. So, each conversation is carried on a different frequency. 1G allowed only voice communication.

ADDITIONAL INFO

In telecommunications, multiplexing is a method by which multiple analog or digital signals are combined into one signal over a shared medium, e.g., several telephone calls may be carried using one wire.

Second Generation (2G)

The second generation (2G) emerged in the 90's with two types of technologies - Code Division Multiple Access (CDMA) and Time Division Multiple Access (TDMA). Unlike, the FDMA in which a specific frequency band is given solely to one signal, CDMA allows numerous signals to occupy a single transmission channel, thus allowing extensive use of available bandwidth.

TDMA allows several users to share the same frequency channel by dividing the signal into different time slots. The users transmit in rapid succession, one after the other, each using its own time slot. TDMA was mostly used by the Global System for Mobile communication (GSM) telephony standards. The 2G technology allowed SMS along with voice communication.

Third Generation (3G)

3G refers to the third generation of mobile technology, sometimes also referred to as the cellular technology. It enhances the features that were already available in 1G and 2G technologies and at the same time infusing further advanced features to it.

The limited range and quality of 2G led to newer innovations and the birth of 3G technology in early 2000's. It promised increased bandwidth, efficient mobile wireless network, support for MMS along with SMS and various other applications. For these applications, it uses GSM and packet switched data transmission.

Features of 3G over the previous generations

- Low cost
- Faster connectivity.
- Greater data speed.
- High speed internet access.
- Supports voice data, SMS, MMS, web browsing and video conferencing.

Various applications of 3G

1. **Location Based Services (LBS)** like check-ins at various places or events like ordering food or booking a cab, especially on Facebook, Google Maps, etc.
2. **Online Services** like virtual banking and shopping are supported by 3G network.
3. **Roaming Service** on the mobile phones.
4. **Multimedia Services** like video conferencing, online presentations, video streaming, etc., have brought a revolution in the field of advertising and online gaming.

Moreover, it allows the user to be online all 24 hours. So, the above services can be enjoyed anytime.

Fourth Generation (4G)

The present technology is the 4G or the fourth generation of mobile communication technology, which represents a significant evolution over the 3G standards.

4G wireless technology is also referred to as **"MAGIC"** which stands for Mobile multimedia, Any-where, Global mobility solutions over, Integrated wireless and Customised services.

If using 4G, the minimum standard data transfer rate for high mobility communication like cars and trains is 100 megabits/sec and for low mobility communications like in offices or at home or while walking, is 1 gigabits/sec. It is a packet switched wireless system which uses the OFDM (Orthogonal Frequency Division Multiplexing) method, in which a single data stream is split across several separate narrowband channels at different frequencies. This helps to achieve clean data transmission in situations prone to interference and signal corruption.

Features of 4G

- 4G provides increased data transfer rates.

- The customer can move smoothly from one network to the other.
- No limit on the IP address whereas 3G had a limited IP address accessibility.
- The 4G facilitates IP telephony which uses broadband internet access for transmission of voice. This communication can be between computer-computer, computer-telephone or telephone-computer.
- This generation has ultra-broadband internet access.
- Gaming services and High Definition multimedia are easily streamed using 4G.
- Roaming connectivity without a call drop or signal interference is possible in 4G.

Fifth Generation (5G)

The fifth generation of mobile technology is ready to sweep the world due to its following advanced features as compared to the 4G:

- The ability to carry larger data volume
- The capability to have connectivity for more devices
- The lower power consumption
- Better and reliable connectivity
- Low cost
- Above all the data transmission speed which will be several Gbps.

KEY TERMS

SMS or Short Message Service A communication technology that allows an exchange of short alphanumeric text messages between mobile devices like mobile phones.

MMS or Multimedia Messaging Service A wireless communication technology that allows exchange of multimedia communications between mobile phones and other devices.

Store and Forward method A method of data transmission where data packets are stored and forwarded only when the further route is available.

Multiplexing A method by which multiple analog or digital signals are combined into one signal over a shared medium before transmitting

FDMA In Frequency Division Multiplexing Access technology, the frequency band is divided into channels of equal bandwidth and a specific frequency band is given to a single user.

CDMA Code Division Multiple Access technology allows numerous signals to occupy a single transmission channel.

TDMA Time Division Multiple Access technology allows several users to share same frequency channel by dividing the signal into different time slots.

LBS (Location Based Services) The services which use the location of a place or event to provide a service.

OFDM Orthogonal Frequency Division Multiplexing technology splits a single data stream across several separate narrow band channels at different frequencies.

POINTS TO REMEMBER

- One SMS can hold up to 160-character alphanumeric characters.
- SMS sent by E-commerce companies and banks for transactions alerts are called Transactional SMS.
- Promotional SMS are used by companies to promote their business.
- SMS like notifications and alerts from government departments or other organisations to several people together are called Bulk SMS.
- 3G technology is low in cost, has great data speed and internet access speed, supports SMS, MMS, web browsing and video conferencing.
- Location Based Services, Online Services, Roaming service and Multimedia services are some of the applications of 3G mobile technology.
- 4G wireless technology is also referred to as "MAGIC" which stands for Mobile multimedia, Any-where, Global mobility solutions over, Integrated wireless and Customised services.
- 4G has made data transfer quite fast, provided easy moving from one network to the other, smooth facility of IP telephony and less probability of call drop and signal interference.

SOLVED QUESTIONS

Q1. Varun's parents received a SMS from his school regarding the due date of fee payment. Under which category would you place this SMS?

Ans. Since such SMS are sent to the parents of all the students of the school, it is a type of the Bulk SMS.

Q2. Amita wants to send her address to her brother. Should she use SMS or MMS?

Ans. As the address is in simple text, so SMS should be used to send it.

Q3. What kind of SMS does the following picture show?

> Nothing is better than having Pizza Hut's Tastier Pan Pizzas with Cricket.
>
> Now get 2 personal pizzas starting @ 99 each
>
> Walk in/order @PH99.in
>
> T&C apply

Ans. This is a promotional SMS.

Q4. Anjali has bought a puppy and wants to inform her friend about it. She also wants to send a video of the puppy playing with her. Which service would she use?

Ans. She would use MMS as the message contains text and video both.

Q5. Which generation of mobile technology supports web browsing and video conferencing?

Ans. The support for web browsing and video conferencing started with 3G.

Q6. Which generation of technology has made mobile network portability possible?

Ans. Moving from one network to another has been made possible with 4G.

Q7. Was e-shopping possible with 2G?

Ans. No, 2G did not support e-shopping.

Exercises

I. Very Short Answer Type Questions

Multiple Choice Questions:

1. SMS sent by the bank to inform one about online payment made by him/her is
   (a) Bulk SMS (b) Transactional SMS
   (c) Promotional SMS (d) MMS
2. SMS sent by a company to its customers informing them about a newly launched product and other discount offers is
   (a) Promotional SMS (b) Transactional SMS
   (c) Bulk SMS (d) both (a) and (c)
3. Online services like banking and shopping started with
   (a) 1G (b) 2G (c) 3G (d) 4G
4. The facility of making or receiving calls, while you are travelling across the globe is called the
   (a) Online Service (b) Location-based Service
   (c) Transactional Services (d) Roaming Service

Fill in the blanks:

1. An SMS can hold up to .... alphanumeric characters.
2. SMS sent by the government department to the citizens to inform them about an important event is the .... type of SMS.
3. Wireless communication technology that allows the exchange of multimedia communication is termed as ....
4. Videos and images sent on the Facebook or WhatsApp are a form of .... (SMS/MMS).
5. Facebook check-in is .... type of service.
6. The mobile technology generation, which has allowed the user to smoothly move from one network to the other is the ....

II. Short Answer Type Questions

1. Differentiate between transactional SMS and bulk SMS.
2. How is 4G better than 3G?
3. How is MMS different from SMS?
4. What are Location Based Services? Give an example.
5. State any two online services which are possible due to 3G technology.

III. Long Answer Type Questions

1. State four features of 3G technology.
2. Explain store and forward method of message transmission.
3. Explain three types of SMS with examples.

Hypertext Markup Language and Its Elements

5

- Introduction to Web Page Designing using HTML, Creating and saving an HTML document, accessing a web page using a web browser
- Container and Empty elements, Designing web pages using the following elements: HTML, HEAD, TITLE, BODY (Attributes: BACKGROUND, BGCOLOR, TEXT, LINK, ALINK, VLINK, LEFT MARGIN, TOP MARGIN), FONT (Attributes: COLOR, SIZE, FACE), BASEFONT (Attributes: COLOR, SIZE, FACE), CENTER, BR (Break), HR (Horizontal Rule, Attributes: SIZE, WIDTH, ALIGN, NOSHADE, COLOR), COMMENTS, ! for comments, H1..H6 (Heading), P (Paragraph), B (Bold), I (Italics), U (Underline), UL & OL (Unordered List & Ordered List Attributes: TYPE, START), LI (List Item), Description lists

5.1 INTRODUCTION TO HTML

The amount of information present on the Internet on various websites and web pages is just enormous. One can easily access this information by surfing the Internet. But, how exactly is this information floated on the Internet? This is the part where the HTML or Hypertext Markup Language comes into play.

The HTML or **Hypertext Markup Language** is a language, which provides a means of organising and formatting the content on web pages, and linking the pages. HTML pages include both text and graphics with sound and various animation effects. The aim is to design the web page in such a way that it is attractive as well as informative. The tools to achieve this are many, the rest is up to the programmer as to how far he/she can exploit them to achieve his/her objective.

HTML is basically a subset derived from SGML, *i.e.*, Standard General Markup Language which includes many specialised languages like one for printing and publishing, another for library indexing, etc. HTML is also a specialised language used for the internet interface. SGML is powerful but complex and very difficult to understand. HTML on the other hand is simple and any person even without the knowledge of programming can learn it with ease. The latest version of HTML is HTML5. For explaining the html tags, HTML4 is being used here, since many tags are not supported by HTML5.

A description of HTML5 and the tags it supports and those it does not support is given at the end of next chapter.

5.2 CREATING A WEB PAGE AND ITS HTML FILE

To a layman, a web page may look like an ordinary document however, what looks like a simple page to the others, can actually be a page with a combination of text and pictures from various computer files, located in different parts of the world. The HTML helps us in arranging these text and pictures on our web page to make it more informative.

An HTML file is basically a text file which can be read and edited with any text editor such as, Windows Notepad, Microsoft Word or Word Perfect. All that needs to be done is to save the file with an extension of **.htm** or **.html**.

To view a web page or an html file, we need a web browser such as Internet Explorer or Netscape Navigator. These browsers display the information on the web page according to the HTML commands written in the file. In this book, Notepad has been used as the text editor and Google Chrome has been used as the web browser.

STEPS To create a web page:

1. Open Notepad and type the HTML code.
2. Save the code in a file with extension .html.
3. Open Internet Explorer and in the address bar, type the address of the above file and press Enter.
4. The code will be executed and the web page will be displayed.

5.3 COMPONENTS OF AN HTML DOCUMENT

Before we start creating a web page, there are certain things we need to learn about the structure of the HTML document.

HTML is not **case sensitive** which means it does not differentiate between upper case and lower case letters.

An HTML document has two parts—head and body. The **Head** is the part where a title for the document and the heading of the web page is given. The **Body** is the part where the code for the actual working is written. The text along with the required tags and elements is written in body part. Let us now learn about these tags and elements.

5.3.1 Elements and Tags in HTML Document

The **HTML element** is the collection of a **start tag**, its **attributes**, an **end tag** (may or may not be there) and everything in between.

HTML tags are the keywords which tell the browser how to format and display the contents on the web page.

An **HTML tag** (either opening or closing), is used to mark the start or end of an element. Tags are enclosed in angle brackets <>.

e.g. <HEAD> </HEAD>

Attributes define additional properties of an element. For example, a **paragraph**, which is represented by the **p element**, would be written as:

<p	**text**	**=**	**"red"**	**> Let us learn about HTML elements and tags**	**</p>**
(opening tag)	(attribute)		(value of attribute)	(text displayed)	(closing tag)

Anything which is not within the angle brackets (<>) is taken as simple text by the web browser and is displayed on the web page.

The tags do not appear on the web page. Enclosing value of most of the attributes in double quotes is optional except in the case of ROWSPAN, COLSPAN and when the value of the attribute is a file name.

5.3.2 Container Elements

These elements appear twice in every HTML document, once within simple <> symbols; this is called **ON tag**, or **opening tag** and second time also within <> but with a '/' after < symbol; this is called **OFF tag** or **closing tag**. *For example*, <HEAD> is an ON tag and </HEAD> is an OFF tag.

Example 1

Container Elements

Head part

Body part

```
<HTML>
<HEAD>
<TITLE> WELCOME TO THE WORLD OF WEB PAGE DESIGNING </TITLE>
</HEAD>

<BODY>
This is the first step towards designing your own web page
</BODY>
</HTML>
```

In the above example, the HTML, HEAD, TITLE and BODY elements have their counterparts with a '/'. So these elements are called **container elements** as they have closing tags. When viewed using a web browser, the above document will appear as shown in Fig 5.1.

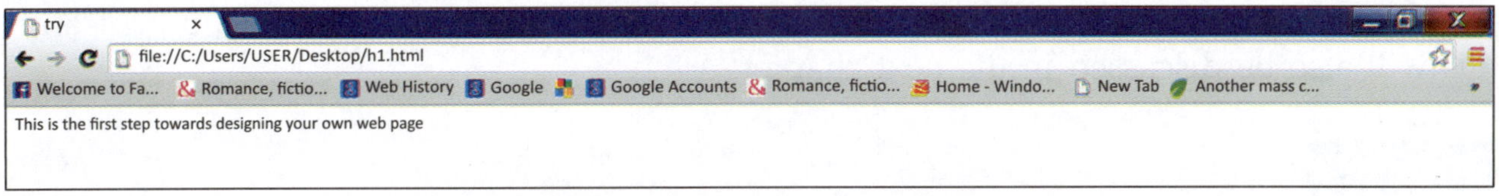

Fig. 5.1: Result of Example 1 as seen using web browser

5.3.3 Empty Elements

The elements which do not require an OFF tag are called **empty elements**. They appear alone as ON tags in the document.

 is an example of empty elements. The following example shows the usage of empty elements.

Example 2

```
<HTML>
<HEAD>
<TITLE> WELCOME TO THE WORLD OF WEB PAGE DESIGNING
</TITLE>
</HEAD>
<BODY>
This is the first step towards <BR>
designing your own web page.
</BODY>
</HTML>
```

Use of empty tag

When viewed using a web browser, the above document will appear as shown in Fig. 5.2.

Now let us study what these tags mean and what is their usage in an HTML document.

> This is the first step towards
> designing your own web page.

Fig. 5.2: Result of Example 2

5.3.4 HTML Element [<HTML>.........</HTML>]

This is a container element and its tags appear at the beginning and end of each HTML document. It has no specific role in the appearance of the document. This tag just lets the web browser know that the document is an HTML document. For example,

```
<HTML>
..........
..........
</HTML>
```

5.3.5 HEAD and TITLE Elements [<HEAD>......</HEAD> & <TITLE>......</TITLE>]

The **HEAD element** is also a container element. As already mentioned, every HTML document has a head and a body. In the head section, we can link the external files like CSS (which will be learnt in the next chapter). The head portion includes another element, *i.e.*, the **TITLE** which is also a container element and encloses the heading given to the document. This heading does not appear on the web page but it appears on the title bar of web browser. Another element which can be used in <Head> element is <style>.

The <style> element is used to define style information for an HTML document and this will also be discussed in the next chapter.

Example 3

```
<HTML>
<HEAD>
<TITLE> This is the title </TITLE>
</HEAD>
<BODY> Say No To Polybags
</BODY>
</HTML>
```

This title does not get displayed on the web page but appears on the title bar of the web browser.

This text gets displayed on the web page.

This example when viewed by web browser would look like as shown in Fig. 5.3.

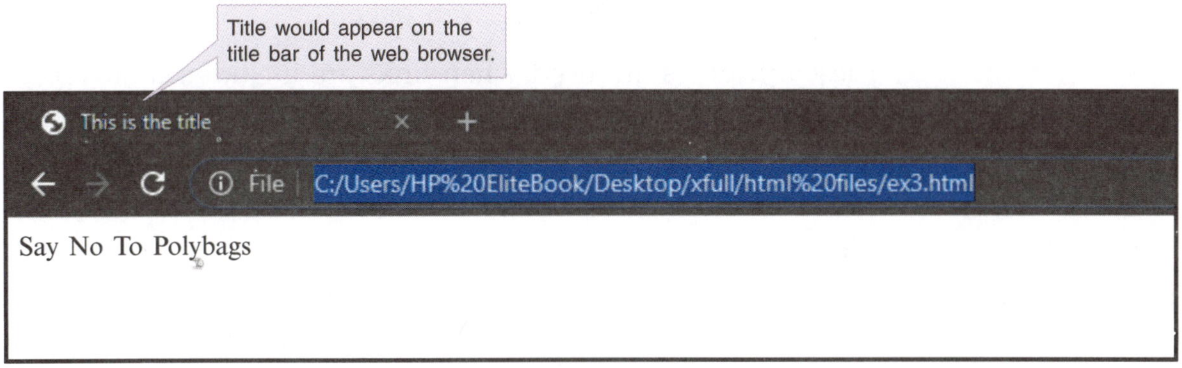

Fig. 5.3: Result of Example 3

5.3.6 Body Element [<BODY>......</BODY>]

The <**BODY**> tag indicates the beginning of the actual text to be printed or displayed and other elements to be executed. The <**/BODY**> tag indicates the end of the text.

Example 4

```
<HTML>
<HEAD>
<TITLE> This is the title </TITLE>
</HEAD>
<BODY> SAY NO TO POLYBAGS
Government has decided to put a ban on the use and manufacturing of recycled polybags.
This would help in reducing pollution and other health hazards.
</BODY>
</HTML>
```

The above HTML document would appear on web as shown in Fig. 5.4.

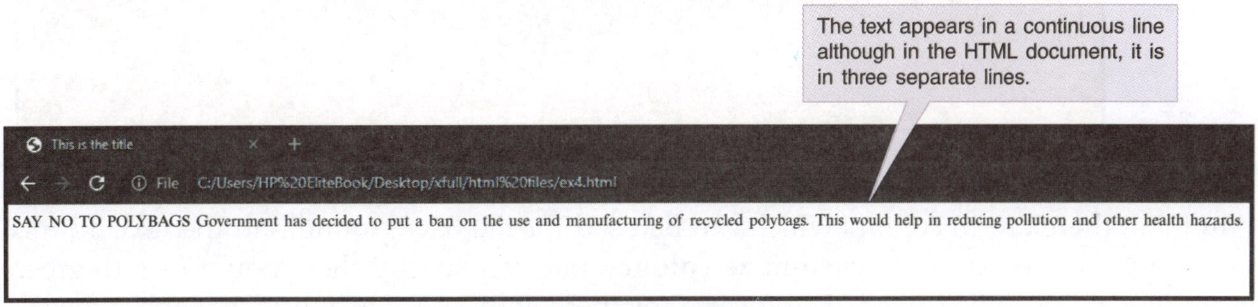

Fig. 5.4: Result of Example 4

Following attributes can be used with <Body> tag:

bgcolor: To set the background colour of the web page.

text: To set the colour of the text on the web page.

background: To set an image as a background for a web page.

leftmargin: To set the left margin on the web page.

topmargin: To set the margin from the top of the web page.

alink, vlink and link: These attributes are used when links are included in a web page and these will be discussed in the next chapter.

Let us learn the usage of these attributes with some examples:

Background and Text Colour

There are various colours like black, white, red, green, blue, yellow, magenta, cyan, purple, gray, lime, maroon, navy, olive, silver and teal (16 to be precise) from which one can choose the colour of the background and of the text. To change the background colour and the text colour, attributes **bgcolor** and **text** are to be used respectively.

Example 5

```
<HTML>
   <HEAD>
      <TITLE>"DISPLAY OF BACKGROUND AND TEXT"</TITLE>
   </HEAD>
   <BODY bgcolor=yellow text =red>
      Mary had a little lamb
      It's fleece was white as snow
   </BODY>
</HTML>
```

Text colour is red

Fig. 5.5: Result of Example 5

In total, there are 16 colours which can be used for the background and the text. To mix one's own colours or say to **customize colours**, one can specify the amount of red, green and blue colour, to be mixed. The format for the colour specification is #rrggbb, where

rr, gg, bb represent the hexadecimal values for red, green and blue colours respectively.

ff — stands for full brightness	00 — stands for 0% of the colour
cc — means 80% of brightness	99 — means 60% of brightness
66 — means 40% of brightness	33 — means 20% of brightness

Therefore #ff0000 would mean bright red and #009999 would mean bluish green.

Example 6

```
<HTML>
  <HEAD>
    <TITLE>"DISPLAY OF BACKGROUND AND TEXT"</TITLE>
  </HEAD>
    <BODY bgcolor=#009999 text =#ff0000>
      Mary had a little lamb
      It's fleece was white as snow
    </BODY>
</HTML>
```

Fig. 5.6: Result of Example 6

Background

An image can be used to form the background of the document by specifying the file name and the path. Such a file name should have either an extension .gif or .jpg. The web browser makes the images in the file appear in the background in tiled pattern. Care should be taken not to choose a bold background as this would suppress the text.

Example 7

```
<HTML>
  <HEAD>
    <TITLE>"DISPLAY OF BACKGROUND IMAGE"</TITLE>
  </HEAD>
    <BODY text = red background="C:\Users\HP EliteBook\Pictures\lamb1.jpg" >
      Mary had a little lamb
      It's fleece was white as snow
    </BODY>
</HTML>
```

Example 7 would appear as shown in Fig. 5.7.

Fig. 5.7: Result of Example 7

Left Margin and Top Margin

The attribute leftmargin sets the left margin of the document.

<BODY leftmargin = 150>

This would set the left margin 150 pixels away from the LHS of the page and the text enclosed between **<BODY>** tags will also be displayed 150 pixels away from the left side of the page.

When the top margin of the document is to be set, we use the following attribute:

<BODY topmargin = 75>

The above statement would make the text in the body of the document appear 75 pixels away from the top.

Example 8

```
<HTML>
  <HEAD>
      <TITLE>"Display of left and top margins"</TITLE>
    </HEAD>
    <BODY topmargin=75  leftmargin=150>
      Mary had a little lamb
      It's fleece was white as snow
    </BODY>
</HTML>
```

Example 8 would appear as shown in Fig. 5.8.

Fig. 5.8: Result of Example 8

5.3.7 Paragraphs [<P>......</P>]

Type the following in an HTML document.

Example 9

```
<HTML>
<HEAD>
<TITLE> PLAY IT COOL WHEN TOUGH TIMES COME </TITLE>
</HEAD>
<BODY> PLAY IT COOL WHEN TOUGH TIMES COME
As fears of an economic downturn grow, cost cutting has become the order of the day and staff
benefits are one of the first expenses to face the axe.
Some large companies are curbing the contributions they make to staff pension funds, and the
city's lifestyle has become less lavish.
</BODY>
</HTML>
```

When viewed using web browser, the above document would appear as shown in Fig. 5.9.

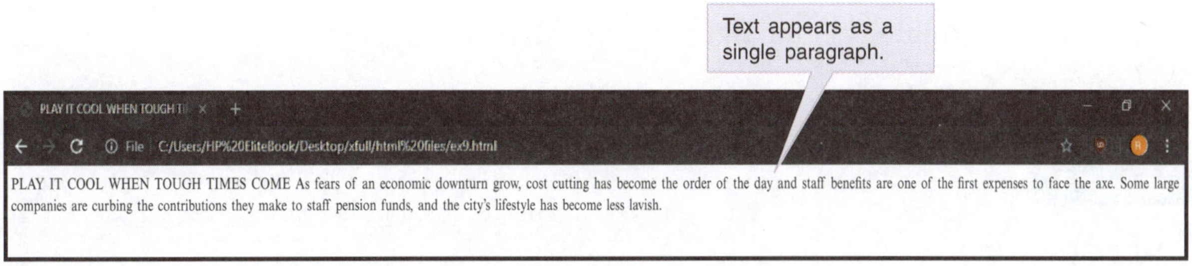

Fig. 5.9: Result of Example 9

Here you might have noticed that in the original HTML document, the body contains two separate paragraphs, but the web browser displays them as a single paragraph. To introduce paragraph breaks, you must use the HTML tag <P> at the beginning of each paragraph and </P> at the end of each paragraph. Let us rewrite our HTML document.

Example 10

```
        <HTML>
        <HEAD>
        <TITLE> PLAY IT COOL WHEN TOUGH TIMES COME </Title>
        </Head>
Para 1 ——<BODY> <P> PLAY IT COOL WHEN TOUGH TIMES COME </P>
Para 2 ——<P> As fears of an economic downturn grow, cost cutting has become the order
        of the day and staff benefits are one of the first expenses to face the axe. </P>
Para 3 ——<P> Some large companies are curbing the contributions they make to staff
        pension funds and the city's lifestyle has become less lavish. </P>
        </BODY>
        </HTML>
```

When the HTML document in the above example is viewed as a web page, the paragraph breaks will appear as shown in Fig. 5.10.

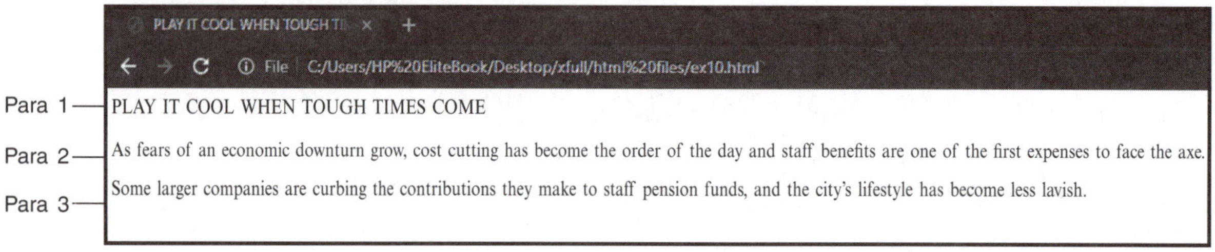

Fig. 5.10: Result of Example 10

The text in the paragraph can be aligned using the align attribute as discussed below:

Text Alignment Attribute

The text can be displayed towards the left margin, the right margin or the centre of the page. To align a paragraph use one of the following attributes inside **<P>** tag at the beginning of the paragraph.

<P align = left>	for left alignment
<P align = right>	for right alignment
<P align = center>	for centre alignment

Example 11

```
<HTML>
<HEAD>
<TITLE> Text Alignment </TITLE>
</HEAD>
<BODY>
```

```
<P align = left> Plants are just as useful indoors as they are outdoors. Naturally, they should be well cared for and appear strong and healthy. Potted plants and freshly cut flowers create a more pleasant environment. Potted indoor plants are a very good option for gifting. </P>
<P align = center> Good quality artificial plants are also effective, but they must be kept dusted and clean. Dried flowers of course should be avoided as they have all the water drained from them. This creates strong negative ch'i. So plants that give out more oxygen should be preferred indoors to purify the air. </P>
<P align = right> As well as encouraging ch'i, plants symbolize life, growth and upwards progress. Plants can be used to remove potential shars created by sharp angles, square columns and long hallways. Thus plants play an important role in our life by keeping our surrounding environment clean and fresh. </P>
</BODY>
</HTML>
```

The above example would appear as shown in Fig. 5.11.

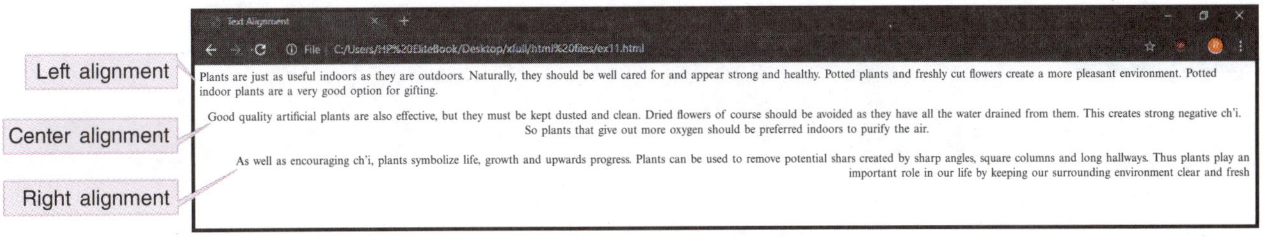

Fig. 5.11: Result of Example 11

5.3.8 Line Break [
]

When the HTML page is displayed by a web browser, it does not take care of carriage returns (end of line) and the number of blank spaces between the words. When the text reaches the edge of the screen, it is wrapped on to the next line. All blank spaces, more than one are reduced to single blank space.

Example 12

```
<HTML>
<HEAD>
<TITLE> MARY'S LAMB </TITLE>
</HEAD>
<BODY> <P> MARY'S LAMB </P>
Mary had a little lamb
Its fleece was white as snow
And everywhere that Mary went
The lamb was sure to go
</BODY>
</HTML>
```

Text in four separate lines

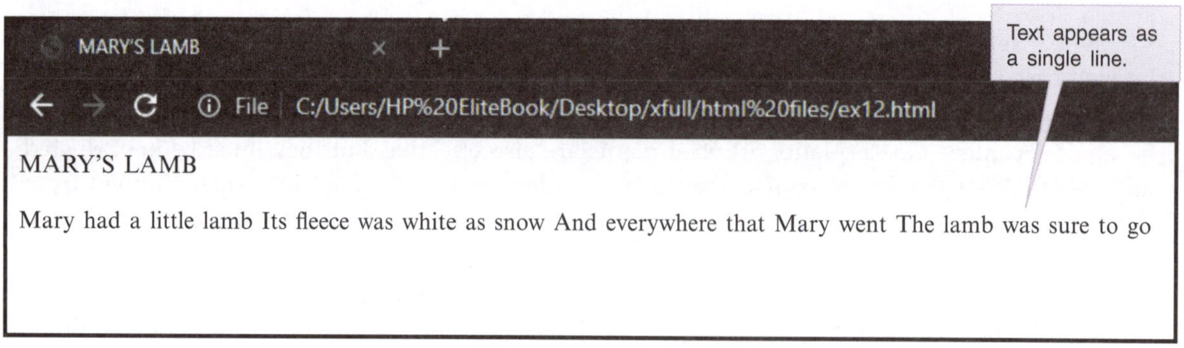

Fig. 5.12: Result of Example 12

Although we have four separate lines in the body of the document, still the text when viewed using a browser, appears as a single line.

One remedy to the problem is to use a paragraph marker, *i.e.*, <**P**> and <**/P**> tags. Let us see how that helps us.

Example 13

```
<HTML>
<HEAD>
<TITLE> Mary's lamb </TITLE>
</HEAD>
<BODY> <P> MARY'S LAMB </P>
<P> Mary had a little lamb </P>
<P> Its fleece was white as snow </P>
<P> And everywhere that Mary went </P>
<P> The lamb was sure to go </P>
</BODY>
</HTML>
```

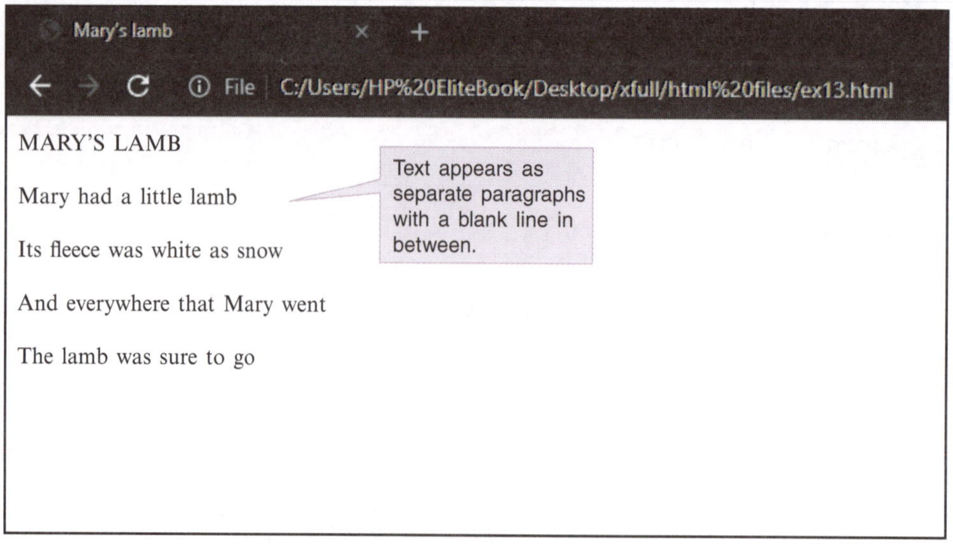

Fig. 5.13: Result of Example 13

In Fig. 5.13 more than one carriage return has occurred between every two lines resulting in blank lines. To avoid blank lines within the text we have another tag called the line break tag **
**. This is an empty tag and thus does not require an OFF tag. Whenever a line break is required (generally at the end of a line)
 is put.

Example 14

```
<HTML>
<HEAD>
<TITLE> MARY'S LAMB </TITLE>
</HEAD>
<BODY> <P> MARY'S LAMB </P>
Mary had a little lamb <BR>
Its fleece was white as snow <BR>
And everywhere that Mary went <BR>
The lamb was sure to go <BR>
</BODY>
</HTML>
```

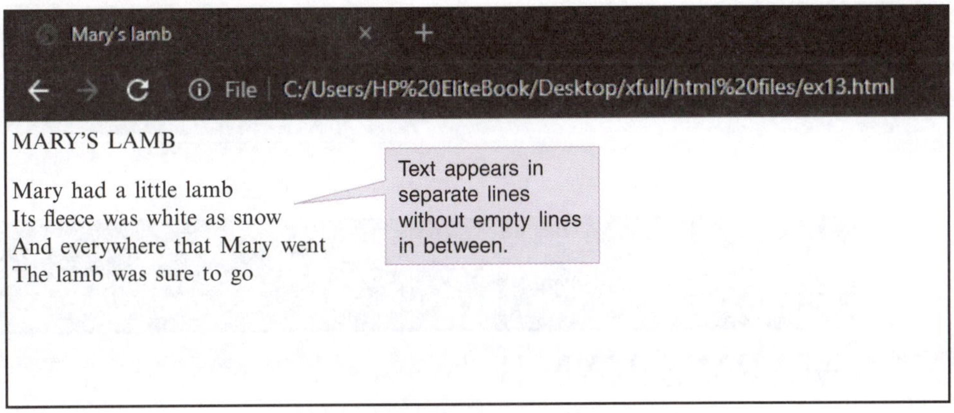

Fig. 5.14: Result of Example 14

5.3.9 Font [<Font>......</FONT>]

This is a container element used to specify the size, colour and font of the text it encloses. It has the following attributes:

Size: It specifies the size of the text.

Color: It specifies the colour of the text.

Face: It specifies the font of the text.

(i) Size

By default the font size of the text within the BODY of the document is 3. You can change the size as per the need by setting the size values between 1 and 7.

Example 15

```
<HTML>
<HEAD>
<TITLE> Mary's lamb </TITLE>
</HEAD>
<BODY>
<FONT SIZE = 6>
MARY'S LAMB <BR>
</FONT>
<FONT SIZE = 4>
Mary had a little lamb <BR>
Its fleece was white as snow <BR>
And everywhere that Mary went. <BR>
The lamb was sure to go <BR>
</FONT>
</BODY>
</HTML>
```

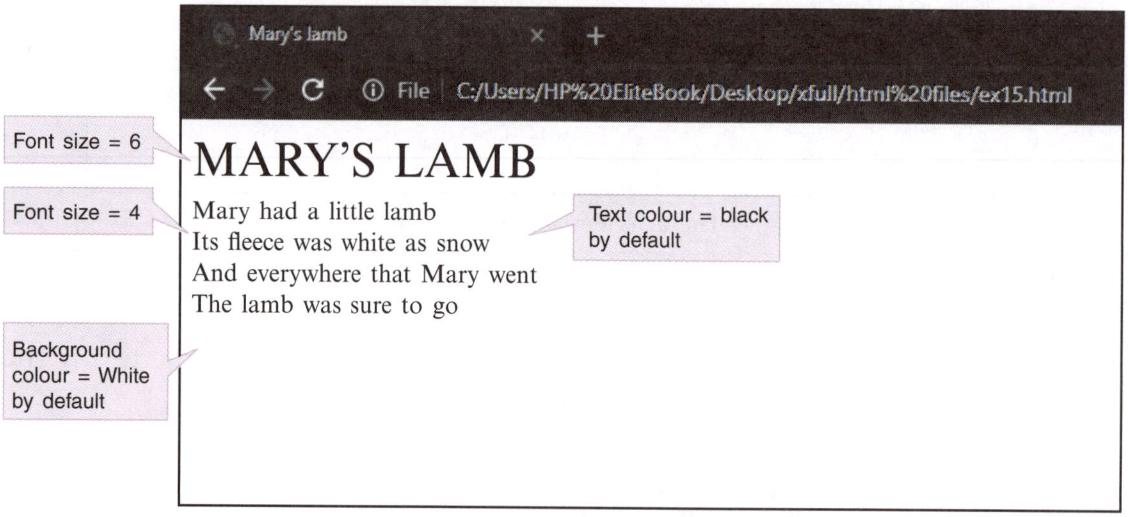

Fig. 5.15: Result of Example 5.15
(No background colour or text colour has been set)

(ii) Colour

The colour of the text can be changed by specifying the standard colour name specified by browser or by giving the hexadecimal values for customised colour selection.

Example 16

```
<HTML>
<HEAD>
<TITLE> MARY'S LAMB </TITLE>
</HEAD>
<BODY>
<FONT SIZE = "6" COLOR = "red">
MARY HAD A LITTLE LAMB <BR>
</FONT>
<FONT SIZE = "4" COLOR = "green">
Mary had a little lamb <BR>
Its fleece was white as snow <BR>
And everywhere that Mary went. <BR>
The lamb was sure to go <BR>
</FONT>
</BODY>
</HTML>
```

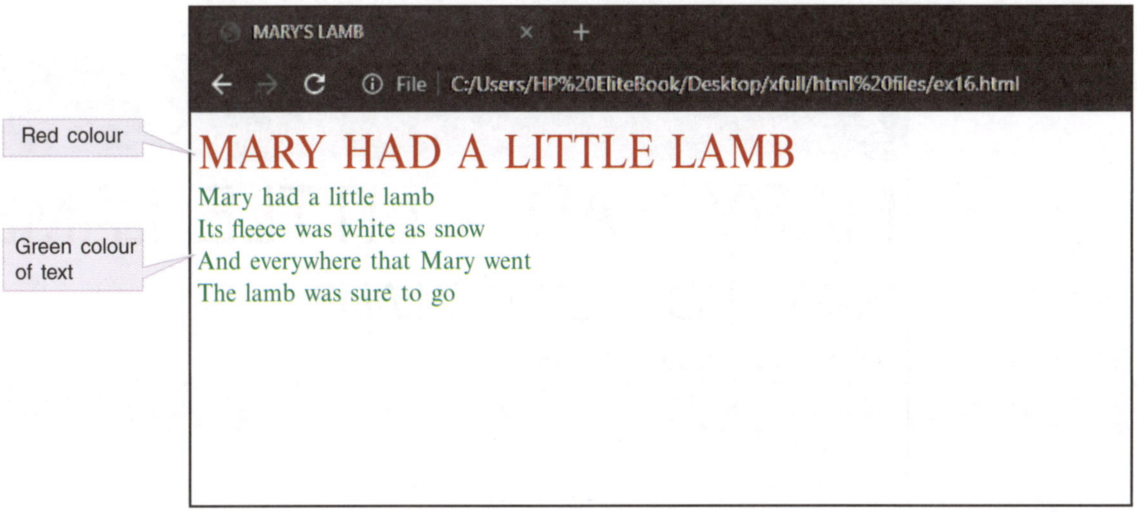

Fig. 5.16: Result of Example 16

(iii) Face

The style in which text is to be written is specified by Face attribute. For example,

<font face = Arial, Comic Sans, Lucida handwriting>

The text enclosed in the font tag will appear as Arial. In case, Arial font is not available then the browser will look for Comic Sans and then for Lucida handwriting, if Comic Sans is also not available. In case none of the specified fonts are available on your computer, browser will display the text using the default font which is usually Times New Roman.

Example 17

```
<HTML>
<HEAD>
<TITLE> MARY'S LAMB </TITLE>
</HEAD>
<BODY>
<FONT  FACE = Arial COLOR = RED SIZE = 8>
MARY HAD A LITTLE LAMB <BR>
</FONT>
<FONT SIZE = 6 COLOR = GREEN>
<FONT FACE = Tahoma>
MARY HAD A LITTLE LAMB <BR>
</FONT>
<FONT FACE = Times New Roman SIZE = 4 COLOR = BLUE>
MARY HAD A LITTLE LAMB <BR>
</FONT>
</BODY>
</HTML>
```

Fig. 5.17: Result of Example 17

5.3.10 BASEFONT [<BASEFONT>]

The <basefont> tag specifies a default text-colour, font-size, or font-family for the text in a document for which no other font-settings are specified. If a new tag affecting the attributes is encountered, basefont becomes dormant. The attributes of the <basefont> tag are size, color and font, similar to the FONT element.

The Example 18 will set the size of the text in the whole web page as 3, in red colour and in the font Arial. But when it encounters <font>, it lets font attributes take over till </font> is encountered. After that BASEFONT attributes again becomes active.

Example 18

```
<html>
  <body  >
    <basefont size=3  color=red  face=Arial>
    <p>Mary had a little lamb <br>
      its fleece was white as snow</p>
    <font  size=5  color=green>
      And everywhere that Mary went<br>
    </font>
    The lamb was sure to go
</body>
</html>
```

Fig. 5.18: Result of Example 18

5.3.11 Bold Face [<b>......</b>]

This is a container tag that lets the text enclosed in it appear as bold text. For example, <**b**> MARY'S LAMB </**b**> will make the text MARY'S LAMB bolder than the rest of the text.

Example 19

```
<html>
<body >
<p>Mary had a little lamb
<b>its fleece was white as snow</b></p>
</body>
</html>
```

Fig. 5.19: Result of Example 19

5.3.12 Italics [<i>...</i>]

For italicized text, you can use **<i>** and **</i>** tags to enclose the text. For the text to be both bold and in italics, use both the tags as done in Example 20.

Example 20

```
<HTML>
<HEAD>
<TITLE> Mary's lamb </TITLE>
</HEAD>
<BODY>
<b> <i> MARY'S LAMB </i> </b> <BR><BR>
Mary had a little lamb <BR>
Its fleece was white as snow <BR>
And everywhere that Mary went <BR>
The lamb was sure to go <BR>
</BODY>
</HTML>
```

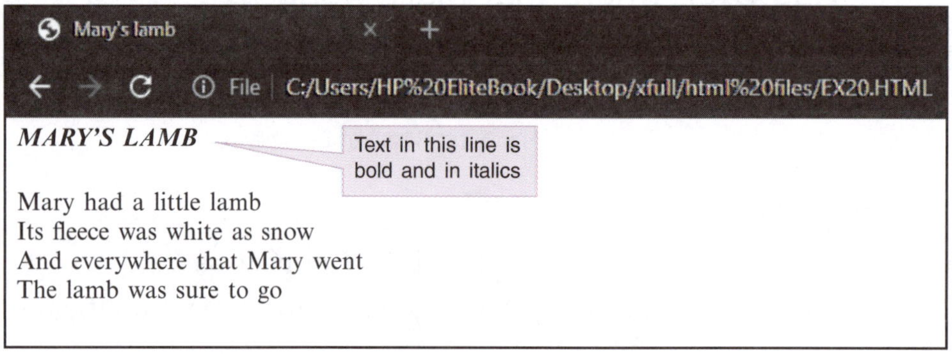

Fig. 5.20: Result of Example 20

5.3.13 Superscript Tag [^{...}]

This container tag **^{** and **}** lets the text enclosed in it appear as superscript as compared to the rest of the text. The superscripts appear a little above the line of text.

Example 21

```
<HTML>
<BODY> <FONT SIZE = "6">
This <sup> example </sup> displays <sup> the </sup> use <sup> of </sup> supscript <sup>
tag </sup>
</FONT>
</BODY>
</HTML>
```

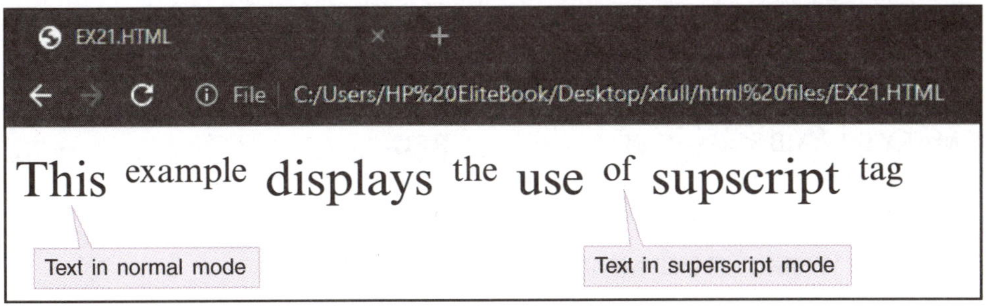

Fig. 5.21: Result of Example 21

5.3.14 Subscript tag [_{...}]

This container tag <**sub**> and <**/sub**> makes the enclosed text appear as subscript. The subscripts appear a little below the line of text.

Example 22

```
<HTML>
<BODY> <FONT SIZE = 6>
This <sub> example </sub> displays <sub> the </sub> use <sub> of </sub> subscript <sub>
tag </sub>
</FONT>
</BODY>
</HTML>
```

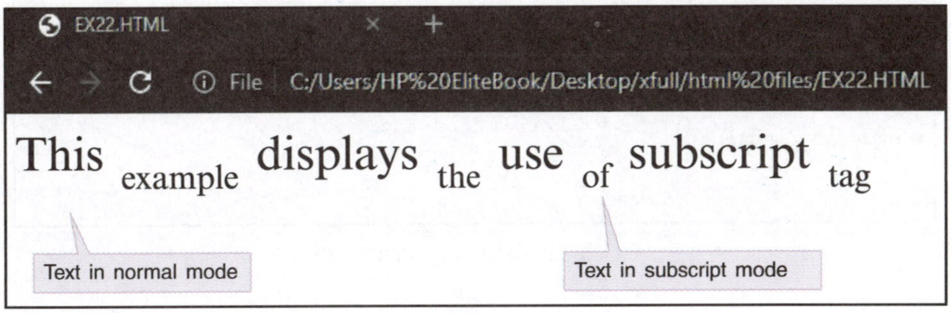

Fig. 5.22: Result of Example 22

5.3.15 Headings [<Hn>...</Hn>]

Sometimes different levels of information have to be displayed on a web page. For this purpose, HTML provides six types of headings ranging from H1 to H6. Of these, H1 is used for the most important heading and H6 for the least important heading.

The heading is a container tag.

Example 23

```
<HTML>
<BODY> MARY'S LAMB <BR> <FONT COLOR = RED>
<H1> MARY HAD A LITTLE LAMB </H1>
<H2> ITS FLEECE WAS WHITE AS SNOW </H2>
<H3> AND EVERYWHERE THAT MARY WENT </H3>
<H4> THE LAMB WAS SURE TO GO </H4>
<H5> SEE THE DIFFERENCE IN </H5>
<H6> THE SIZE AND BOLD TYPE </H6> </FONT>
</BODY>
</HTML>
```

The above example would appear as shown in Fig. 5.23.

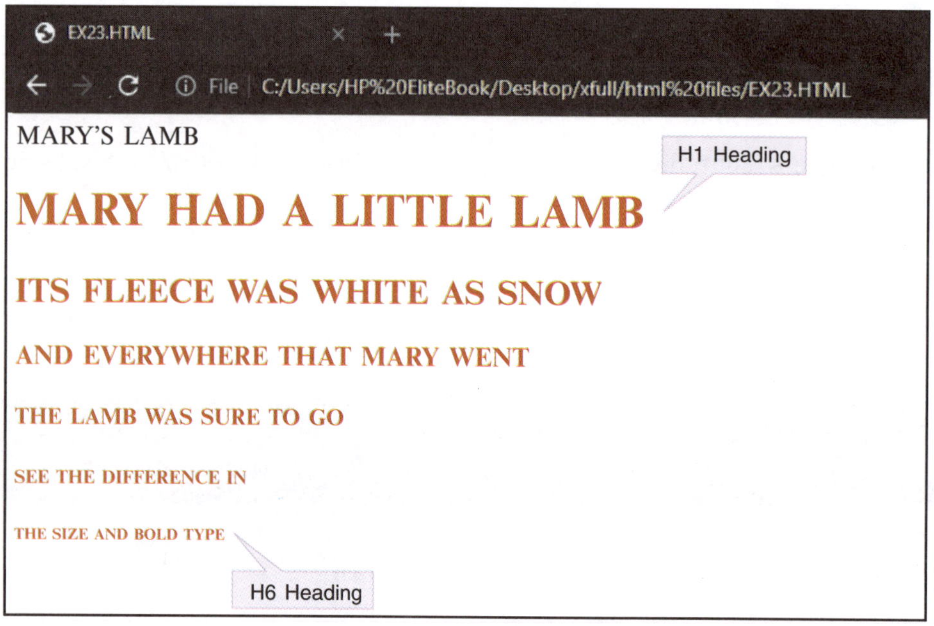

Fig. 5.23: Result of Example 23

5.3.16 HTML Lists

Lists are among the most extensively used elements of the HTML. Lists are used to group together related sections of information in a structured form. They are a way of grabbing the attention of the web page visitor by facilitating him/her to read and scan the content quickly. There are three kinds of HTML lists, namely, **unordered**, **ordered** and **description** lists.

(i) Unordered list [<ul><li>...</li>...</ul>]

Each item of unordered list has a special bullet symbol in front of it. The whole list is enclosed in **<ul>** and **</ul>** tags. Here, <ul> stands for unordered list and the tag used to mention each item of the list is <li>, where <li> stands for list item. Each item of the list should be enclosed within the **<li>** and **</li>** tags for clarity, however </li> closing tag is **optional**.

Example 24

```
<HTML>
<HEAD>
<TITLE> GOOD FORTUNE </TITLE>
</HEAD>
<BODY>
For the Chinese, good fortune is not limited to some chance occurrence of luck,
such as winning a lottery. It also includes <BR>
<ul>
<li> a long and healthy life
<li> a good reputation
<li> a happy marriage
<li> a successful career
</ul>
</BODY>
</HTML>
```

Tags for unordered list

Tags for list items

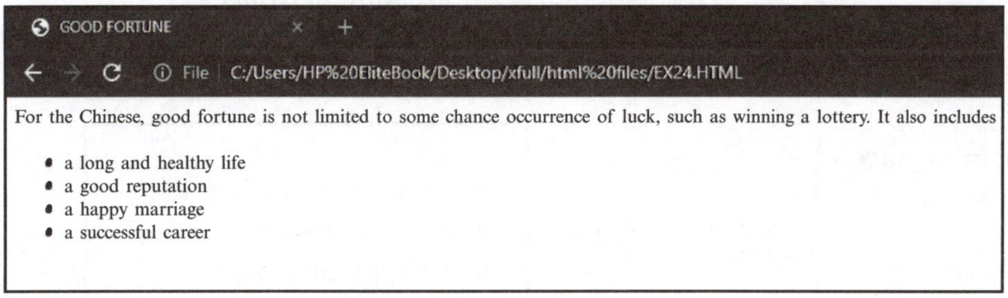

Fig. 5.24: Result of Example 24

(ii) Ordered list [<ol><li>...</li>...</ol>]

The ordered list has number or alphabet in front of each element instead of bullet. The list is enclosed in <ol> and **</ol>** tags, where <ol> stands for ordered list. Each item begins with <li> and ends with **</li>**. Here too, closing tag </li> is **optional**.

Example 25

```
<HTML>
<HEAD>
<TITLE> GOOD FORTUNE </TITLE>
</HEAD>
<BODY>
For the Chinese, good fortune is not limited to some chance occurrence of
luck, such as winning a lottery. It also includes <BR>
<ol>
<li> a long and healthy life
<li> a good reputation
<li> a happy marriage
<li> a successful career
</ol>
</BODY>
</HTML>
```

Tags for ordered list

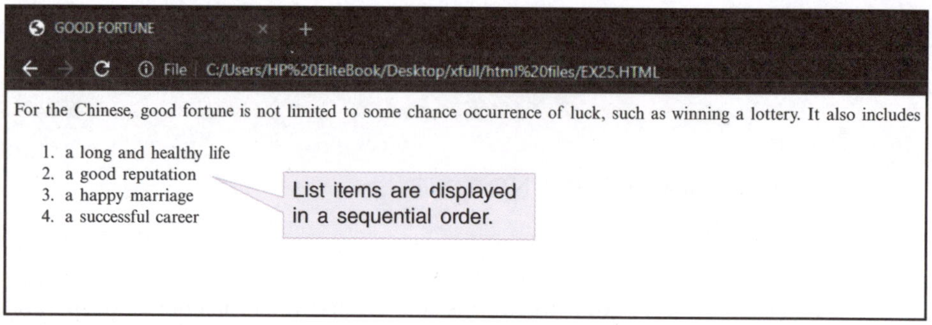

Fig. 5.25: Result of Example 25

Type attribute of <ol> and <ul>

By default, each item of an unordered list is preceded with a bullet. To change the type of bullet from circle to square, disc or none, following commands can be written accordingly:

```
<ul TYPE = DISC>
..........
..........
</ul>
```

for using disc as bullet

- a long and healthy life
- a good reputation
- a happy marriage
- a successful career

```
<ul TYPE = square>
..........
..........
</ul>
```

for using square as bullet

▪ a long and healthy life
▪ a good reputation
▪ a happy marriage
▪ a successful career

In an ordered list, each item can be preceded by either counting numbers (by default starting from one) or Roman numerals or upper case/lower case letters.

A is for upper case letters.

a is for lower case letters.

I is for upper case Roman numbers.

i is for lower case Roman numbers.

For example,

```
<ol TYPE = i>
..........
..........
</ol>
```

The output will be

i. a long and healthy life
ii. a good reputation
iii. a happy marriage
iv. a successful career

The counting in the ordered list can be started from any number even other than one. For this, **START** attribute is used with **TYPE** attribute.

For example,

```
<ol START = 8  TYPE = i>
..........
..........
</ol>
```

The list in the output will be

viii. a long and healthy life
ix. a good reputation
x. a happy marriage
xi. a successful career

(iii) Description or Definition lists [<dl><dt>....<dd>......</dl>]

This is another variety of list in which items are not marked with bullets or numbers but are marked with pattern of **indentation**. The whole list is enclosed in <**dl**> and </**dl**> tags where <dl> stands for description lists. Each item in the list begins with the **description title** tag <**dt**> followed by **description details** tag <dd>. The <dd> tag provides the definition or other related text associated with the term specified using <dt>. Multiple <dt> elements together indicate several terms that are all defined by the immediate next <dd> element.

Example 26

```
<HTML>
<HEAD>
<TITLE> USE OF DESCRIPTION LIST</TITLE>
</HEAD>
<BODY>
<h2>Services provided by Internet</h2>
<dl>
<dt>www:
<dd> commonly known as world wide web, it is the information space
<dd> where web resources are identified by URL
<dt> email:
<dd> message distribution through internet to one or more recipients
</dl>
</BODY>
</HTML>
```

Example 26 would appear as shown in the following figure.

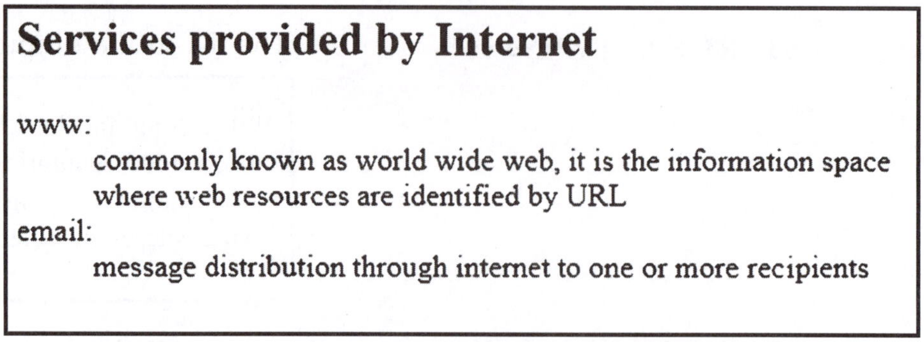

Fig. 5.26: Result of Example 26

5.3.18 Horizontal Rule [<HR>]

The <hr> or horizontal rule tag draws a horizontal line across the page. It is used to separate the sections of a web page. Horizontal rule is an empty tag and allows the following attributes:

align : It controls the alignment (left, right and center).

noshade : It displays the rule as a solid colour.

size : It fixes the thickness of the line in pixels.

width : It fixes the width of the line.

color : It specifies the colour of the line.

The usage of above mentioned attributes is displayed using the following examples.

Example 27

```
<HTML>
<BODY> <FONT COLOR = RED> SIZE = 6
<HR> SAY NO TO PLASTIC BAGS </FONT>
</BODY>
</HTML>
```

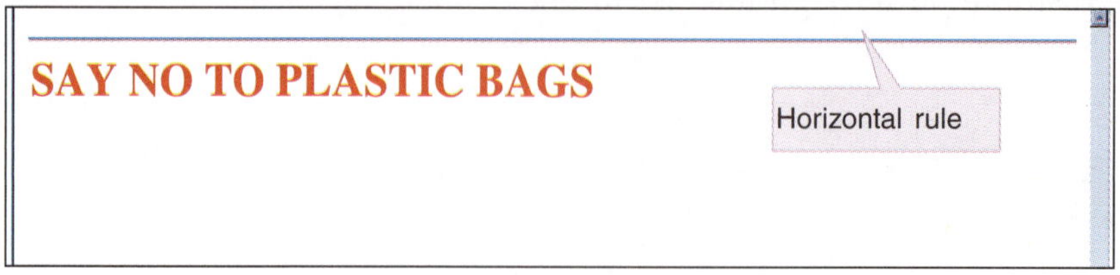

Fig. 5.27: Result of Example 27

Example 28

```
<HTML>
<BODY>
<HR SIZE = 6> <FONT COLOR = RED SIZE = 6>
SAY NO TO PLASTIC BAGS </FONT>
</BODY>
</HTML>
```

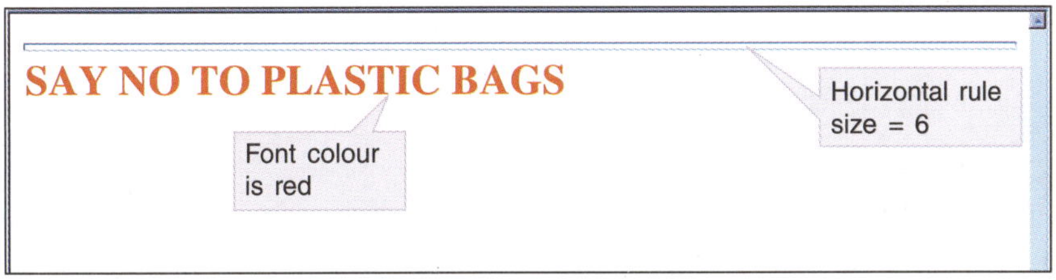

Fig. 5.28: Result of Example 28

Example 29

```
<HTML>
<BODY BGCOLOR = "BLACK">
<HR WIDTH = 75% SIZE = 10> <FONT COLOR = RED SIZE = 6>
SAY NO TO PLASTIC BAGS
</FONT>
</BODY>
</HTML>
```

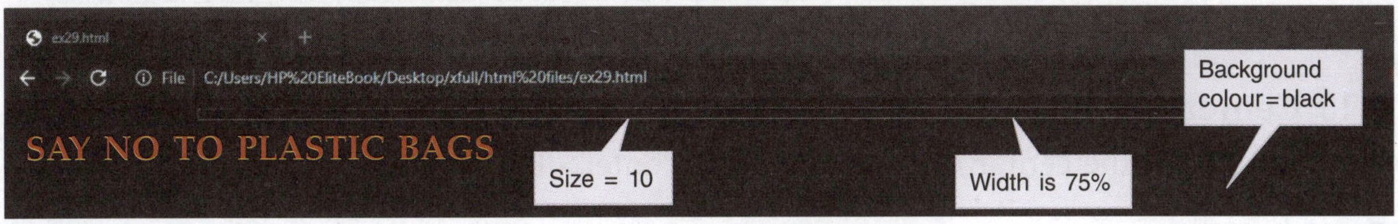

Fig. 5.29: Result of Example 29

Example 30

```
<HTML>
<BODY BGCOLOR = PURPLE>
<FONT SIZE = 6>
<HR ALIGN = LEFT WIDTH = 50%>
SAY NO TO PLASTIC BAGS
</FONT>
</BODY>
</HTML>
```

The above example would appear as shown in Fig. 5.30.

Fig. 5.30: Result of Example 30

Example 31

```
<HTML>
<BODY>
<HR WIDTH = 50% SIZE = 10>
<FONT COLOR = RED>
<H2>SAY NO TO PLASTIC BAGS </H2><BR>
<HR WIDTH = 50% NOSHADE SIZE = 10>
SAVE ENVIRONMENT </FONT>
</BODY>
</HTML>
```

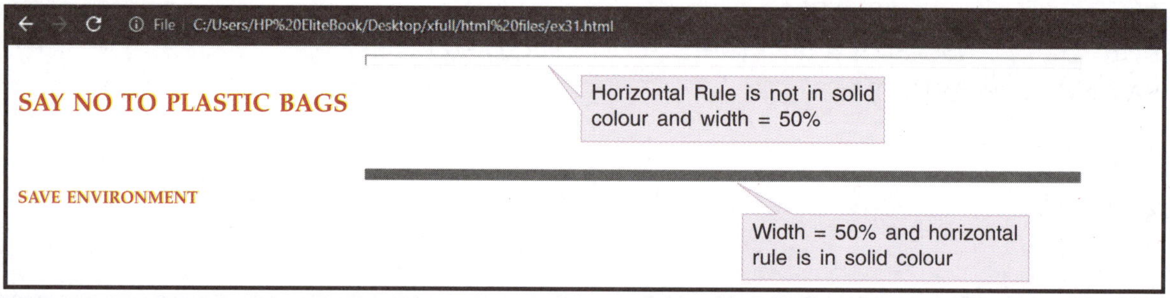

Fig. 5.31: Result of Example 31

5.3.19 Center tag [<Center>......</Center>]

To align a text in the center of the page, the <center> tag is used. It is a container tag.

Example 32

```
<html>
<body bgcolor=pink>
<h1><font color=blue>
<center> Say No to Plastic Bags</center>
</font></h1>
   </body>
</html>
```

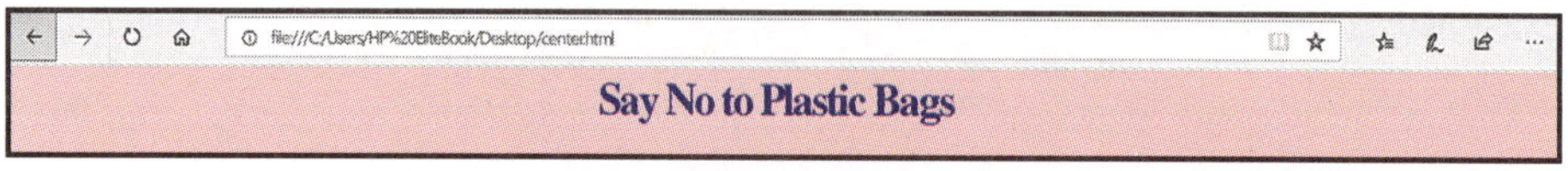

Fig. 5.32: Result of Example 32

5.3.20 Comment Tag

Comments are included in the HTML documents by the user for his/her own understanding. Comments are neither executed nor displayed by the browser. The comment tag is also a container tag and the comment is enclosed in <!– and –> tags.

Example 33

```
<HTML>
<BODY>
<! COMMENTS ARE ONLY FOR EASY UNDERSTANDING OF THE DOCUMENT->
<FONT COLOR = RED>
TEXT ENCLOSED IN BODY TAG IS PRINTED ON THE WEB PAGE
</FONT>
</BODY>
</HTML>
```

The above example would appear as shown in Fig. 5.33.

Fig. 5.33: Result of Example 33

KEY TERMS

HTML tags The keywords which tell the browser how to display and format the contents of the web page.

Attributes The additional specifications used with tags and related to the tag.

Container elements The elements having an opening tag and a closing tag.

Empty elements The elements which do not have a closing tag.

Lists To group together related sections of information in a structured form.

Unordered list Displays the items in a list with a bullet like symbol in front of them.

Ordered list Displays the items in a list with a serial number.

Description lists or definition lists Display the description of some terms in a list.

POINTS TO REMEMBER

- Web pages are written using Hyper text Markup Language (HTML) which allows organising and formatting the text and linking the pages.
- Any text editor like Notepad, MS Word, etc. can be used to write an HTML document.
- The HTML document has an extension .htm or .html.
- To view the output of an HTML document we need a web browser like Google Chrome.
- HTML document has a head and a body.
- HTML tags are enclosed in angle brackets <> and do not appear on the web page.
- Every container element appears twice in a document and empty elements do not require the OFF tag.
- The HTML, HEAD and TITLE elements appear in the head part of the document.
- Many tags have attributes, e.g., FONT has attributes like SIZE, COLOR, FACE, etc.
- Text can be displayed towards left margin, right margin or centre of the page.
- HTML provides six types of heading ranging from H1 to H6.
- HTML document can create unordered, ordered or definition list on the web page.
- Horizontal rule draws a horizontal line across the page to separate the section of a web page.
- Comments are included in the HTML documents by the users for their own understanding.

SOLVED QUESTIONS

Q1. How will you display ($C_6H_{12}O_2$) on a web page?

Ans. C ₆ H ₁₂ O ₆.

Q2. Differentiate between Homepage and Website.

Ans. Homepage is the introductory page of a website which has links to other pages of the website or external web pages. It acts like an index for the website.

Q3. What do you mean by 'source code' of the current page viewed in a Web Browser?

Ans. Source code is the HTML code written using a text editor.

Q4. How can we start a list with S. No. 3?

Ans. <OL start = 3>

Q5. While writing a HTML code, how can one find out what the web page would look like?

Ans. The file having HTML code can be opened in a web browser to find out what the web page would look like.

Q6. Which of the given attributes is not supported by <HR> tag?

Size, color, length, width

Ans. <HR> tag does not support length attribute.

Q8. What is the error in the following code?

<UL type = a start = 8 >

Ans. <UL> is used with unordered list where members of the list are not preceded by any serial number so start attribute does not work with it.

Q9. Identify at least one tag used at the marked points in the following web page.

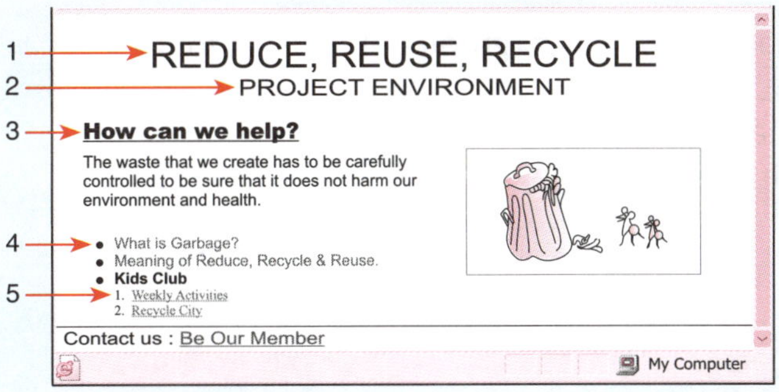

Ans. 1. <h1> is used along with <center>.
2.<h2> is used along with <center>.
3.<b> is used to make the text bold.
4.<u> is for underlining the text.
5.<ul> is used for unordered list.
6.<ol> is used for ordered list.

Q10. Write an HTML code to display the following description list.

Homonyms:

Each of two or more words having the same spelling or pronunciation but different meanings and origins.

Bark -
- a tree's out layer
- the sound a dog makes

Bat -
- an implement used to hit a ball
- a nocturnal flying mammal

Bright -
- Very smart or intelligent
- filled with light

Ans.
```
<html>
<body bgcolor=pink>
 <dl><h3><font  color=red> Homonyms : </font></h3><br>
<font leftmargin=25   color=blue>Each of two or more words having the same <br>
spelling or pronunciation but different meanings and origins.</font><br><br>
<dt><font  leftmargin=50  color=green > Bark - </font>
<ul>
<dd><li>a tree's out layer
      <li>the sound a dog makes
</ul>
<dt><font  leftmargin=50  color=green >Bat -</font>
<ul>
<dd><li> an implement used to hit a ball
      <li> a nocturnal flying mammal
```

```
</ul>

<dt><font leftmargin=50 color=green >Bright - </font>
<ul>
<dd><li>very smart or intelligent
     <li>filled with light
</ul>
</dl>
</boby>
</html>
```

EXERCISES

I. Very Short Answer Type Questions

Multiple Choice Questions:

1. HTML stands for .
   (a) Hyper Text Makeup Language (b) Hyper Text Markup Language
   (c) Hyper Text Machine Language (d) Heavy Text Making Language
2. Hypertext is the text stored in
   (a) Encoded form (b) Electronic form (c) Capital letters (d) Pictorial form
3. HTML documents include
   (a) Text (b) Graphics (c) Sound (d) Animation effects
   (e) All of the above
4. HTML file can be edited with
   (a) Windows Notepad (b) MS Word
   (c) Word Perfect (d) Any of the above
5. To break text into paragraphs, we use
   (a) <P> tag (b)
 tag (c) <L> tag
   (d) Write the text in different paragraph
6. The format for colour specification in HTML is
   (a) *rgbrgb (b) #rrggbb (c) /rrggbb (d) rrggbb
7. #ff0000 would mean
   (a) bright red colour (b) bright blue colour
   (c) bright green colour (d) a mixed colour
8. Top margin = 45, here 45 means
   (a) 45 mm (b) 45 cm (c) 45 pixels (d) 45 rows
9. FACE attribute specifies
   (a) style of text i.e., font (b) size of text
   (c) boldness of text (d) all of the above
10. The most important headings in HTML document are given using the tag
    (a) H1 (b) H6 (c) H3 (d) H4
11. In an unordered list, it is necessary to enclose each item in
    (a) <li> tag (b) <ul> tag (c) <i> tag (d) <ol> tag

Fill in the blanks:

1. The HTML stands for ....
2. Any HTML document can be created using .... or .... package.
3. The HTML document has an extension .... or ....
4. The output of an HTML document can be viewed using the ....
5. An HTML document has two parts .... and ....
6. The title of the page is entered in .... part of an HTML document.
7. The title of page is enclosed in .... and .... tags.
8. The head section of an HTML page is enclosed in .... and ....
9. The body section of an HTML page is enclosed in .... and ....
10. HTML has two types of elements— .... and ....
11. The container elements are enclosed in .... and .... tags.
12. The elements with only one tag (ON tag) are called ....
13. The beginning and end of an HTML document is delimited by .... element.
14. The title of the document .... (is/is not) displayed in the text of the document.
15. The body element is a .... element.
16. If an image is to be included in an HTML document, it should have .... or .... extension.
17. While using LEFT MARGIN attribute, the number represents ....
18. With font size attribute, ... is the default value of the font size and the valid values range from .... to ....
19. The name of the font can be changed using .... attribute.
20. The line break is given through .... element.
21. The <HR> element draws a .... across the page.
22. .... tag is used to underline the text.
23. .... element is used to show a list item.
24. <H1> tag is an .... tag.
25. For displaying an unordered list, ... tag is used.
26. FACE attribute specifies ....
27. .... are enclosed in angle brackets and do not appear on the web page.
28. Anything written in < > in an HTML document is called a ....
29. .... elements appear twice in an HTML document, once within < > and second time within </ >.
30. .... tag lets the browser know that the document is an HTML document.
31. .... tag is a container tag and appears in the head portion of an HTML document.
32. .... tag encloses the heading which appears on the title bar of web browser.

33. To introduce paragraph breaks, we must use the HTML tag .... at the beginning and .... at the end of each paragraph.
34. HTML provides the heading ranging from .... to ....
35. HTML lists are basically of ...., ... and .... types.
36. <li> tag in an .... list will display sequence numbers.
37. <li> tag in an .... list will display bullets.

II. Short Answer Type Questions

1. What is HTML?
2. Which software can be used to create an HTML document?
3. What should be the extension of an HTML document?
4. Which software is used for viewing an HTML document as a web page?
5. What are the three basic tags of an HTML document?
6. What is contained in the Head section of an HTML document?
7. What are the two types of HTML elements?
8. How can a picture be used as a background for a document?
9. What is the use of the <FONT> tag? Write any two attributes used with this tag.
10. How can the font size of a single line or a web page be changed?
11. How can a horizontal line be inserted in a web page?
12. What is the method of using headings in HTML?
13. What is the difference between <P> and <BR> tag?
14. How can the style of numbering in an ordered list be changed?
15. What is the purpose of:
    (i) <BODY> tag (ii) Type attribute used with lists?
16. How can you view the source code of current page in web browser?

III. Long Answer Type Questions

1. Differentiate between container and empty element.
2. What are the three modes of text alignment? How are they achieved?
3. What is the use of the comment element? How is it used?
4. Differentiate between an ordered list and an unordered list. Specify the tags used for them.
5. Which tag do we use to change the size and style of the text of an HTML file viewed on a web browser? Also, explain any two attributes used with this tag.
6. What are attributes? How do they differ from elements?

IV. Application Based Questions

1. Mr. Sharma noticed a lot of water getting wasted in his surroundings.

   He wants to design a web page which would look somewhat like the one shown in figure alongside. Write an HTML document for designing the web page.

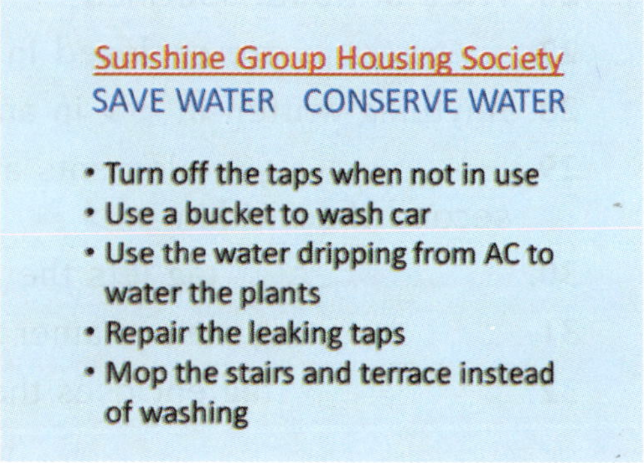

2. Identify three tags used in the HTML code for the following web page:

3. Write ane HTML code for the following: (2)

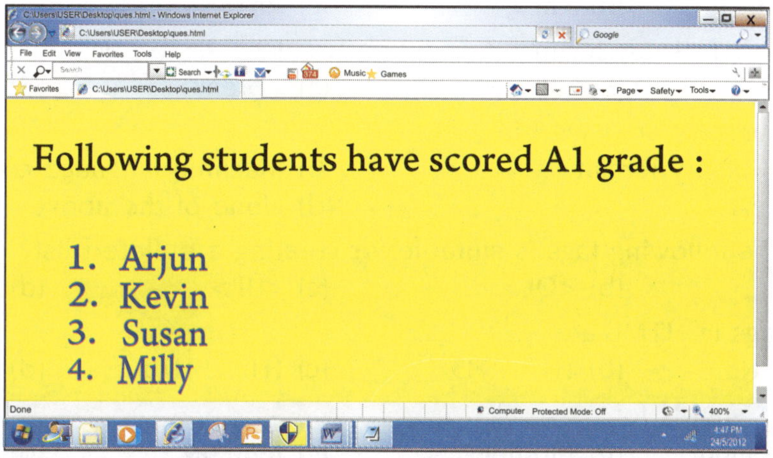

4. Write an HTML code to make the following list:

Components of a Computer System:

Input Unit:

This unit takes input from the user with the help of any of the following input devices:

Keyboard

Mouse

Scanner

Central Processing Unit:

This unit is responsible for controlling the units of a computer system. It also stores data temporarily while performing the arithmetic and logical operations on it. It has the following sub-units:

Control Unit

ALU

Memory

Output Unit:

This unit provides the user with the output which may be on:

Printer

VDU

Previous Years' Solved Examination Questions

I. Very Short Answer Type Questions

Multiple Choice Questions:

1. HTML tag to convert a regular text into heading:
   (a) H1...H6 (b) <HEADING> (c) <HEAD> (d) <TITLE> (2017)
2. FACE and SIZE are the attributes of .... tag(s). (2018, 2018C)
   (a) FONT (b) BASEFONT (c) H1...H6 (d) Both (a) and (b)
3. What is the correct HTML tag for adding a background colour? (2017)
   (a) <body color = "yellow"> (b) <body bgcolor = "yellow">
   (c) <background > yellow </background> (d) <body background = "yellow">
4. Choose the correct HTML tag for the smallest size heading. (2017)
   (a) <heading> (b) <h6> (c) <h1> (d) <head>
5. What is the HTML tag for inserting a line break? (2017)
   (a)
 (b) <lb> (c) <break> (d) <newline>
6. HTML documents are saved in .... (2017)
   (a) Special binary format (b) Machine language code
   (c) ASCII text (d) None of the above
7. Which of the following tags is suitable for creating a bulleted list? (2011,2016)
   (a) <BL> (b) <OL> (c) <UL> (d) <DL>
8. Heading tags in HTML are .... (2019)
   (a) H1 .... H6 (b) H1 ... H5 (c) H1 ... H10 (d) H1 ... H8
9. M in HTML stands for .... (2019)
   (a) Management (b) Modified (c) Markup (d) Machine
10. <HR> tag inserts .... in a web page. (2016)
    (a) a straight line (b) a circle (c) a border (d) none of these
11. Choose HTML tag for the largest heading. (2016)
    (a) H1 (b) H6 (c) <Big heading> (d) <H size = 1>
12. Which attribute is not valid for <body> tag? (2016)
    (a) Bgcolor (b) color (c) Text (d) Top margin
13. A total of how many headings are there in HTML?
    (a) 4 (b) 7 (c) 6 (d) 8
14. How can we make attributes with multiple values? (2017)
    (a) <myElement myAttribute = "value1 value 2">
    (b) <myElement myAttribute = "value1" myAttribute = "value2">
    (c) <myElement myAttribute = "value1, value 2">
    (d) Attributes cannot have multiple values.
15. To create an HTML document, you require a (2017)
    (a) web page editing software (b) High powered computer
    (c) just Notepad software (d) None of the above

Answers: **1.** (a) **2.** (d) **3.** (b) **4.** (b) **5.** (a) **6.** (a) **7.** (c) **8.** (a) **9.** (c) **10.** (a) **11.** (a) **12.** (b) **13.** (c) **14.** (d) **15.** (c)

Fill in the blanks:

1. A tag that requires an opening as well as a closing tag is called a .... tag.(2017)
2. The .... tag provides additional information including title, scripts used, etc. about a web page. (2017)

3. <HR> tag is used for .... (2014)
4. .... tag is used to insert line break on a web page. (2013)
5. .... tag is used to create a subscript. (2011)
6. .... tag creates a bulleted list. (2011)
7. .... attribute with <HR> tag is used to define the thickness of the line. (2015)

Answers:

1. Container 2. <title> 3. Horizontal Rule 4.
5. <SUB> 6. <UL> 7. WIDTH

True/False:

1. An attribute defines a property of an element. (2017)
2. HTML tags tell a web browser how to render a web page. (2017)
3. <I> tag displays text in bold. (2016)
4. <Head> defines the HTML header and does not affect the appearance of the document if CSS is not used. (2016)

Answers:

1. True 2. True 3. False 4. True

II. Short Answer Type Questions

1. Write the full forms of: (2016C, 2013)
   (i) <DL> (ii)
 (iii) <SUP> (iv) <P>
2. Identify which of the following is a tag or an attribute. (2016C)
   (i) HR (ii) BR (iii) P (iv) Align
   (v) Text
3. Identify which of the following is a tag or an attribute. (2017)
   (i) Align (ii) Color (iii) Font (iv) Noshade
4. Write HTML code to generate the web page as shown below having lists in the given style. (2018)

   Stream Options
   1. Science
      ◦ With Maths
      ◦ Without Maths
   2. Commerce
   3. Humanities
5. Differentiate between <OL> and <UL> tag with suitable examples. (2018, 2018C)
6. Differentiate between ^{...} and _{.....}tags with suitable example of each. (2019)

Answers:

1. (i) <DL> – Description List
   (ii)
 – Break
   (iii) <SUP> – Superscript
   (iv) <P> – Paragraph
2. (i) <HR> – tag
   (ii)
 – tag
   (iii) <P> – tag
   (iv) Align – Attribute
   (v) Text – Attribute

3. (i) Align – Attribute
   (ii) Color – Attribute
   (iii) <Font> – tag
   (iv) Noshade – Attribute

4.
```
<H3> Stream options </H3>
<OL>
<li> Science>
<ul type = circle>
<li> With Maths
<li> Without Maths
</ul>
<li> Commerce
<li> Humanities
</OL>
```

5. <OL> stands for Ordered List which can be either numerical or alphabetical while <UL> stands for Unordered List which can be either disc, square or circle.
   Code examples containing <OL> and <UL> is given below with their respective outputs:

HTML CODE AND OUTPUT	HTML CODE AND OUTPUT
Code	**Code**
Hobbies	Hobbies
<OL>	<UL>
<LI>Games	<LI>Games
<LI>Programming	<LI>Programming
<LI>Dramatics	<LI>Dramatics
</OL>	</UL>
Output	**Output**
Hobbies	Hobbies
1. Games	• Games
2. Programming	• Programming
3. Dramatics	• Dramatics

6. The <sup> tag defines superscript text. Superscript text appears half a character above the normal line, and is displayed in a smaller font.
   For example:
   a ² + b ² will be displayed as $a^2 + b^2$.
   The <sub> tag defines subscript text. Subscript text appears half a character below the normal line, and is displayed in a smaller font.
   For example:
   H ₂ + O will be displayed as H_2O.

HTML Continued

6

Insertion of images using the element IMG (Attributes: SRC, WIDTH, HEIGHT, ALT, ALIGN), Superscript SUP, Subscript SUB, Creating Table TABLE (BACKGROUND, BGCOLOR, WIDTH, CELLSPACING, CELLPADDING, BORDER), TR, TD, ROWSPAN, COLSPAN, Internal and External Linking between Web Pages: Significance of linking, A - Anchor Element (Attributes: NAME, HREF, TITLE, ALT MAILTO), Target attribute, Embed audio and video, HTML forms: Textbox, radio buttons, checkbox, password, list, combobox, Cascading style sheets (CSS)

In the previous chapter the basic elements of HTML were discussed which were mainly related to text. A web page does not have only text, it can have images, tables, audio and video links, hyperlinks, mailing links and forms. This chapter deals with all these features that help in making the web page more attractive, informative and interactive. The later part of the chapter explains the use of CSS that are used to control the layout of a single web page or multiple web pages all at once.

6.1 INSERTION OF IMAGES [<IMG>]

Images with the extension **.gif** or **.jpg** can be inserted on a web page but they should be stored in the same folder as the HTML file. To insert an image, we use **<IMG> tag**.

The following attributes are used with <IMG> tag.

(i) SRC

This attribute has a pathname of the image file enclosed in double quotes as its value and should always be enclosed in <IMG> tag.

Example 1

```
<HTML>
<BODY>
<H1> A BEAUTIFUL SUNSET </H1>
<IMG SRC = "SUNSET.JPG"><BR><BR><BR>
</BODY>
</HTML>
```

Source of image

Pathname of image

OUTPUT:

Fig. 6.1: Result of Example 1

(ii) ALT

As graphic images take a bit longer to appear or may not appear, due to some problem; we can meanwhile display a message, i.e., some text about the image at the place where the image is to appear. This is done by using **ALT attribute**. In the following example, SUNSET is the alternate text which gets displayed when we move the mouse pointer in the image placeholders.

Example 2

```
<HTML>
<BODY>
<IMG SRC="SUNSET.JPG" ALT="SUNSET">
<H1> A BEAUTIFUL SUNSET </H1>
</BODY>
</HTML>
```

(iii) Width and Height

The width and height of an image can be specified within <IMG> tag. In case you do not have any idea about the dimensions of the image, you can use PaintShop to view the image and know its exact height and width.

Example 3

```
<HTML>
<BODY>
<IMG SRC = "SUNSET.JPG" WIDTH = 30% HEIGHT = 30%>
<FONT COLOR = RED>
<H1> A BEAUTIFUL SUNSET</H1> </FONT>
</BODY>
</HTML>
```

OUTPUT:

Fig. 6.2: Result of Example 3

(iv) Align

An image can aligned with the text by using the align attribute which can take the following:

TOP: image will be aligned with the top of the tallest letter of the text in the line

BOTTOM: image will be aligned with the bottom of the lowest letter of the text in the line

MIDDLE: image will be aligned w.r.t the middle of the top of the tallest letter of the text in the line

LEFT: image will be aligned with the left margin of the page

RIGHT: image will be aligned with the right margin of the page

CENTER: image will be aligned with the centre of the page

Example 4.1 displays the use of left attribute, example 4.2 uses top, middle and bottom attributes and example 4.3 shows the use of center attribute.

Example 4.1

```
<HTML>
<BODY>
<BR>
<H1>A BEAUTIFUL SUNSET</H1>
<IMG SRC="SUNSET.JPG"  ALIGN="LEFT"   HEIGHT="20%"  WIDTH="20%">
Sunset, also known as sundown, is the daily disappearance of the Sun <BR> below the horizon
due to Earth's rotation. As viewed from the Equator, the <BR> equinox Sun sets exactly due
west  in both spring and fall. As viewed from the<BR> middle latitudes, the local summer Sun
sets to he northwest for the Northern<BR> Hemisphere, but to the southwest for the Southern
Hemisphere.
</BODY>
</HTML>
```

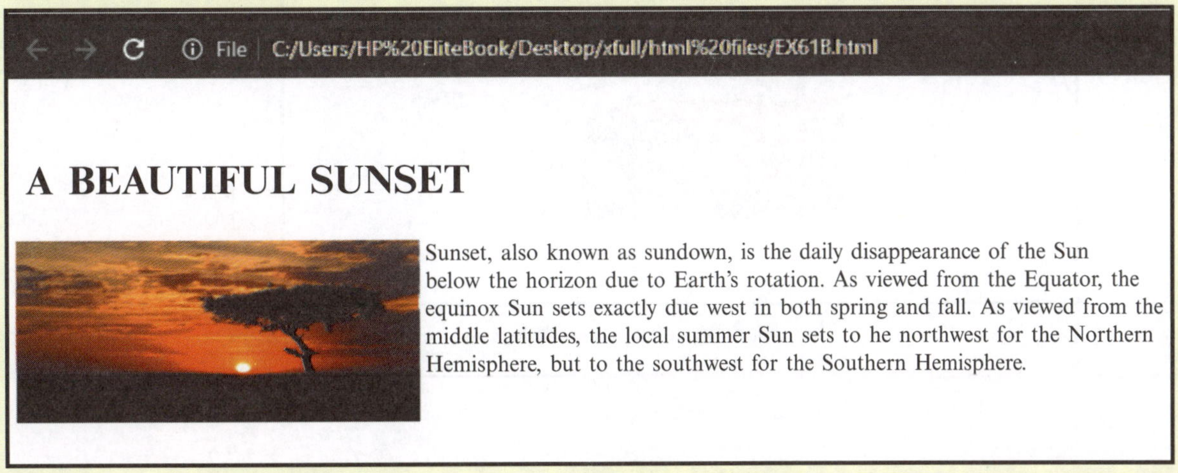

Fig 6.3: Left aligned

Example 4.2

```
<HTML>
<BODY>
<BR><BR><BR><BR><BR><BR>
<H1>A BEAUTIFUL <IMG SRC="SUNSET.JPG" WIDTH ="10%" HEIGHT="10% "
ALIGN="TOP">SUNSET</H1>
<BR><BR><BR><BR>
<H1>A BEAUTIFUL <IMG SRC="SUNSET.JPG" WIDTH ="10%" HEIGHT="10% "
ALIGN="BOTTOM">SUNSET</H1>
<BR><BR><BR><BR>
<H1>A BEAUTIFUL <IMG SRC="SUNSET.JPG" WIDTH ="10%" HEIGHT="10% "
ALIGN="MIDDLE">SUNSET</H1>
<BR><BR><BR><BR>
</BODY>
</HTML>
```

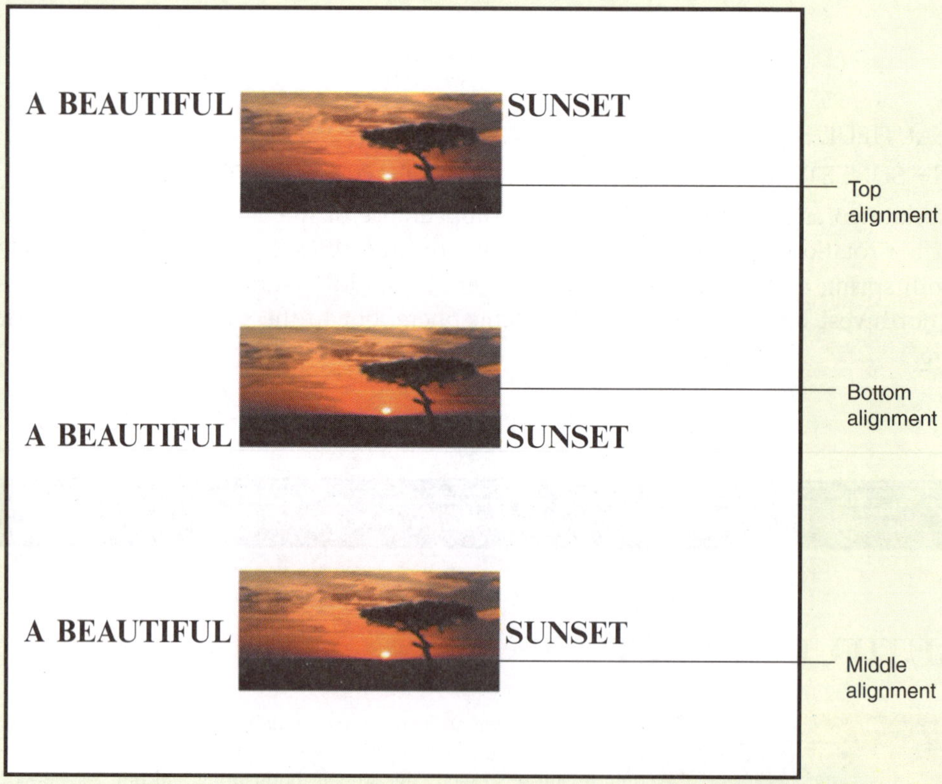

Fig. 6.4 Alignment of image with text

Example 4.3

```
<HTML>
<BODY>
<BR>
<H1 ALIGN="CENTER">A BEAUTIFUL SUNSET</H1>
<CENTER>
<IMG SRC="SUNSET.JPG"  HEIGHT="50%"  WIDTH="50%">
</CENTER>
<P  ALIGN="CENTER" >Sunset, also known as sundown, is the daily disappearance of the Sun
<BR>
below the horizon due to Earth's rotation. As viewed from the Equator, the <BR>
equinox Sun sets exactly due west  in both spring and fall. As viewed from the<BR>
middle latitudes, the local summer Sun sets to he northwest for the Northern<BR>
Hemisphere, but to the southwest for the Southern Hemisphere.</P>

</BODY>
</HTML>
```

Fig. 6.5: Center aligned

(v) Border

You can also apply/set a border around the image to be inserted. The image can also have a border of various widths. Like height and width attributes, the **BORDER attribute** is also enclosed in <IMG> tag. The following example displays two copies of the same picture, one with a thin border and other with a thick border. You can adjust the width of the border according to your own requirement.

Example 5

```
<HTML>
<BODY>
<IMG SRC="SUNSET.JPG" WIDTH=30% HEIGHT=30%
BORDER=10>
<BR>
<BR>
<BR>
<IMG SRC="SUNSET.JPG" WIDTH=30% HEIGHT=30%
BORDER=4>
</BODY>
</HTML>
```

OUTPUT:

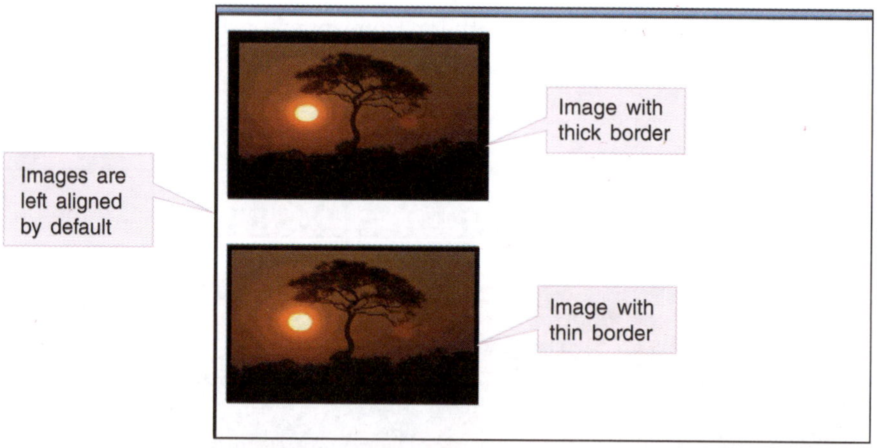

Fig. 6.6: Result of Example 5

6.2 INTERNAL AND EXTERNAL LINKING BETWEEN WEB PAGES

Sometimes you may come across a document which is very lengthy. It may have information related to many topics and presenting such informtion in the form of a single web page might prove to be very cumbersome and unattractive. HTML provides two different ways to view such documents. We can display the topic headings in one main document and their related information on another single document or on separate documents. Clicking on one of the headings from the main document will then lead us to its related information by opening the related document. This is called **linking**.

Linking is achieved by using the **Anchor tag**, i.e., **<A> </A>** with **HREF**, **NAME**, **mailto** and **TARGET** as its attributes.

6.2.1 Anchor Tag [<A>...</A>]

This is a container tag and the address of the link is displayed between **<A>** and **</A>** using **HREF**. *For example,*

```
<A HREF="SAMPLE.HTML"> click here </A>
```

The web browser will display **click here** in blue. This text will act as a link to the file Sample.html. When you click on this text, the document named Sample.html will be opened, provided it exists in your directory.

The attributes used with anchor tag are explained below:

(i) HREF

HREF stands for hypertext reference. This reference could be the URL (Uniform Resource Locator) which is the Internet address or the name of an HTML document which exists in your directory or full address of the HTML document existing in another folder of another directory. *For example,*

```
<A HREF="http://yahoo.com/animals/dengo.html"> click here </A>
```

OR

```
<A HREF="Sample.html"> enter </A>
```

Example 6 H321.HTML (External Linking: Links to external HTML files)

```
<HTML>
<HEAD>
<TITLE>ACADEMIC STRUCTURE OF OUR SCHOOL</TITLE>
</HEAD>
<BODY> <FONT COLOR = RED>
<H1>ACADEMIC STRUCTURE OF OUR SCHOOL</H1>
Our school has classes from LKG to XII. Each class from LKG to X has 4 sections.<BR>
Classes XI & XII have 5 sections each.
Subjects taught to <A HREF = "PRIMARY.HTML"> Classes I to V </A> and to <BR>
<A HREF = "MIDDLE.HTML"> Classes VI to VIII </A> are <BR>
according to the syllabus prescribed by Directorate of Education <BR>
<A HREF = "SECONDARY.HTML"> Classes IX & X </A> have a system of 5+1 subjects strictly
according to the CBSE pattern.
In Classes <A HREF = "SENIOR.HTML"> XI & XII </A> there are 3 streams - Humanities,
Commerce and Science </FONT>
</BODY>
</HTML>
```

When H321.HTML is opened by Internet Explorer, it will display links like Classes I to V, Classes VI to VIII, Classes IX & X and XI & XII in blue colour.

OUTPUT:

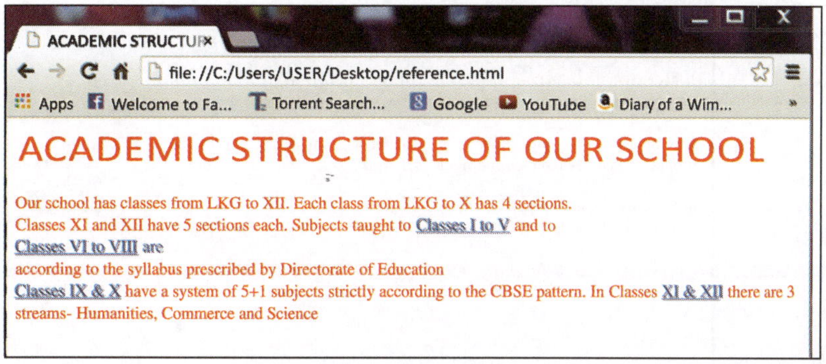

Fig. 6.7: Result of Example 6

Classes I to V when clicked will open the document PRIMARY.HTML and the colour of text **Classes I to V** will change from blue to purple. This implies that the link has been visited.

OUTPUT:

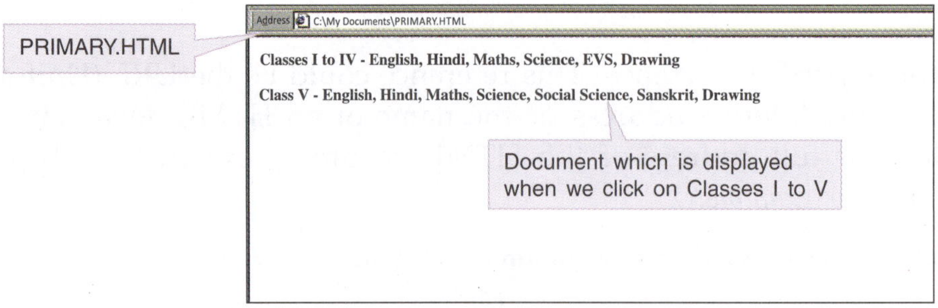

Fig. 6.8: Contents of PRIMARY.HTML

Similarly, **Classes VI to VIII** when clicked will display the document MIDDLE.HTML.

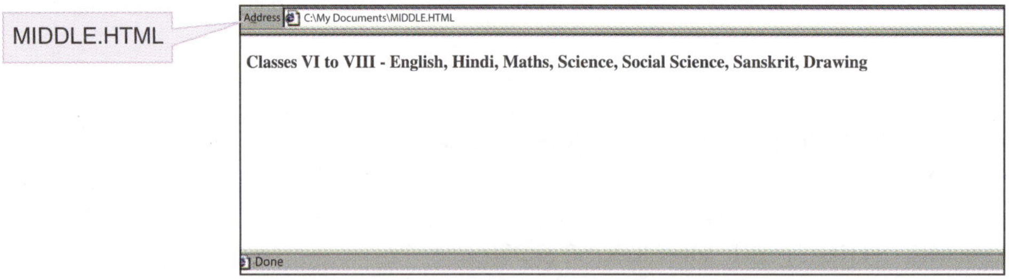

Fig. 6.9: Contents of MIDDLE.HTML

On clicking **Classes IX & X** you can see the following contents of SECONDARY.HTML.

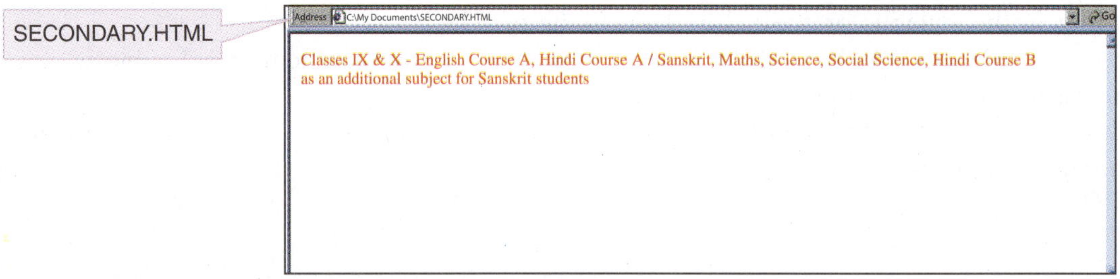

Fig. 6.10: Contents of SECONDARY.HTML

Similarly, on clicking **XI & XII** in the main document, SENIOR.HTML document will be displayed as shown in Fig. 6.11.

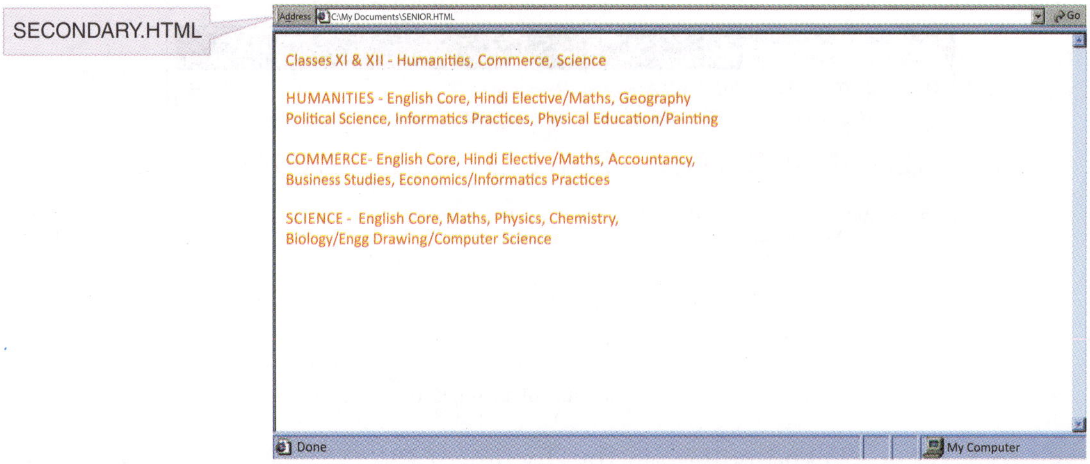

Fig. 6.11: Contents of SENIOR.HTML

NOTE

When a link has been clicked, its colour in the main document changes from blue to purple. This indicates that the link has been visited by the user at least once.

(ii) Name Attribute (Internal Linking) For Creating Link on the Same Page

Links can be created between various sections of the same page. Also in such a case clicking on a text in blue in one section of the document will display the related text written in another section of the same document.

This is done using the **NAME attribute**. *For example,*

```
<A HREF="#PRIMARY"> Classes I to V </A>
```

This will make Classes I to V as a link and appear in blue colour. **'#' implies that reference is in the same document**. Type the following in another section of the document to create a link.

```
<A NAME="PRIMARY">
<B> Classes I to V </B>
Subjects—English, Maths, EVS, Hindi, Science, Sanskrit (only for Class V)
</A>
```

Whenever 'Classes I to V' is clicked, the section showing related information is displayed. This link is formed by matching

```
<A HREF="#PRIMARY">
        with
<A NAME="PRIMARY">
```

The following example displays the creation of links in the same document (Internal linking).

Example 7 H24.HTML

```
<HTML>
<HEAD>
<TITLE>ACADEMIC STRUCTURE OF OUR SCHOOL</TITLE>
</HEAD>
<BODY> <FONT COLOR = "RED">
<H1>ACADEMIC STRUCTURE OF OUR SCHOOL</H1>
Our school has Classes from LKG to XII. Each Class from LKG to X has 4 sections.<BR>
Classes XI & XII have 5 sections each<BR>.
Subjects taught to <A HREF = "#PRIMARY"> Classes I to V </A> and for <BR>
<A HREF = "#MIDDLE"> Classes VI to VIII </A> are <BR>
according to the structure prescribed by Directorate of Education <BR>
<A HREF = "#SECONDARY"> Classes IX & X </A> have a system of 5+1 subjects strictly <BR>
according to the CBSE pattern <BR>
```

Internal link

Internal link

Internal link

```
In Classes <A HREF = "#SENIOR"> XI & XII </A> there are 3 streams —
Humanities, Commerce and Science <BR>
<HR>
<A NAME = "PRIMARY">
<B> PRIMARY </B>
<P> SUBJECTS OFFERED- <BR>
ENGLISH, HINDI, MATHS, EVS, SCIENCE, DRAWING <BR>
SANSKRIT (FOR CLASS V ONLY) <BR> </A>
</P>
<A NAME = "MIDDLE">
<B> MIDDLE </B>
<P> SUBJECTS OFFERED- <BR>
ENGLISH, HINDI, MATHS, SOCIAL SCIENCE, SCIENCE, DRAWING <BR>
& SANSKRIT <BR> </A>
</P>
<A NAME = "SECONDARY">
<B> SECONDARY </B> </A>
<P> SUBJECTS OFFERED - <BR>
ENGLISH-A, HINDI-A/SANSKRIT , MATHS, SOCIAL SCIENCE, <BR>
SCIENCE,  HINDI-B (ONLY WITH SANSKRIT AS 6th SUB) <BR>
</P>
<A NAME = "SENIOR">
<B> SENIOR </B>
<P> SUBJECTS OFFERED- <BR>
HUMANITIES - ENGLISH, HINDI/MATHS, POL. SCIENCE, GEOGRAPHY <BR>
PHY. EDN./PAINTING, INFORMATICS PRACTICES <BR>
COMMERCE - ENGLISH, HINDI/MATHS, ECONOMICS/INF. PRACT, <BR>
BUSINESS STD., ACCOUNTANCY <BR>
SCIENCE - ENGLISH, PHYSICS, MATHS, CHEMISTRY, BIO/COMP. SC <BR>
/ENGG. DRAW. <BR> </A> </FONT>
</P>
</BODY>
<HTML>
```

Internal link

Section linked to PRIMARY in the same document

Section linked to MIDDLE in the same document

Section linked to SECONDARY in the same document

Section linked to SENIOR in the same document

OUTPUT:

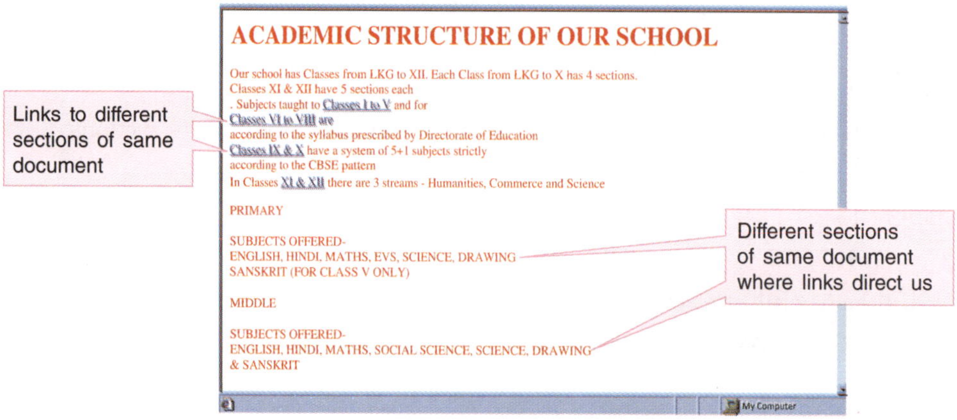

Fig. 6.12: Result of Example 7

6.2.2 Link, Alink and Vlink

These are the attributes of the Body tag but have been discussed here since this section of the chapter deals with linking.

In case a link is present in the document, it may appear in any one of the following three colours:

Blue—in case the link has not been visited.

Red—when the link is being clicked.

Purple—in case the link has been visited.

You can change these colours according to your wish using the following attributes:

Link—for unvisited links.

Alink—for links being clicked.

Vlink—for links already visited.

The following HTML code changes the colour of Link to black, Alink to green and Vlink to purple.

Example 8 ECLIPSE.HTML

```
<HTML>
<BODY BGCOLOR = "AQUA"  TEXT="RED" LINK= "BLACK"   ALINK="GREEN"
VLINK="PURPLE">
<H1> REALITY & MYTHS ABOUT ECLIPSES </H1>
<P>
<H4>ECLIPSES OCCUR EVERY FEW DAYS. SOMETIMES IT IS THE SOLAR ECLIPSE AND
AND SOMETIMES IT IS THE LUNAR ECLIPSE. MOST PEOPLE INSPITE OF BEING EDUCATED
STILL BELIEVE IN MANY MYTHS RELATED TO ECLIPSES. TO UNDERSTAND HOW AN
ECLIPSE
ACTUALLY OCCURS <BR><BR><BR>
CLICK ON THE FOLLOWING PICTURES ONE BY ONE <BR>
</P>
<P  ALIGN="LEFT" >  LUNAR ECLIPSE</P>
<A HREF="H26.HTML#E1">
<IMG SRC="LUNAR.JPG"  BORDER ="4" ALIGN="LEFT">
</A>
<P  ALIGN ="RIGHT"    >
SOLAR ECLIPSE</P>
<A HREF="H26.HTML#E2">
<IMG SRC="SOLAR.JPG"  BORDER = "4" ALIGN="RIGHT">
</A>
</BODY>
</HTML>
```

OUTPUT:

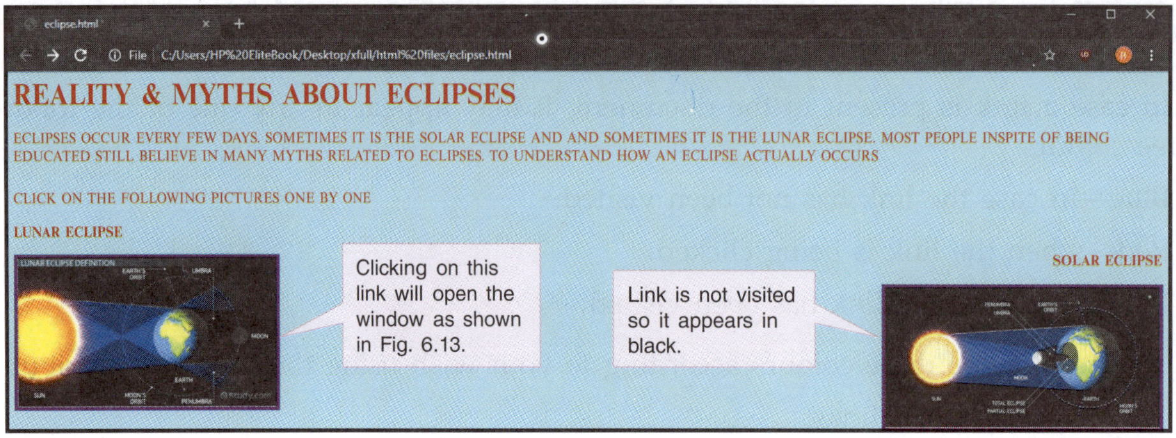

Fig. 6.13: Result of Example 8

Example 9 H26.HTML

```
<HTML>
<BODY> <FONT COLOR = "RED">
<H4> LUNAR ECLIPSE </H4>
<A NAME = "E1">          internal link name
<IMG SRC = "LUNAR.WMF" BORDER = "4" HEIGHT = "37%"  WIDTH = "37%">
</A>
<BR>
<BR>
<H4> SOLAR ECLIPSE </H4>
<A NAME = "E2">          internal link name
<IMG SRC = "SOLAR.WMF" BORDER = "4" HEIGHT = "37%" WIDTH = "37%">
</A> </FONT>
</BODY>
</HTML>
```

Execution of HTML code in Example 8 will take you to specific links E1 or E2 in the external H26.HTML file depending on whether the link for Lunar eclipse or link for Solar eclipse is clicked in Example 8.

OUTPUT:

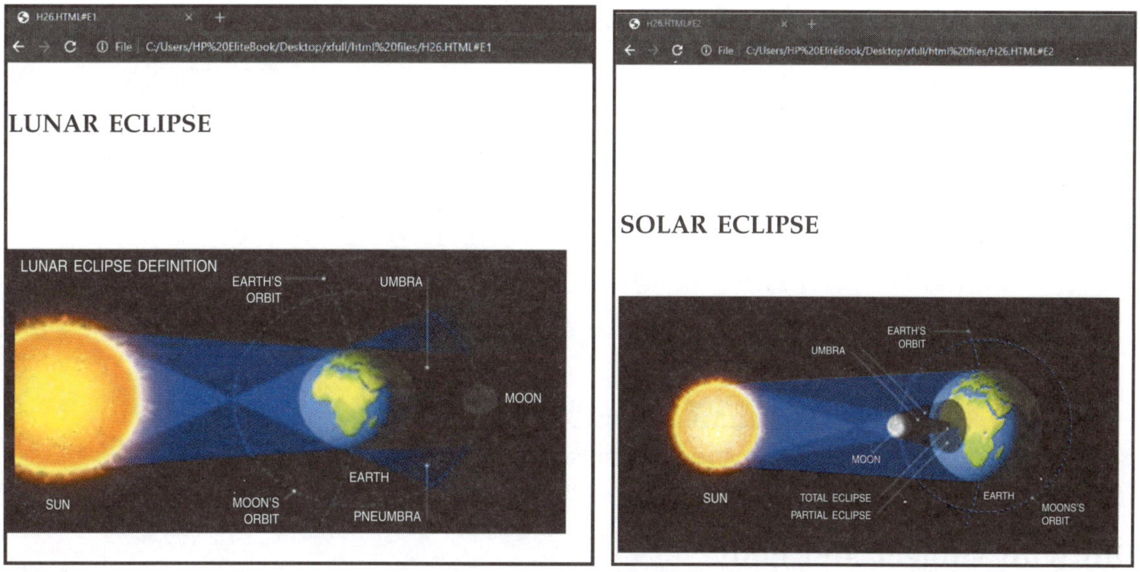

Fig. 6.14: Result of Example 9

(iii) Mailto

HTML Mailto has a prerequisite according to which the person visiting your website should have configured with an e-mail client. Outlook Express, Netscape Messenger, etc. are the most used e-mail clients. Mailto is an easy and fast way by which a visitor at your website can either send a feedback to your e-mail id or can send the information on the website directly to a friend.

Syntax: <a href=“mailto:email address”> message </a>

For example, <a href=“mail to:twilight@hotmail.com”> you can send your comments </a>

The result displayed will be:

<u>you can send your comments</u>

When the above link is clicked, the configured e-mail client is set to work. New Message window is opened up (Fig. 6.16) where the mail message can be typed and then sent.

Example 10

```
<html>
<title>
</title>
<body>
<a href="mailto:soodranju@hotmail.com">
you can send your comments</a>
</body>
</html>
```

OUTPUT:

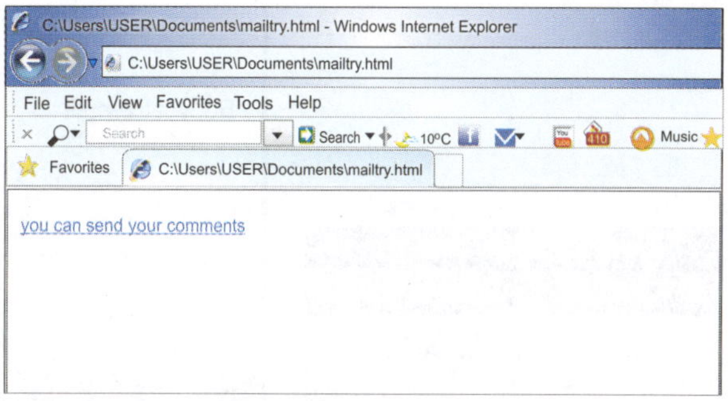

Fig. 6.15: Result of Example 10

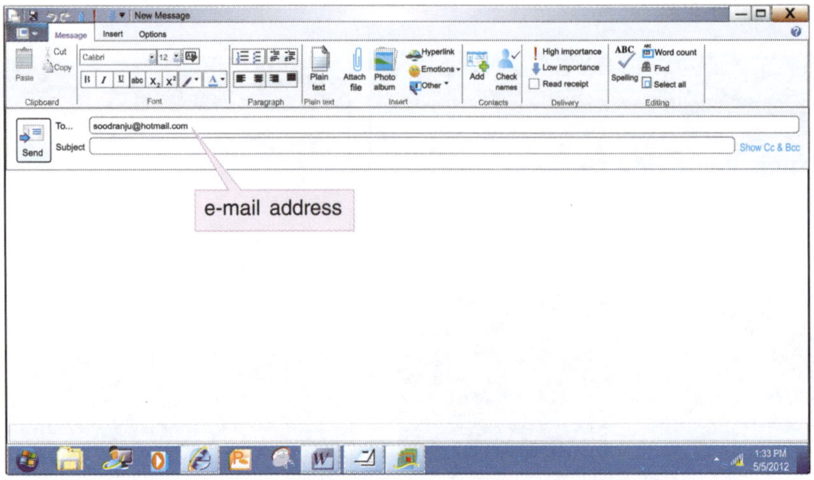

Fig. 6.16: An e-mail can be created at the given address

Mailto with subject and body

To add a subject and body to an e-mail we can use the following format:

E-mail address | Subject line

```
<a href="mailto:soodranju@hotmail.com?subject=Feedback on Magical Numbers &body=
    The information about the Magical Numbers is amazing" > you can send your
    comments </a>
```

Message | Linking text

Observe how **?** and **&** are used in the above format.

The following figures show the result of the mailto tag with subject and body:

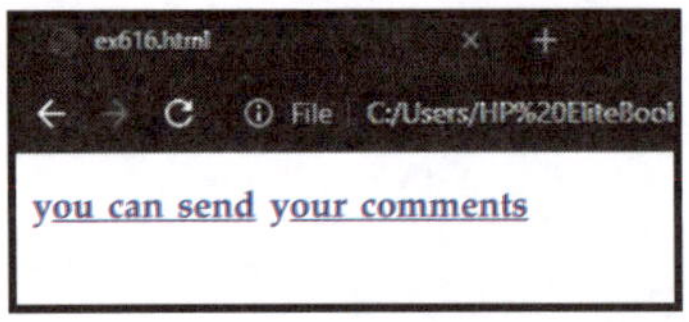

Fig. 6.17(a): Webpage with link

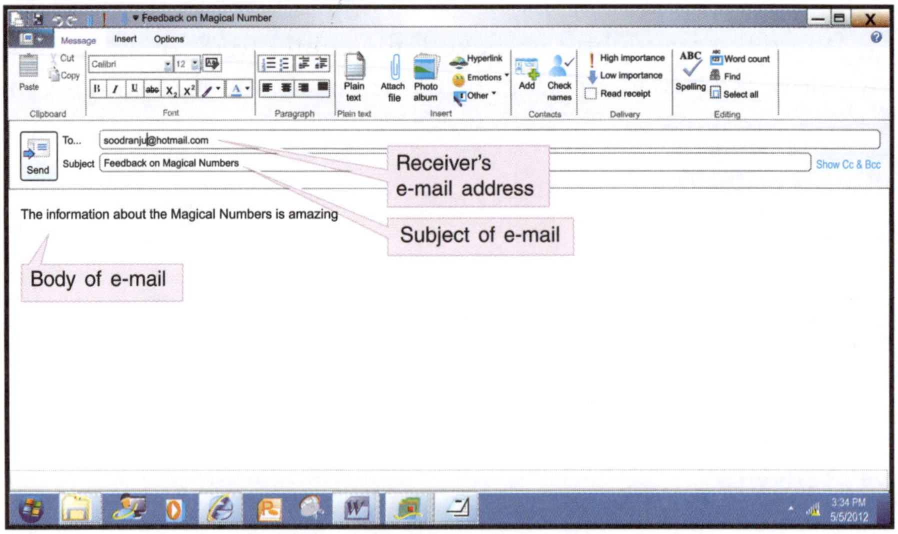

Fig. 6.17(b): Mailto with subject and body

Mailto with Cc and Bcc

To send a copy of mail and a blind carbon copy of mail, type the following code:

Example 11

```
<html>
<title>
</title>
<body>
<a href="mailto:soodranju@hotmail.com?subject=Feedback on Magical Numbers
&body=The information about the Magical Numbers is amazing&cc=pourush@
gmail.com&bcc=soodherschel@ymail.com">you can send your comments</a>
</body></html>
```

On execution, the above code will generate the following web page with a clickable link (Fig. 6.18a). This link will open the e-mail creation page (Fig. 6.18b).

Fig. 6.18a: Clickable link

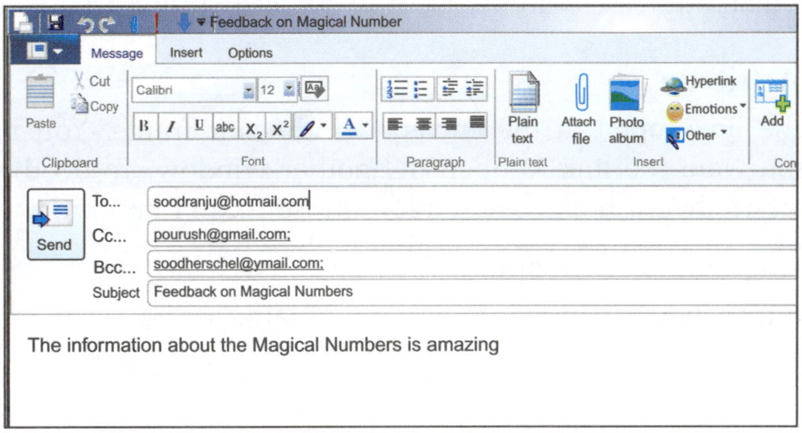

Fig. 6.18b: Mailto with Cc, Bcc (Result of Example 11)

Sending a page to a friend

You can also give the provision where the visitor to your website can send the link of your website to his friends using the following code:

```
<a href="mailto:?subject=visit www.interestingfacts.com&body=For interesting
facts in mathematics visit this website">
Send this page to a friend </a>
```

Here, e-mail address has been left blank so that the visitor can enter the e-mail address of his/her own choice. The execution of the given code will generate the output as follows:

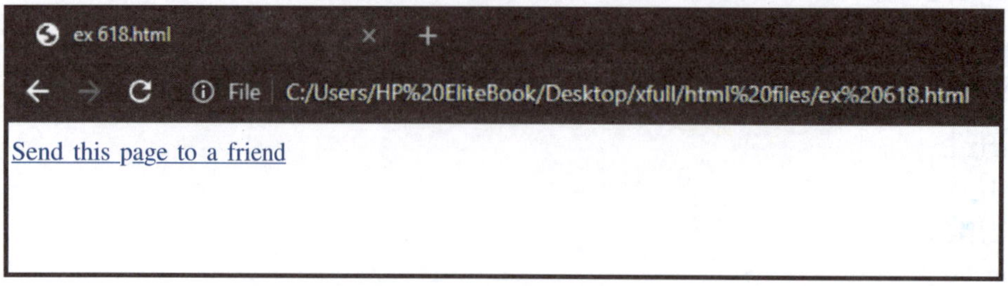

Fig. 6.19a: Clickable link

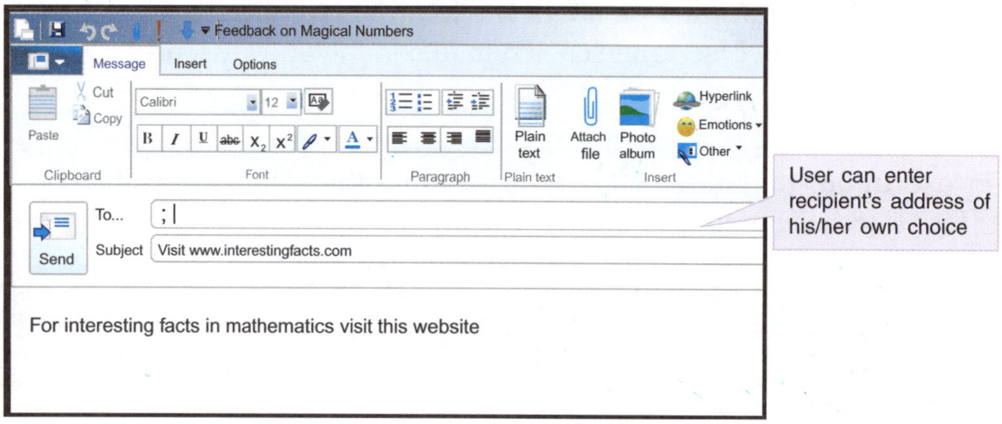

Fig. 6.19b: Mailto with variable e-mail address

The disadvantages of using mailto are:

(i) The user has to configure with an e-mail client.

(ii) The e-mail addresses can be used by spamsters to send spam mails.

(iv) Target Attribute

By default, the links open in the current window or frame. You need to add a target attribute if you want the link to open in another window. To do this, you simply add a target attribute to the <a href>. The target attribute can't be used without href attribute.

The following example will open Yahoo in a new window:

<a href="http://www.yahoo.com" target="_blank"></a>

The following code will open the home page in another tab:

<a href="/" target="_blank"> </a>

Syntax: <a ref="link" target="_blank|_self|_top">

_blank : loads in the new window or tab

_top : loads in full body of the window

_self : loads the link in the current window

If no target is specified, the link will open in the current window. Blank target is used to open the offsite links. So, the user can click on a reference to open it in a new tab and go to it as and when required without leaving the current page.

6.3 INSERTING TABLE

A table is made up of rows and columns. A cell is where a row and a column intersect.

- A data cell may contain text, images, lists, paragraphs, tables, etc. A table with three rows and two cells in each row would be

R1C1	R1C2
R2C1	R2C2
R3C1	R3C2

The tags used within Table element are described below. In new versions of HTML, the closing tag may not be used with some opening tags such as <TH><TR><TD>.

- Tables are defined with the **<TABLE>** tag.
- Rows are defined by **<tr>** tag and each row has data cells.
- The tag **<td>** is used to define the data cell, also called table data.
- The tag **<th>** defines the table header.

Example 12

```
<table border = 1>
<tr>
<th> Name
<th> Class
<tr>
<td> Manju
<td> VII
<tr>
<td> Arun
<td> IX
</table>
```

Table heading	Name	Class
Table data for first row	Manju	VII
Table data for second row	Arun	IX

Fig. 6.20: Result of Example 12

So, if there are 2 <tr> tags that means there are two rows and if there are 3 such tags that means the table has 3 rows. Similarly, if there are 2 <td> tags it means there are 2 data cells in each row.

Table Attributes

- *border = n:* This attribute is used for the border of the table where n is the value. "0" represents no border.
- *bordercolor:* Along with the border size, we can enter *bordercolor* also, which can be any hex colour.
- *bgcolor:* This attribute is used for setting the background color of the table.

  So, <table border = 3 bordercolor = ff9900

  bgcolor = cc99ff>

  will create a table with border width = 3, colour = orange and background = mauve.

- ***Align:*** It aligns the table on the web page.

  <Table align=LEFT> will align the table with the left margin of the page. The other values can be right and center.

- ***Background:*** An image can be set as a background for the table by using background attribute.

  <Table background="C:\PICTURES\FLOWER.JPG">

- ***Cell Spacing and Cell Padding:*** Cell spacing attribute adjusts the space between the cells. Cell padding adjusts the space within the cell.

  <table border = 4 cellspacing = 10

  cellpadding = 3>

  This will increase the space between two cells substantially but the cell size will be 3. Fig. 6.21 shows increased cell spacing as compared to Fig. 6.20.

NAME	CLASS
MANJU	VII
ARUN	IX

Fig. 6.21: Normal cell spacing

NAME	CLASS
MANJU	VII
ARUN	IX

Fig. 6.22: Increasing the spacing between the cells

- ***Column Span*** (with <TH> and <TD>): Cells may stretch to or span several rows or columns which is also called **Spanning**. The number of columns spanned by a cell is set by **colspan attribute** for <TH> and <TD> elements. The following code designs a table where the fourth row and the third column span two cells.

  e.g., <TD COLSPAN="2">DATA NOT AVAILABLE></TD>

NAME	CLASS	MARKS OBTAINED	RANK
MANJU	VII	450	II
ARUN	IX	495	I
TARUN	X	*DATA NOT AVAILABLE*	

Spanning over 2 columns

Fig. 6.23: Column Span (Result of Example 13)

Example 13

```
<HTML>
<HEAD>
<TITLE> USING TABLE</TITLE>
</HEAD>
<BODY>

<TABLE BORDER=8 BORDERCOLOR=ff0000 BGCOLOR=ffff00 cellspacing=10 cellpadding=5>
<TR>
<TH> NAME
<TH> CLASS
<TH> MARKS OBTAINED
<TH> RANK

<TR>
<TD> MANJU
<TD> VII
<TD> 450
<TD> II
<TR>
<TD> ARUN
<TD> IX
<TD> 495
<TD> I
<TR>
<TD> TARUN
<TD> X
<TD   COLSPAN="2"> DATA NOT AVAILABLE
</TABLE>
</BODY>
</HTML>
```

Merging of 2 cells

Row Span

A row span is similar to a column span except for the fact that here the cell may span more than one row. The row span is set by **rowspan attribute** for <TH> and <TD> elements. The use of row span is shown below.

<TD ROWSPAN = "3">500

Caption <CAPTION> </CAPTION> To give a heading to a table caption tag is used immediately after the table tags:

e.g. <caption>ANNUAL RESULT </caption> will print a heading above the table as in Fig. 6.24.

ANNUAL RESULT

NAME	CLASS	MARKS OBTAINED	MAXIMUM MARKS
MANJU	VII	450	*500*
ARUN	IX	495	
TARUN	X	367	

Cells of 3 rows have been merged

Fig. 6.24: Row Span (Result of Example 14)

Example 14

```
<HTML>
<HEAD>
<TITLE> USING TABLE</TITLE>
</HEAD>
<BODY>
<TABLE BORDER="8 BORDERCOLOR="ff0000 BGCOLOR="ffff00cellspacing="10"
cellpadding=5>
<CAPTION>ANNUAL RESULT</CAPTION>
<TR>
<TH> NAME
<TH> CLASS
<TH> MARKS OBTAINED
<TH> MAXIMUM MARKS
<TR>
<TD> MANJU
<TD> VII
<TD> 450
<TD ROWSPAN=3>500
<TR>
<TD> ARUN
<TD> IX
<TD> 495
<TR>
<TD> TARUN
<TD> X
<TD>367
</TABLE>
</BODY>
</HTML>
```

Spanning over 3 rows

6.4 EMBED AUDIO AND VIDEO

In the beginning of the chapter, you have learned to embed an image in an HTML page. You can also embed an audio and a video clip from a file, in the HTML page using audio and video tags respectively. The use of these tags is explained below:

6.4.1 Audio Tag [<Audio>...</Audio>]

To embed an audio file in an HTML document, the **<audio> tag** is used. It is a container tag. The commonly used attributes of <audio> tag are:

- **src:** It specifies the URL address of the audio file.
- **loop:** It makes the audio file to play repeatedly.
- **autoplay:** It plays the audio file as soon as it is loaded.
- **controls:** It displays the audio controls.

In the following example, an audio file from the music directory of the computer is embedded in an HTML document which plays when the play button is clicked.

Example 15 Embedding an audio file

```
<HTML>
<BODY>
<p>SONG "WE ARE THE WORLD"</p>
<p>CLICK ON PLAY BUTTON</p>
<AUDIO CONTROLS>
<SOURCE SRC = "C:\Users\HP EliteBook\
Music\USA for Africa- We are the World.mp3">
</AUDIO>
</BODY>
</HTML>
```

OUTPUT:

Fig. 6.25: Result of Example 15

6.4.2 Video Tag [<video>...</video>]

A video tag specifies a video file or a movie clip to be embedded in an HTML document. It is also a container tag. The attributes used with video tag are:

- **src:** It specifies the source of the video file.
- **loop:** It plays the video repeatedly.
- **height and width:** It specifies the height and width of the video player. It can be adjusted by giving the value in pixels.
- **controls:** It displays the video controls.
- **muted:** It does not play the audio while video is running.

The following example will display the video file showing the life cycle of a butterfly. The file is stored in the video directory of the computer.

Example 16 Embedding a video file

```
<HTML>
<BODY>
<p>VIDEO "AMAZING LIFE CYCLE OF A BUTTERFLY"</p>
<p>CLICK ON PLAY BUTTON</p>
<VIDEO   width=320 height=240 CONTROLS>
<SOURCE SRC = "C:\Users\HP EliteBook\Videos\Amazing Life Cycle of a Monarch Butterfly.
mp4">
</VIDEO>
</BODY>
</HTML>
```

OUTPUT:

Fig. 6.26: Result of Example 16

6.5 HTML FORMS

Many a times when we visit a website, we are asked to create an account or fill a form with details like name, address, email address and then submit it. Such forms are called **web forms** or **HTML forms**. The data taken by these forms is transferred to the server for processing. HTML uses <form> tag to create such forms. It is a container tag. There are various controls which are used to create HTML forms. Each of these controls has its own attributes.

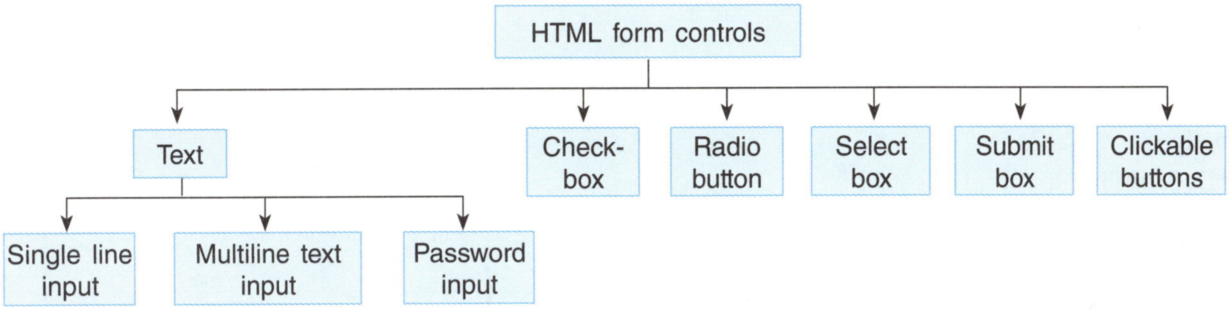

1. **Text input:**

   (a) **Single line input control:**

   Syntax: <input type = "text">

   <input name = "first name" type = "text" value = "*******">

   The above code displays asterisks as default value for **first name** field and waits for the user to give the input of type text.

Example 17

```
<html>
<body>
<H2>Text Input</H2>
<form>
   Enter your name:
      <input name="firstname" type="text" value="*******">
      <br>   <br>
      <input type="Submit">
</form>
</body>
</html>
```

OUTPUT:

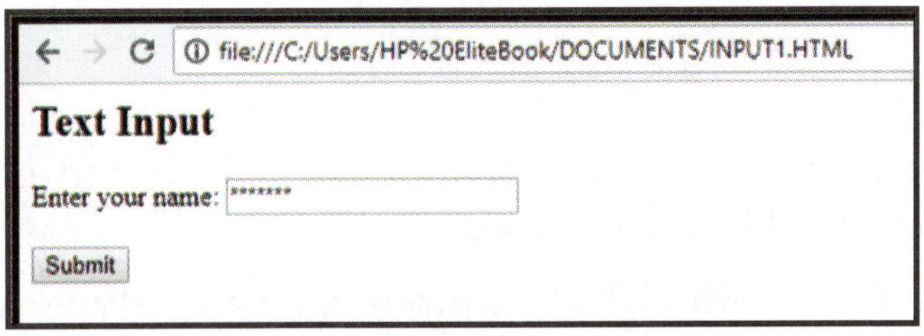

Fig. 6.27: Result of Example 17

(b) **Multiline text input:** When more than one line of the text has to be entered, multiline attribute is used. But this control uses **<textarea>** as attribute instead of <input>.

<textarea> is a container tag.

name, **rows** and **cols** are the attributes used with this tag.

Syntax: <textarea row=value1 cols=value2>

Example 19

```
<html>
<body>
<H2>Multiline Input</H2>
<br><br><br>
Enter Description:
<form>
   <textarea name="Description" rows="5" cols="20">
   </textarea>
   <br>   <br>  <br>
   <input type="Submit">
</form>
</body>
</html>
```

OUTPUT:

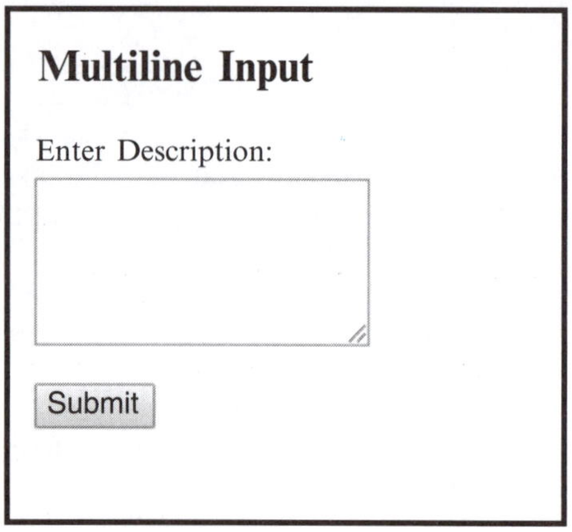

Fig. 6.28: Result of Example 18

(c) **Password input control:** This control is used to take a password as input.

Syntax: <input type="password">

Example 19

```
<html>
<body>
<H2>Password Input</H2>
<form>
   Enter your password:
      <input name="Password"  type="password" >
      <br>  <br>
      <input type="Submit">
</form>
</body>
</html>
```

OUTPUT:

Fig. 6.29: Result of Example 19

2. **Checkbox input:** When several options for input are given and more than one can be selected by the user, checkboxes are used.

   Attributes that can be used with checkbox input are **name**, **type**, **value** (to be used when checkbox is selected) and **checked** (if checkbox has to be selected by default).

   Syntax: <input type="checkbox">

Example 20

```
<html>
<body>
<H2>Checkbox Input</H2>
<form>
   <input type =“checkbox” name =“gender1” value=“male”>MALE<br>
   <input type =“checkbox” name =“gender2” value=“female”>FEMALE<br>
   <input type=“Submit”>
</form>
</body>
</html>
```

OUTPUT:

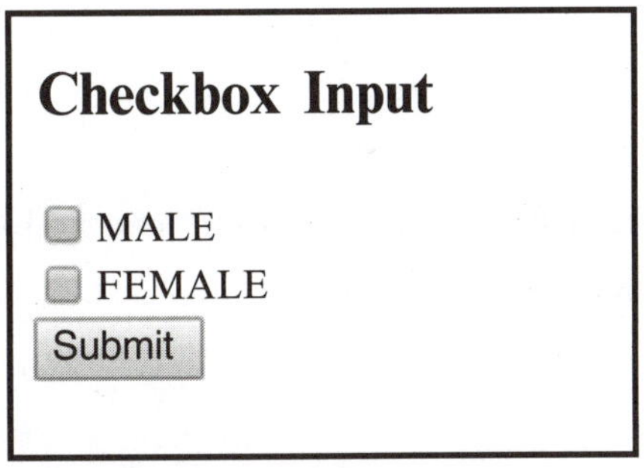

Fig. 6.30: Result of Example 20

3. **Clickable button:** When a button on a form is clicked and it initiates another event, such a button is called **Click button**. The attributes used with this button are:
   - Submit (creates a button that submits the form)
   - Button (creates a button that triggers another event)

   Syntax: <input type = “button”> or

   <input type = “submit”>

Example 21

```
<html>
<body>
<H2>Clickable Button Input</H2>
<form>
   <input type ="button"onclick="alert(‘Are you Sure?’)"  value="Click Me">
</form>
</body>
</html>
```

OUTPUT:

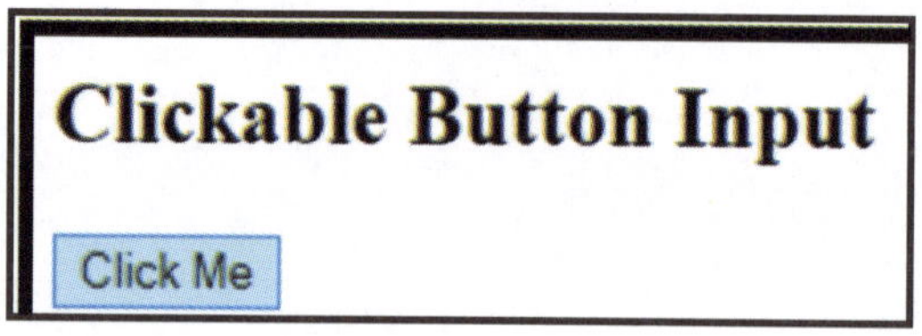

Fig. 6.31: Result of Example 21

4. **Radio Button:** When there are many options but only one has to be selected, radio buttons are used. The attributes are same as that of checkbox.

   Syntax: <input type = "radio">

Example 22

```
<html>
<body>
<H2>Radio Button Input</H2>
<form>
    <input type ="radio" name ="four wheeler" value="four" checked>Four Wheeler<br >
    <input type ="radio" name ="three wheeler" value="three">Three Wheeler<br >
    <input type ="radio" name ="two wheeler" value="two">Two Wheeler<br >
    <input type="Submit">
</form>
</body>
</html>
```

OUTPUT:

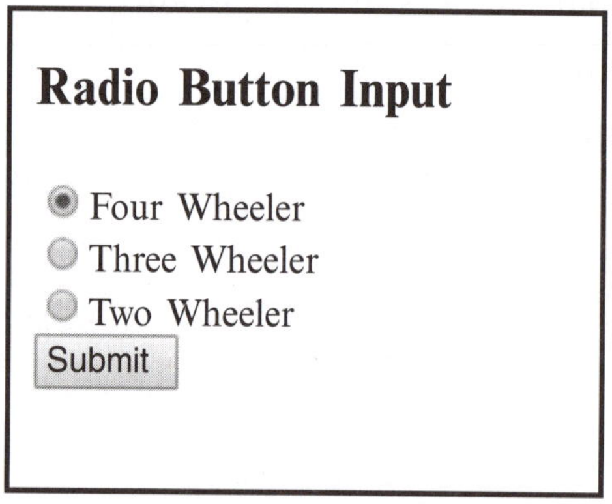

Fig. 6.32: Result of Example 22

5. **Select box:** A select box provides a drop down list of options from which one can be selected. In the following example, any one subject has to be chosen from the list.

Example 23

```
<html>
<body>
<H2>Select Input</H2>
<form>

<select>
<option value = "Maths"> Maths</option>
<option value = "Biology"> Biology</option>
<option value = "Computer Sc">Computer Science</option>
<option value = "P T">Physical education</option>
</select>
<br><br><br><br><br><br>
<input type="Submit">
</form>
</body>
</html>
```

OUTPUT:

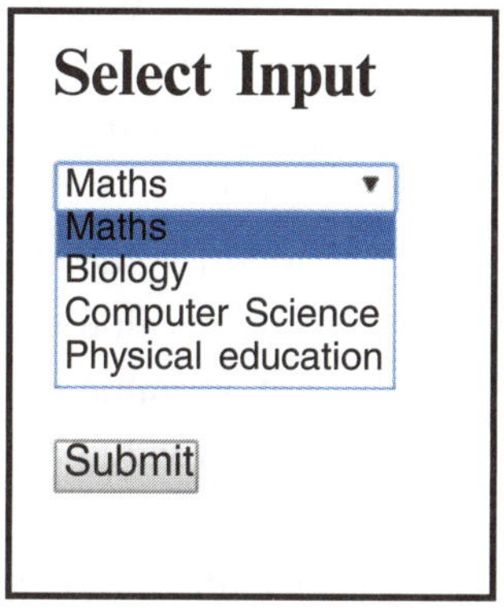

Fig. 6.33: Result of Example 23

6. **Submit/Reset box:** When the data entered in the form has to be erased and default values have to be taken, **Reset** box is used.

   Syntax: <input type = reset>

   Submit button transfers the data of the form to the server. Submit button has been used in all the examples of the HTML forms.

Example 24

The following code uses almost all the input controls to enter the data in a vehicle registration form.

```
<html>
<body>
<H2>Data Input Form for Vehicle Registration</H2>
<form>
Enter your name:
<input name = "firstname" type = "text">
<br><br>
Enter Address
<textarea name ="Description" rows="5" cols="20">
</textarea>
<br><br>
    <input type ="checkbox" name ="gender1" value="male">MALE<br>
    <input type ="checkbox" name ="gender2" value="female">FEMALE<br>
<br><br>
<p>You want to register for</p>
```

```
    <input type ="radio" name ="four wheeler" value="four" checked>Four Wheeler<br>
    <input type ="radio" name ="three wheeler" value="three">Three Wheeler<br>
    <input type ="radio" name ="two wheeler" value="two">Two Wheeler<br>
<br><br>
<p> Select the region for registration
<select>
<option value = "east"> East</option>
<option value = "west"> West</option>
<option value = "north">North</option>
<option value = "south">South</option>
</select>
<br><br><br>br><br><br>
<input type="submit">
</form>
</body>
</html>
```

OUTPUT:

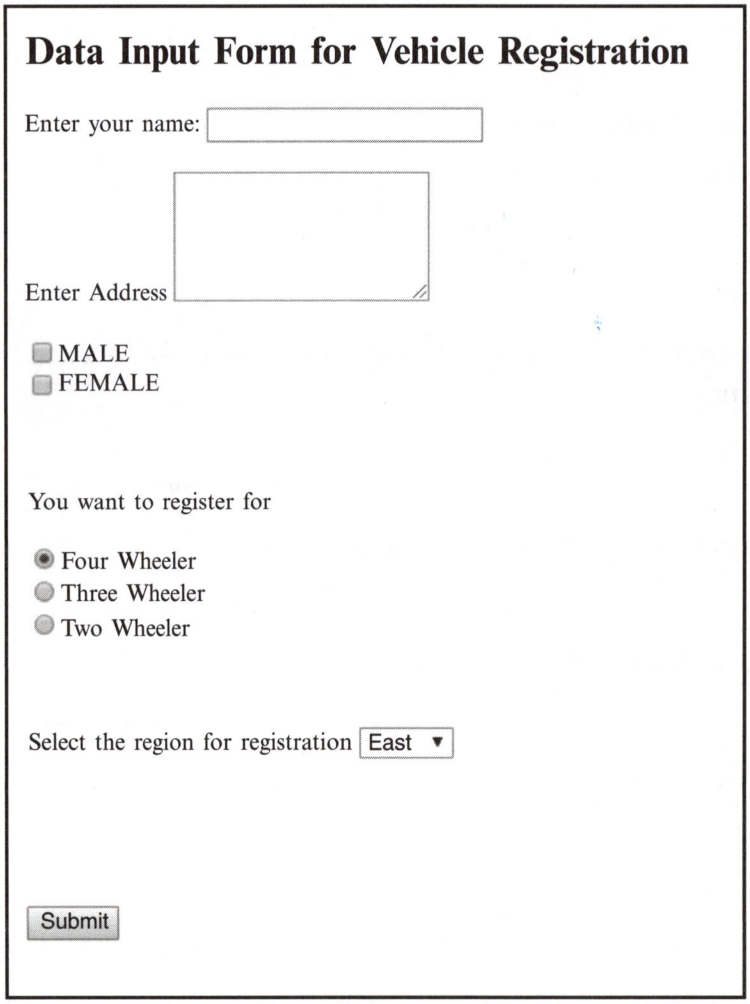

Fig. 6.34: Result of Example 24

6.6 CASCADING STYLE SHEETS (CSS)

CSS is a language that describes the style of an HTML document. It describes how HTML elements should be displayed when an HTML page is opened. Different stylesheets can change the layout of the HTML page.

CSS can control the layout of multiple web pages all at once. Style can be set internally in the HTML code or in an external file having an extension .css.

Suppose, for example, the H1 command appears 20 times in a code. Each time the heading appears, its attributes such as colour have to be defined. If the colour has to be changed, it will have to be changed at all the 20 occurrences of H1. To save time and effort, a style sheet in a css file can be created in which the common attributes for the commands can be specified. When the browser will read a style sheet it will format the HTML document according to the information given in CSS file. Let us now learn to write CSS code.

6.6.1 CSS Selectors

In CSS, selectors play a major role and are the patterns used to select the element(s) to be styled. CSS code is enclosed in <style> </style> tag if written in the same HTML document. Some of the various selectors used are:

Selector	Example	Example description
.class	.display	Selects all elements with class="display"
#id	#one	Selects the element with id="one"
*	*	Selects all elements
element	p	Selects all <p> elements

Syntax: Selector {property1: value1; property2: value2; ....;}

CSS declaration always ends with a semicolon and is enclosed in curly brackets.

Let us study these selectors one by one.

1. **Use of element as selector:** The following is an example where elements are used as selectors:

   e.g., H1 {color: Red; text-align: center;}
   (selector) (Property1) (value 1) (Property2) (value 2)

   The above code makes the heading H1 appear in red colour and centrally aligned on the web page whenever H1 tag is executed in the HTML code.

   If more than one selector have to be assigned the same value then, they can be grouped together, *e.g.,*

   H1, H2, P {color: Red; text-align: center;}

   The headings H1, H2 and the <P> tag wherever they will be executed in the HTML document, their text will be in red colour and centrally aligned on the web page.

2. **Use of class as selector:** In the above example we have seen that multiple elements have been given the same look. It is also possible to give an HTML element multiple looks with CSS.

   For example, sometimes the font has to be large and red, while other times the font is preferred to be small and black. CSS allows this with the use of classes.

   Using classes is simple. Only an extension needs to be added to the typical CSS code and one has to specify this extension in the HTML document body. In the following CSS code, 'one' and 'two' are the classes for which style attributes are defined by style element. This style has been linked with HTML code by specifying the class name one and two. This example is just to give an idea as to how multiple looks can be given to the same element.

   CSS Code:

   p.one {background: yellow;}

   p.two {background: pink;}

Example 25

```
<!DOCTYPE html>
<html>
<head>
<style>
p.one {background: yellow;}
p.two {background: pink;}
</style>
</head>
<body>
<p>This is normal text</p>
<p class=one>this text follows p.one css style</p>
<p class=two>this text follows p.two css style</p>
</body>
</html>
```

OUTPUT:

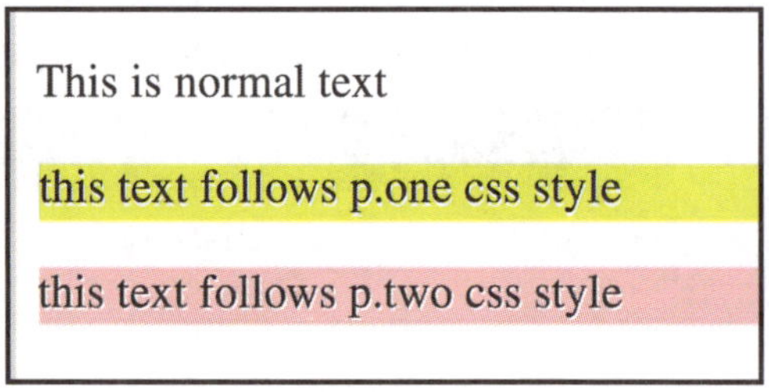

Fig. 6.35: Result of Example 25

3. **Use of #id as selector:** The #id selector styles the element with the specified id. It does not use the element name or class for identification. Look at the following CSS code which has to be enclosed in <head> tag.

Example 26

```
<style>
#one { background: yellow;}
#two { background: pink;}
</style>
```

The selector will be linked in the body tag as follows:

In this code #one is applied to <p> element and #two is applied to <H1> element. The output will be

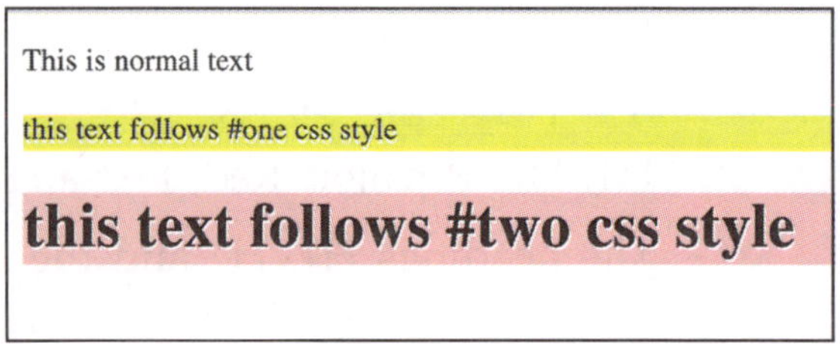

Fig. 6.36: Result of Example 26

```
<body>
<p>This is normal text</p>
<p id=one>this text follows #one css style</p>
<H1 id=two>this text follows #two css style</p>
</body>
```

4. **Use of * as selector:** The * is a universal selector and applies to all elements of HTML document. The code given below will set the background for all elements and the whole web page to yellow.

```
<style>
* { background-color: yellow;}
</style>
```

6.6.2 Types of CSS

Cascading Style Sheets come in three types: internal, external and inline.

- **Internal CSS:** When using internal CSS, a new tag, <style>, inside the <head> tag is used. The HTML codes above illustrate the usage of <style>. Further examples in this chapter use internal CSS in most cases.
- **External CSS:** When using CSS, it is preferable to keep the CSS separate from the HTML code. Placing CSS in a separate file allows the web designer to completely differentiate between content (HTML) and design (CSS). External CSS is a file that contains only CSS code and is saved with a ".css" file extension. This CSS file is then referenced in the HTML document using the <link> instead of <style>. This topic is dealt in the later part of this chapter.
- **Inline CSS:** It is possible to place CSS right in the body of the HTML code, and this method of CSS usage is referred to as inline CSS. Inline CSS has the highest priority out of the three ways of using CSS: external, internal and inline. This means that you can override styles that are defined in external or internal by using inline CSS. However, inline CSS detracts from the true purpose of CSS, to separate design from content, so it is not used frequently.

  Syntax:

  ```
  <ON tag style =property1:value1; property2:value2;> text </OFF tag>
  ```

Example 27

```
<!DOCTYPE html>
<html>
<body>
<h1 style=color:blue;>This is inline
    CSS styling a Heading</h1>
</body>
</html>
```

OUTPUT:

This is inline CSS styling a Heading

Fig. 6.37: Result of Example 27

6.6.3 CSS Properties

1. *COLOR:* The colour of the text on the web page can be set using color property as in the example given below:

   Syntax: selector {color: value;}

   Here, value can be colour name (*e.g.*, red) or hexadecimal code (*e.g.*, FF0000) or rgb value (*e.g.*, rgb 255,0,0)

Example 28

```
<!DOCTYPE html>
<html>
<head>
<style>
H1 {color:red}
p {color:blue}
</style>
</head>
<body>
<h1>Heading is in red</h1>
<p>The color of the text in paragraph is blue</p>
</body>
</html>
```

OUTPUT:

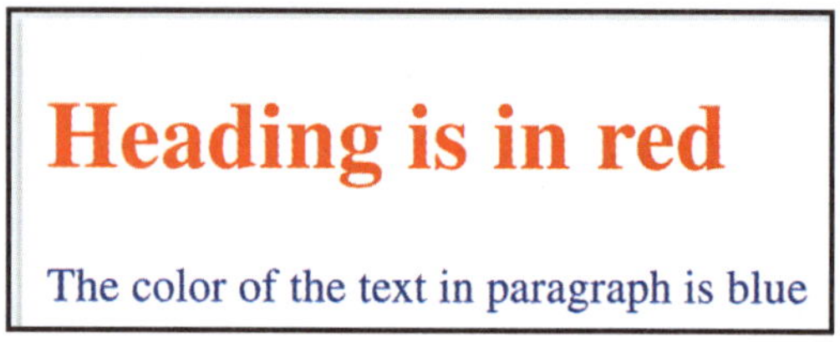

Fig. 6.38: Result of Example 28

2. *Background Color:* The background-color property sets the background-colour of an element.

   The background of an element is the total size of the element, including padding and border but not the margin.

   Syntax: Selector {background-color: value;}

   where value can be colour name or hexadecimal code or rgb value.

   e.g., body { background-color: yellow;}

   p {background-color: pink;}

   The above code will change the background-colour of entire page to yellow and that of paragraph to pink.

3. *Background Image:* This property can be used to insert a background-image on a web page.

   Syntax: Selector{ background-image:url("location and name of image");}

   e.g., body{ background-image:url("C:/User/Desktop/lamb.jpg");}

4. *Font:* It sets all the font properties.

   - In CSS, there are two types of font family names:

     Generic family – a group of font families with a similar look (like "Serif" or "Monospace")

     Font family – a specific font family (like "Times New Roman" or "Comic Sans")

   - The font-family property should hold several font names. If the browser does not support the first font, it tries the next font, and so on.

- Start with the font you want, and end with a generic family, to let the browser pick a similar font in the generic family, if no other fonts are available.
- If the name of a font family is more than one word, it must be in quotation marks, like: "Times New Roman".
- More than one font family is specified in a comma-separated list:

5. *Font Property:*

   Font-family – specifies the font family for text.

   Font-size (xx-small, x-small, small, medium, large, x-large, xx-large) – sets the size of the font.

   Font-style (normal, italic, oblique) – sets the style of the font.

   Font-variant (small caps, normal) – sets font to normal or small caps.

   Font-weight (normal, bold) – sets the thickness of the font.

Example 29

```
<html>
  <head>
    <style>
    p {font-family: "Times New Roman", Times, Serif; font-size: x-large; font-style: italic;}
    </style>
  </head>
  <body>
    <p >This is a paragraph, shown in the Times New Roman font with x-large font size and
    in italic. </p>
    </body>
</html>
```

OUTPUT:

This is a paragraph, shown in the Times New Roman font with x-large font size and in italic.

Fig. 6.39: Result of Example 29

6. *Border:* It sets the border properties for all the four borders.

   Syntax:

   selector {border-width: value; border-style: value; border-color:value;}

   The values of the properties can be:

   Border-width (thin, medium, thick)

   Border-style (none, hidden, dotted, dashed, solid, double)

   Border-color (name, rgb( ), hexadecimal code)

   The following code sets the border properties for all the text between paragraph tags.

Example 30

```
<html>
  <head>
    <style>
      p {border-style: dashed; border-color: red; border-width: thick;}
    </style>
</head>
  <body>
    <h2>learning to set border in CSS</h2>
    <p>The border is set in red color with thick width and dashed style</p>
</body>
</html>
```

OUTPUT:

Fig. 6.40: Result of Example 30

7. ***Outline:*** An outline is a line that is drawn around elements, outside the borders, to make the element "stand out". It also has style, colour and width attributes which can be written in Border property separately or together.

   Syntax: selector{ outline-style:value; outline-color:value; outline-width:value;}

   The properties can have the following values:

   Outline-style: (none, hidden, dotted, dashed, solid, double, groove, ridge, inset, outset)

   Outline-color: (name, rgb(), hex code)

   Outline-width: (thin, thick, medium)

   Note: The values of the attributes of the properties discussed above can also be written one after the other separated by blank space as in the following example:

Example 31

```
<html><head>
    <style>
    h1 {outline: dashed red thick; border: solid blue;}
    </style></head>
  <body>
    <h1>Using Outline Property</h1>
  </body>
</html>
```

OUTPUT:

Fig. 6.41: Result of Example 31

8. ***Margin:*** This property sets the margins for each side of an element (top, right, bottom and left).

   Syntax:

   selector {margin-top: value; margin-bottom: value; margin-left: value; margin-right: value;}

   The all margin properties may be applied or any of margin-top, margin-bottom, margin-left and margin-right. These properties can have the following values:

   - **auto** – the browser places the element in the centre.
   - **length** – specifies a margin in px (pixel).
   - **%** – specifies a margin of the width of the containing element in %.
   - **4 values** – specify one value each for the four margins.
   - **3 values** – specify first value for top, second for both left and right and the third value for the bottom margin.
   - **2 values** – specify first value for both top and bottom margin and second value for both left and right margins.
   - **a single value** – sets all the four margins to the given value.

Example 32

```
<html><head>
    <style>
H1 {border: dashed black thin;
        margin-top: 50px;
        margin-bottom: 100px;
        margin-right: 200px;
            margin-left: 50px;

        background-color: linen;}
</style></head>
<body>
        <H1>Using margin properties</h1>
</body></html>
```

OUTPUT:

Fig. 6.42: Result of Example 32

9. ***Height and Width:*** The height and width properties are used to set the height and width of an element. It can be set to auto/px/% as in margins.

   Syntax: Selector {height: value; width: value;}

Example 33

```
<html><head>
<style>
img {height: 25%; width: 50%;}
</style></head>

<body>
<h2>Set the height and width in % of an image</h2>
<img class="one" src="C:\Users\HP EliteBook\Pictures\Saved Pictures\bday image1.jpg" >
</body>
</html>
```

OUTPUT:

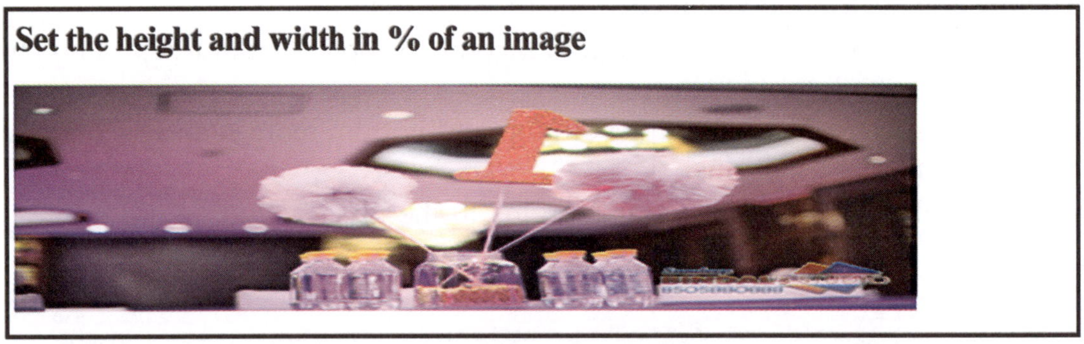

Fig. 6.43: Result of Example 33

10. ***Float:*** The float property is used to position the element. It is very often used to wrap text around images. Images can be placed left or right of the text.

    Syntax:

    Selector {float: value;}

Example 34

```
<html><head>
<style>
img {float: right; height: 25%; width: 25%;}
</style></head>
<body>
<h2>float image to the right of text</h2>
<p><img  src="C:\Users\HP EliteBook\Pictures\grapefruit.jpg">
"The health benefits of grapefruits are many and nearly unmatched by any other fruit. A glass
of chilled grapefruit juice, especially in summer, helps boost levels of vitamin C in your body,
which makes them the most nutritious fruit amongst various citrus fruits. </p>
</body>
</html>
```

OUTPUT:

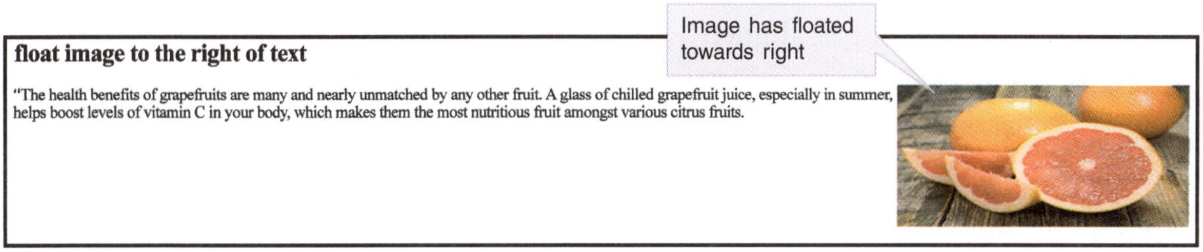

Fig. 6.44: Result of Example 34

11. *Align:* This property is used to align the element. The element may be the text in border, or an image. The text-align property specifies the horizontal alignment of text in an element.

    Syntax: selector {text-align: left/right/center/justify;}

    To align horizontally margin: auto is used. The width should be defined for horizontal alignment.

Example 35

```
<html><head>
<style>
h2 {margin: auto; width: 60%; border: 3px solid blue; text-align: center;}
</style>
</head>
<body>
<h2>Heading is Center Aligned </h2>
</body></html>
```

OUTPUT:

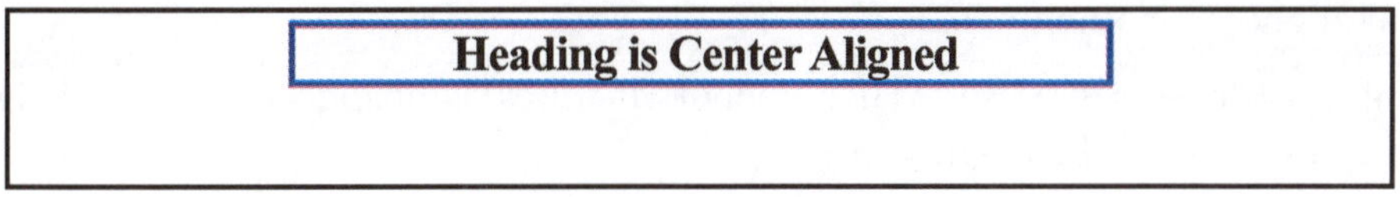

Fig. 6.45: Result of Example 34

12. **Vertical alignment:** The vertical-align property sets the vertical alignment of an element.

    Syntax:

    selector {vertical-align: baseline/sub/sup/top/text-top/middle/bottom/text-bottom;}

    - **sub:** The element is aligned with the subscript baseline of the text.
    - **sup:** The element is aligned with the superscript baseline of the text.
    - **top:** The element is aligned with the top of the tallest element on the line.
    - **text-top:** The element is aligned with the top of the parent element's font.

- **middle:** The element is placed in the middle of the parent element.
- **bottom:** The element is aligned with the lowest element on the line.
- **text-bottom:** The element is aligned with the bottom of the parent element's font.

Example 36

```
<!DOCTYPE html>
<html>
<head>
<style>
img.a {  vertical-align: baseline;}
img.b {  vertical-align: text-top;}
img.c {  vertical-align: text-bottom;}
img.d {  vertical-align: sub;}
img.e {  vertical-align: super;}
</style>
</head>
<body>
<h1>The vertical Property</h1>
<h2>vertical-align: baseline (default):</h2>
<p>An <img class="a" src="C:\Users\HP EliteBook\Pictures\lamb.jpg" width="50" height="50">
image with a default alignment.</p>
<h2>vertical-align: text-top:</h2>
<p>An <img class="b" src="c:\Users\HP EliteBook\Pictures\lamb.jpg" width="50" height="50">
image with a text-top alignment.</p>
<h2>vertical-align: text-bottom:</h2>
<p>An <img class="c" src="C:\Users\HP EliteBook\Pictures\lamb.jpg" width="50" height="50">
image with a text-bottom alignment.</p>
<h2>vertical-align: sub:</h2>
<p>An <img class="d" src="C:\Users\HP EliteBook\Pictures\lamb.jpg" width="50"
height="50"> image with a sub alignment.</p>
<h2>vertical-align: sup:</h2>
<p>An <img class="e" src="C:\Users\HP EliteBook\Pictures\lamb.jpg" width="50" height="50">
image with a super alignment.</p>
</body>
</html>
```

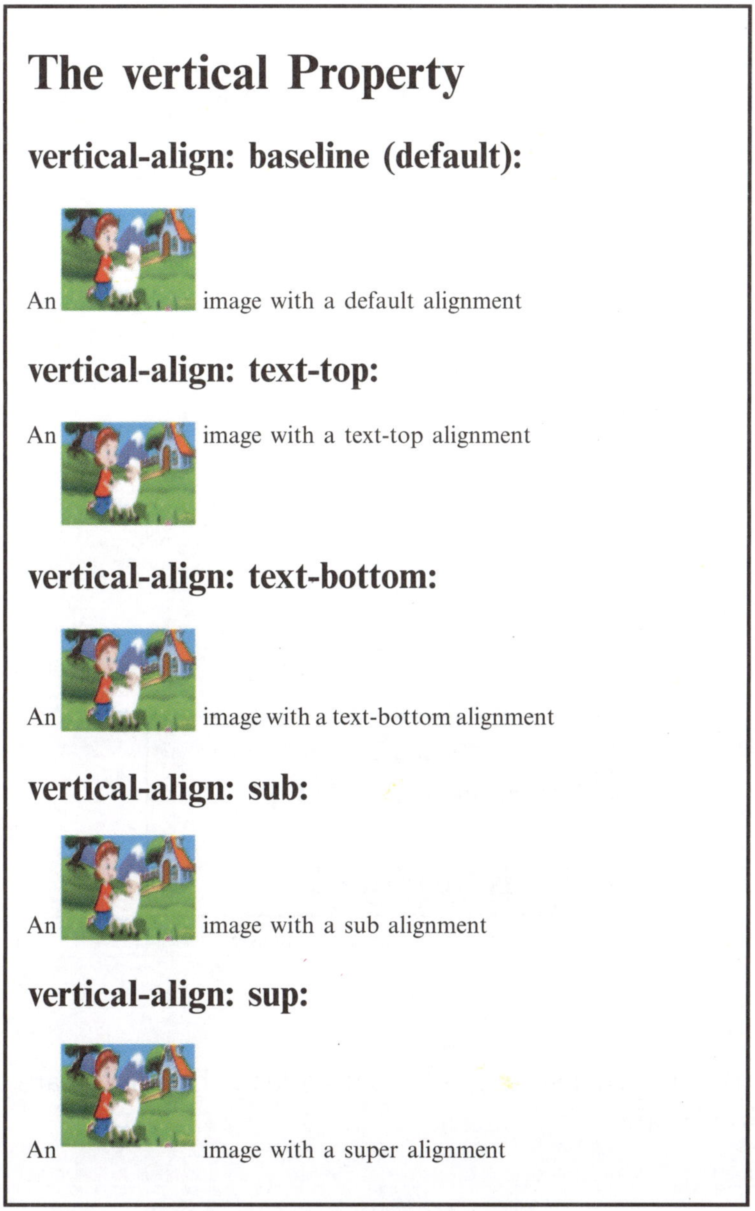

Fig. 6.46: Result of Example 36

13. *Text:* The text-decoration property specifies the decoration added to text, and is a property for:
    - text-decoration-line (required)- (like underline, overline, line-through)
    - text-decoration-color
    - text-decoration-style(like solid, wavy, dotted, dashed, double)

    Syntax:

    selector {text-decoration: *text-decoration-line text-decoration-color text-decoration-style;}*

Example 37

(The following example will not work in Internet Explorer as IE does not support text-decoration property, so use Google Chrome.)

```
<!DOCTYPE html>
<html>
<head>
<style>
h1 {  text-decoration: underline overline dotted red;}
h2 {  text-decoration: underline overline wavy blue;}
</style>
</head>
<body>
<h1>This is heading 1</h1>
<h2>This is heading 2</h2>
</html>
```

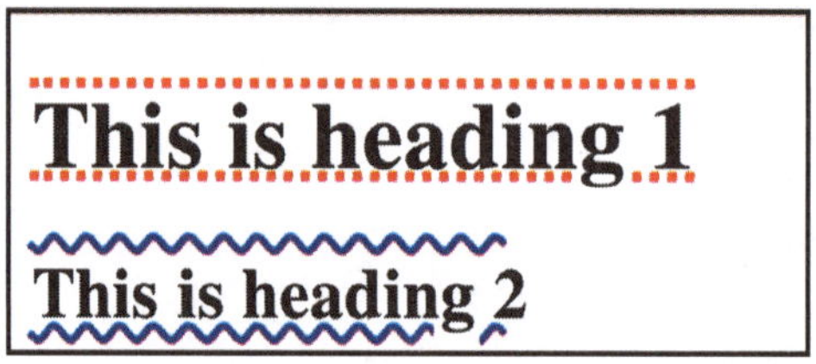

Fig. 6.47: Result of Example 37

6.6.4 Creating external CSS

Till now we have used internal styling, now let us learn how to create an external styling code and store it in CSS file.

STEPS

1. Create an HTML file using any text editor and include the style block in it.
2. Create a new file and save it as *.css in the same directory. Here * is any file name.
3. Move the style block from the HTML file to the *.css file. Don't copy the style tags.
4. Remove the style block from the HTML file.
5. In the HTML file, add a link tag after the closing title tag that points to *.css
   e.g., if the css file is Sheetwithstyle.css then type
   <link href="Sheetwithstyle.css" rel= "stylesheet" type="text/css">
   where href : is the location of the external style sheet
   rel : must be set to "stylesheet" for linking style sheets
   type : must be set to "text/css" for linking to cascading style sheets
6. Open the HTML file in a browser to view the applied style.

Example 38

Link to external CSS file

```
<!DOCTYPE html>
<html>
<head>
<link href="C:\Users\HP EliteBook\Desktop\extry.css"  rel="stylesheet"  type= "text/css"}
</head>
<body>
<h1>Heading is in red</h1>
<p>The color of the text in paragraph is blue</p>
</body>
</html>
```

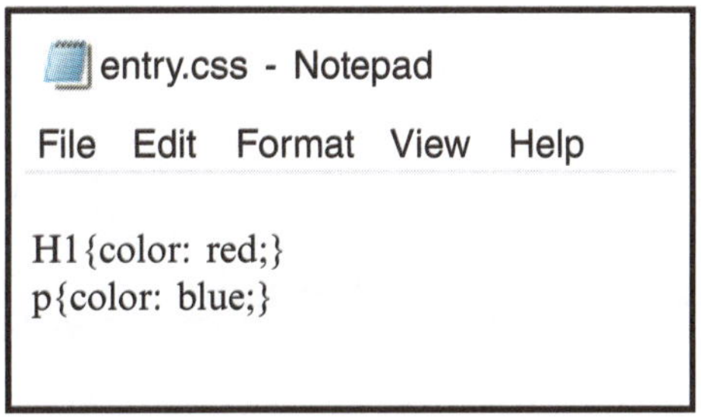

Fig. 6.48: Contents of extry.css file

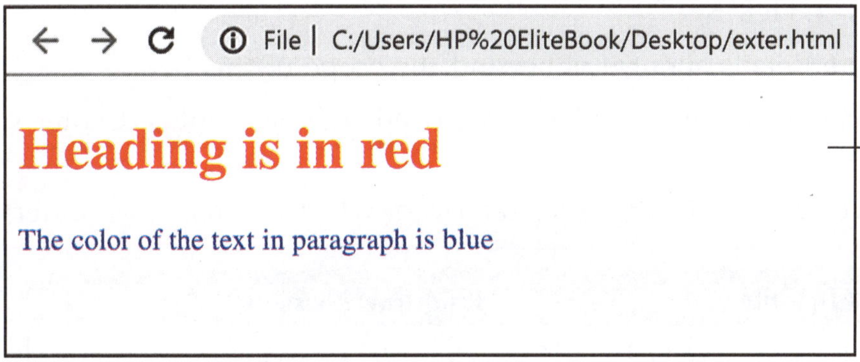

Output of HTML file and CSS file

Fig. 6.49: Result of Example 38

The above example displays linking with external CSS file. The HTML code includes link to the CSS file the contents of which are displayed in Fig. 6.48. Execution of HTML code of Example 38 displays the web page as in Fig. 6.49. To change the formatting of this web page, only the CSS file has to be updated, HTML code remains untouched.

6.7 BASICS ABOUT HTML5

HTML5 is the latest version of the HTML and has many additional features as compared to HTML4. Some of the features and attributes of HTML4 are not supported by HTML5 and these have been listed further in this section.

The structure of HTML5 document is as follows:

1. The HTML syntax requires a **doctype** (document type) to be specified to ensure

that the browser identifies the code as HTML5 code. The doctype has no other purpose.

For example,

```
<!doctype html>
<html  lang="en">
<head>
<meta charset="UTF-8">
<title>Example document</title>
</head>
<body>
<p>Example paragraph</p>
</body>
</html>
```

2. HTML tag has an attribute to specify the language used. If it is English, the attribute is written as lang="en". By default the language is English, so this attribute can be skipped.
3. The meta tag is used within the Head tag to specify the character coding used. In normal case UTF-8 coding is used.

   ```
   <meta charset="UTF-8">
   ```

   Going into more details about it is beyond the scope of this book.
4. The elements that have been completely removed are <Basefont>, <Center>, <Font> and <Underline>.
5. Some tags have only a few attributes removed, which are listed as under:

Removed Attributes	From the Elements
target	link
name	img
align	caption, iframe, img, input, object, legend, table, hr, div, h1, h2, h3, h4, h5, h6, p, col, colgroup, tbody, td, tfoot, th, thead and tr.
alink	body
link	body
vlink	body
text	body
background	body

bgcolor	table, tr, td, th and body
border	table
cellpadding	table
cellspacing	table
noshade	hr
nowrap	td and th
size	hr
type	li, ol and ul
valign	col, colgroup, tbody, td, th, and tr
width	hr, table, td, th, col, colgroup

Cascading Style Sheets (CSS) can be used for getting the same results as that of the attributes that have been made obsolete in HTML5.

KEY TERMS

- **Internal link** Leads to another section of the same document.
- **External link** Leads to a web page of another website.
- **Table** A structure made of rows and columns.
- **Cell space** The space between two cells.
- **Cell padding** The space within a cell.
- **HTML form** A web document for taking user input and transferring it to the server.
- **CSS (Cascading Style Sheet)** A style sheet language used for describing the presentation of a document written in a markup language like HTML.
- **Selectors** The elements to which the defined style is applied.
- **Generic family** A group of font families with a similar look.
- **Font family** Refers to a specific font.

POINTS TO REMEMBER

- Images can be inserted in a web page using IMG tag.
- SRC, WIDTH, HEIGHT, BORDER, ALT are some of the attributes used with IMG tag.
- ALT attribute is used to display a text during the time the image takes to get displayed.
- A link can lead to another section on the same web page or to another web page.
- Linking is done using Anchor tag with HREF, NAME and ALT as attributes.
- Link attribute is used for unvisited links, ALINK for links being clicked and VLINK for links already visited.
- Mailto is an easy and fast way by which a visitor at a website can directly send mail to the website owner or send the information on the website to another e-mail address.
- While inserting a table on a web page, cell spacing is used to adjust space between the cells and cell padding is used to adjust space within the cell.
- Audio and video files can be embedded in an HTML document using Audio/Video tags.
- HTML forms are designed to take input from the user and pass it on to the server
- Text, Checkbox, radio buttons, Select box, Submit box, clickable buttons are some of the HTML form controls.
- Cascading style sheets are used to format the layout of a web page and create a uniform look across several web pages.
- Styling may be Inline, Internal or External.
- Internal styling is declared in Head section using <style> and </style> tags.
- Inline styling is done in the body of the html code inside the element tags.
- External styling is done using .CSS file. A link to the CSS file is declared in the head section of the HTML code.

SOLVED QUESTIONS

Q1. Amita has used IMG element as shown below in her html document to insert an image but the browser is not displaying the image on the web page. What could be the possible reason?

<img src="flower.jpg" width = "30%" height="30%">

Ans. The image file and the html code should be in the same directory or else full pathname or location of the image file should be mentioned.

Q2. What is the function of ALT attribute in img tag?

Ans. The alt attribute provides alternative information for an image if a user cannot view it for some reason.

Q3. What is the difference between the following codes?

(i) <A href="physics.html" > Physics </A>

(ii) <A href="#Physics" > Physics </A>

Ans. (i) This code will provide a link to an html file named physics.html. So, it is external linking.

(ii) This code will provide a link to the section named Physics in the same document, so it is internal linking.

Q4. What is the significance of the following code?
<a ref=mailto:? subject=visit www.healthcaretips.com&body=for health related tips visit this website>

Ans. Here e-mail address has been left blank so the visitor of the web page can enter the e-mail address of his choice to send the mail.

Q5. What will be the output of the following code?
<table border="3" color="red" bgcolor="yellow">

Ans. It will create a table with red coloured border of width = 3 and the background colour of the table will be yellow.

Q6. How does html know the number of rows and columns of a table?

Ans. Number of <tr> tags identifies the rows and number of <td> tags within a <tr> tag represents the column.

Q7. What will be the outcome of the following code?
<TD colspan="3" > Same as above </TD>

Ans. 3 columns will be merged to make a single column in the active row and the text – "Same as above" will be printed in it.

Q8. Which attribute of Audio tag plays the audio repeatedly?

Ans. The loop attribute plays the audio repeatedly.

Q9. Which HTML form controls have been used in the following form?

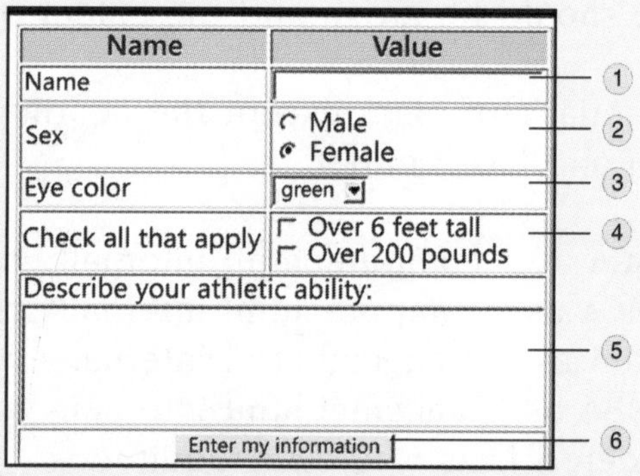

Ans.
1. text
2. radio button
3. select
4. checkbox
5. textarea
6. Submit

Q10. What will be the outcome of the following code?
<style>
H1{ outline: dashed red thick ; border: solid blue ;}
</style>

Ans. The above code will set the style for H1 heading. The heading will be surrounded by solid blue border which will have a thick dashed red outline.

Q11. Write down the HTML code to generate a page in the format and style shown below:

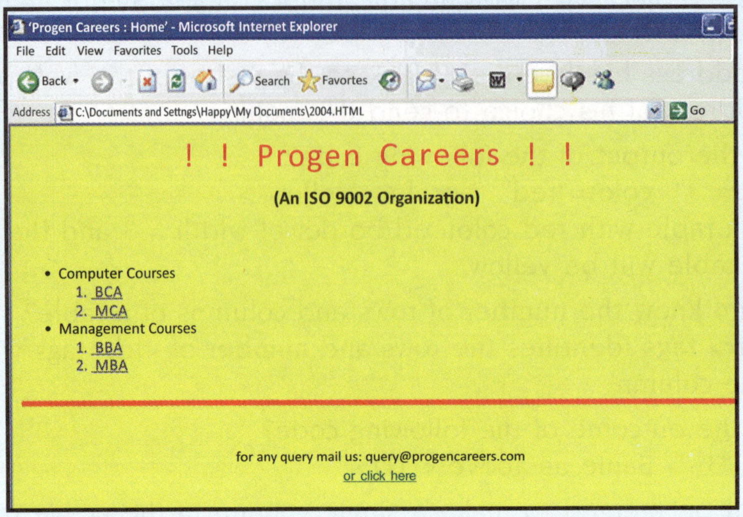

Special notes:

(i) Title of the page is 'Progen Careers'.

(ii) Background colour of the page is yellow.

(iii) Link colour of the page should be green and the colour of the visited links should be blue.

(iv) All font face should be Arial and black except the heading !!Progen Careers!! which should be in red colour and face Courier.

(v) Pages linked with

BCA as	computer.html internally named BCA
MCA as	computer.html internally named MCA
BBA as	mangmnt.html internally named BBA
MBA as	mangmnt.html internally named MBA

(vi) Use Ordered and Unordered Lists wherever required.

(vii) The Horizontal Ruler before the bottom message is of size 5 with Noshade attribute.

(viii) Use mailto tag for the last line.

You can assume any other attribute which is not otherwise mentioned above to produce a similar output.

Ans.

```
<HTML>
<HEAD>
</HEAD>
<BODY BGCOLOR="YELLOW" LINK="GREEN" VLINK="BLUE">
<FONT face="COURIER" COLOR="RED">
<H1 align="centre">! !     Progen Careers     ! !</H1>
</FONT>
<FONT="ARIAL">
<H3 align="centre"> (An ISO 9002 Organization) </H3>
<BR>
<BR>
<UL>
```

```
<li> Computer Courses </li>
<ol>
<li><A HREF="COMPUTER.HTML"> BCA </A></li>
<li><A HREF="COMPUTER.HTML"> MCA </A></li>
</ol>
<li> Management Courses </li>
<ol>
<li><A HREF="MANGMNT.HTML"> BBA </A></li>
<li><A HREF="MANGMNT.HTML"> MBA </A></li>
</ol>
</UL>
<HR COLOR="RED" NOSHADE SIZE=5>
<br>
<br>
<p align="center"> for any query mail us : query@progencareers.com
<a href="mailto: query@progencarrers.com"> or click here </a>
</p>
</FONT>
</BODY>
</HTML>
```

Q12. Write down the HTML code to generate a page in the format and style shown below:

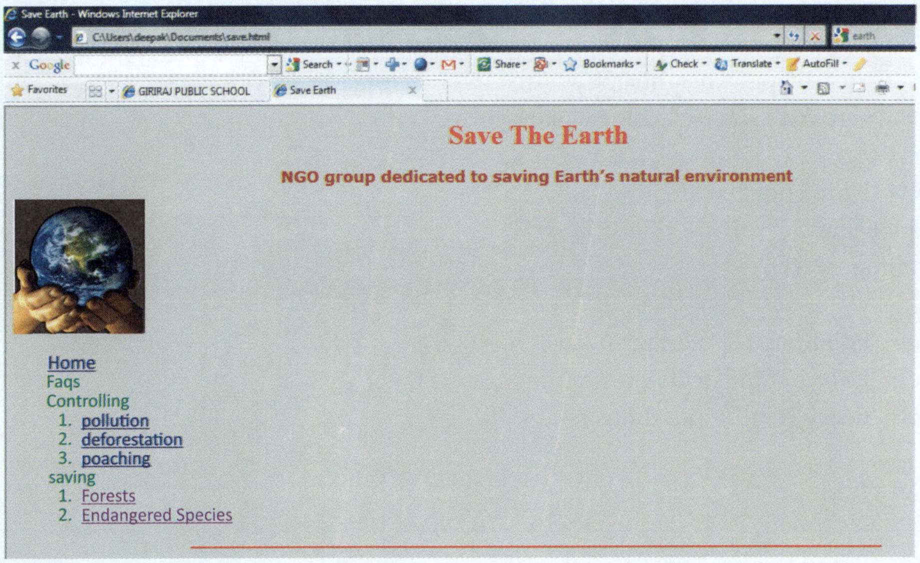

Special notes:

(i) Title of the page is 'Save Earth'.

(ii) Background colour of the page is silver.

(iii) Link colour of the page should be green and the colour of visited links should be blue.

(iv) All font face of text should be Verdana, size 4 and black except the heading which should be in black colour, face Arial and size 6 and the sub heading is in 'Verdana' font, size 4 and colour brown.

(v) Image used is from the file 'dearearth.jpg'.

(vi) Pages linked with

Home	Home.htm
Faqs	Faq.htm
Pollution	Poll.htm
Deforestation	Defores.htm
Poaching	Poach.htm
Forests	Forest.htm
Endangered Species	Specie.htm

(vii) Use Ordered and Unordered Lists wherever required.

(viii) The Horizontal Ruler before the bottom message is of width 820 and height 80.

(ix) Also create a mailto tag for further queries at askusanytime@hotmail.com.
You can assume any other attribute which is not otherwise mentioned above to produce a similar output.

Ans.

```
<html> <head>
</head>
<body bgcolor="silver" >

<h1  align="center">
<font color = "red" face ="arial" > Save The Earth </font>
</h1>
<font size = 4 color="brown" face="verdana">
<h3  align="center"> NGO group dedicated to saving Earth's natural environment </h3>

<img src="dearearth.jpg"  height=150 width=150> </font>
<font face ="verdana" size = 4 color="black">
<ul>
<li><a href="Home.html"> Home </a></li>
<li><a faq="Faq.html"> Faqs </a></li>
<li>Controlling </li>
<ol>
<li><a href="Poll.html"> pollution </a></li>
<li><a href="Defores.html"> deforestration </a></li>
<li><a href="Poach.html"> poaching </a></li>
</ol>
<li> saving</li>
<ol>
<li><a href="Forest.html"> Forests </a></li>
<li><a href="Specie.html"> Endangered Species </a></li>
</ol>
</ul>
<hr color="red"width =820 height=80>
<a href="mailto: askusanytime@hotmail.com"> For futher queries click here </a>
</font>
</body>
</html>
```

EXERCISES

I. Very Short Answer Type Questions

Multiple Choice Questions:

1. Column span specifies
(a) stretching of a cell over more than one column
(b) stretching of a cell over more than one row
(c) duplicating the data in each cell in a row
(d) none of the above

2. Linking is achieved by using
(a) <li> tag (b) <A> tag (c) <HREF> tag (d) none

3. HREF could be
(a) URLs
(b) address or name of an HTML document existing in your directory
(c) address or name of an HTML document existing in some other directory
(d) all of the above

4. A link used to navigate or open other web pages on a website on internet is called
(a) Higher link (b) Hyper link (c) Hydro link (d) Web link

5. Which one of the following is not an attribute of <A> tag?
(a) name (b) href (c) src (d) both (a) and (c)

6. Combining two or more cells in an HTML table is called
(a) Merging (b) Concatenation (c) Joining (d) Spanning

7. Which of the following is the correct way to create an e-mail link?
(a) <A href = "dumdum@abc.com">
(b) <A mail to : "dumdum@abc.com">
(c) <A href = "mailto:dumdum@abc.com">
(d) <A e-mail = "dumdum@abc.com">

8. Colspan attribute can only be added to
(a) <Table> (b) <TH> (c) <TR> (d) <TD>

9. Which of the following is not an HTML form control?
(a) Checkbox (b) Select (c) Password (d) Table

10. Which button on HTML form transfers the data to the server?
(a) Radio button (b) Checkbox (c) Select (d) Submit

11. Which tag in Head section is used for setting the properties of an html document?
(a) <Title> (b) <body> (c) <LOOKS> (d) <style>

12. In HTML file, a link tag is added after .... closing tag to point to *CSS.
(a) Title tag (b) Body tag (c) HTML tag (d) Head tag

13. For linking style sheets, **rel** attribute must be set to
(a) "*CSS" (b) "stylesheet" (c) "*html" (d) "text/CSS"

14. To align horizontally .... value of margin is used.
(a) 50 px (b) auto (c) "horizontal" (d) "align"

15. CSS declaration always ends with a
(a) comma (b) semicolon (c) double quotes (d) square bracket

16. CSS stands for
(a) Computer System Software
(b) Custom Style Sheet
(c) Cascading Style Sheets
(d) Cascading Sheet Style

17. Which is the correct way of defining a link tag for CSS file?
(a) <link href = "LOOK.CSS" rel = "stylesheet" type = "text/CSS">
(b) <link href = "Stylesheet" rel = "Look.CSS" type = "text/CSS">
(c) <link href = "LOOK.CSS" rel = "text/CSS" type = "Stylesheet">
(d) <link href = "LOOK.CSS" rel = "stylesheet" type = "CSS/text">

18. Selector is the .... to which properties are applied.
(a) code (b) attribute (c) element (d) text

19. Inline Styling is done in
(a) Head section
(b) Body section
(c) CSS file
(d) not allowed in HTML

20. Which of the following tags are not included in a CSS file?
(a) <HTML> (b) <Style> (c) <Head> (d) All of the above

Fill in the blanks:

1. .... tag is used for creating hypertext links.

2. Link defines the colour of ....

3. .... defines the colour of link as it is being clicked.

4. .... defines the colour of link after it has been visited.

5. Text to be printed in merged cells is enclosed in .... and .... tags.

6. <th> tag is written for ....

7. Number of <tr> tags represents the number of .... in the table.

8. .... attribute sets the distance between the cells.

9. .... attribute sets the space within the cell.

10. The four attributes that can be used with the Anchor tag are ...., ..., ... and ....

11. HREF stands for ....

12. When a link has been visited its colour in the main document changes from .... to ....

13. .... symbol implies that the reference is in same document.

14. Link refers to .... links, ... refers to links being clicked and .... refers to links visited.

15. .... are used to take input from the user on a web page.

16. <form> tag is a .... tag.

17. .... attribute specifies the URL address of the audio or video file.

18. .... attribute does not play the audio while video is running.

19. By default the width of single line text input control is ....

20. .... tag is used for multiline text input.

21. The lists which uses pattern indentation for elements is ....

22. <dd> tag is used to give .... related to the term specified by ....

23. CSS declaration ends with a .... and is enclosed in ....
24. A group of font families with a similar look is called ....
25. While setting font properties, we should start with a .... and end with a .... family.
26. If only two values for margin properties are given then they represent .... and .... margins.
27. .... property is used to wrap text around images.
28. A style sheet should have an extension ....

II. Short Answer Type Questions

1. What is hyperlink?
2. What is meant by VLINK?
3. What do you understand by option ALINK used with <BODY> tag?
4. The following code is written to align the image in centre of browser's window. However, the desired result is not achieved. Mention the reason.
   <IMG SRC='house.gif' Align=centre>
5. Consider the HTML code <A HREF=#intro> Introduction </A>. What is the purpose of using #? What will happen when the user clicks 'Introduction'? What is the purpose of HREF in tag <A>?
6. Which tag is used to insert a picture in a web page? Write the option used with it.
7. What is the pre-requisite for using mailto tag in HTML?
8. What is the difference between ol list, ul list and description list?
9. Which tags are used with <dl> tag and what do they signify?
10. Which attribute allows us to play, stop or pause an audio or video on a web page?
11. What is the significance of using HTML forms?
12. Name the different input controls for HTML forms.
13. What type of input control is password?
14. What are CSS sheets? What is their use?
15. What are the two locations for setting the styles for web pages?
16. What are the two types of font families?
17. Why is it advisable for font-family to hold several font names?
18. When can several selectors be grouped together?
19. What will be the result of the following code segment?

```
<style>
Body {background-color : blue;}
H1 {color : white; text-align : centre;}
</style>
```

20. Where and why is an outline property used?
21. Write a style statement to float an image towards left with height and width 50% each.
22. Write the statement to link AABB.CSS file to an HTML file.

III. Long Answer Type Questions

1. How can link between different sections of some documents be established?
2. How can a document be linked with another document?
3. How is the internal linking different from external linking?
4. Differentiate between cell padding and cell spacing.
5. Give two advantages and two disadvantages of mailto tag.
6. Differentiate between checkbox, radio button and select input controls.
7. Write the steps to create an external CSS.
8. Which attributes are used to link CSS file to an HTML file? Explain.
9. Write an HTML code with CSS to perform the following:
   (i) Heading 'National Parties in India' should be in centre with a solid red outline.
   (ii) Write a few lines about any one party with an image of its symbol on the right side. The text should be justified and the left margin of the image should be set. Write the text in blue, Georgia and Italic. Draw an outline around the image.
10. Design an HTML form for taking in the following data:

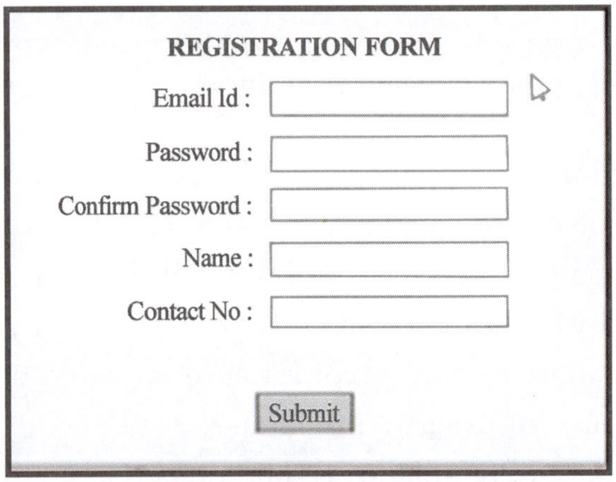

11. Write an HTML code using CSS to make the following list:

    Components of a Computer System:

    1. Input Unit:

    This unit takes input from the user with the help of any of the following input devices:

    - Keyboard
    - Mouse
    - Scanner

    2. Central Processing Unit:

    This unit is responsible for controlling the units of a computer system. It also stores data temporarily while performing arithmetic and logical operations on it. It has the following sub-units:

    - Control Unit
    - ALU
    - Memory

3. Output Unit:

This unit provides the user with the output which may be on:

- Printer
- VDU
- Speaker

12. Design an input form for taking in the following data:

(i) Name : First name [ ]
Middle name [ ]
Last name [ ]

(ii) Address : [ ]

(iii) Type of service required:

[Electrician]
[Plumbing]
[Mason]
[Carpenter]
[Whitewash]

(iv) Convenient time for contacting : [ ]

(v) Phone no. : [ ]

13. Write the HTML code to generate the following output:

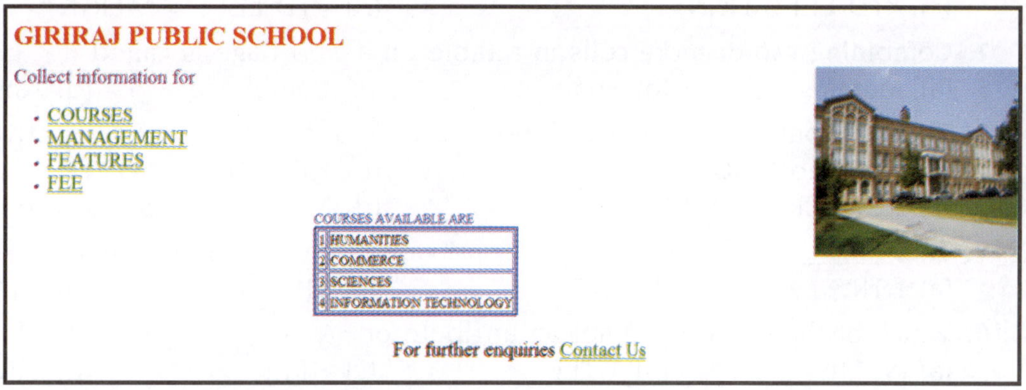

Note the following points while generating the web page:

- Link colour is green, active link colour is blue and visited link colour is red.
- Title of the page is "GIRIRAJ PUBLIC SCHOOL".
- Heading of the page is "School.jpg".
- Caption of table is blue.
- Table border is blue and of size 2.
- The 4 links are one.html, two.html, three.html and four.html.
- The e-mail address for contact is giriraj@abc.com

14. Observe the following table and write the HTML code to generate it:

<table>
<tr><th colspan="6">Time Table</th></tr>
<tr><th rowspan="6">Periods</th><th>Mon</th><th>Tue</th><th>Wed</th><th>Thu</th><th>Fri</th></tr>
<tr><td>Science</td><td>Maths</td><td>Science</td><td>Maths</td><td>Arts</td></tr>
<tr><td>Social Sci.</td><td>History</td><td>English</td><td>Social Sci.</td><td>Sports</td></tr>
<tr><th colspan="5">Lunch</th></tr>
<tr><td>Science</td><td>Maths</td><td>Science</td><td>Maths</td><td rowspan="2">Practicals</td></tr>
<tr><td>Social Sci.</td><td>History</td><td>English</td><td>Social Sci.</td></tr>
</table>

Previous Years' Solved Examination Questions

I. Very Short Answer Type Questions

Multiple Choice Questions:

1. MAILTO and HREF are the attributes of .... tag: (2019)
(a) <MAIL> (b) <A> (c) IMAGE> (d) <TABLE>

2. In VLINK attribute, V stands for (2018)
(a) Visited (b) Victory (c) Very (d) Visitor

3. Which tag allows you to add a row in a table? (2017)
(a) <td> and </td> (b) <cr> and </cr>
(c) <th> and </th> (d) <tr> and </tr>

4. The attribute used to set the border colour of a table is (2011)
(a) BORDER (b) BORDER COLOR (c) COLOR (d) BORDERCOLOR

5. Which of the following is not an attribute of the <TABLE> tag? (2011)
(a) ALT (b) WIDTH (c) BORDER (d) BACKGROUND

6. Choose the correct HTML code to left-align the content inside the table cell. (2011)
(a) <TD ALIGN = "left"> (b) <TD VALIGN = "LEFT">
(c) <TD LEFTALIGN> (d) <TD LEFT = "ALIGN">

7. Combining two or more cells in a table on a web page is called .... (2011)
(a) Merging (b) Spanning (c) Combining (d) None of these

8. The two common attributes of the <IMG> and <TABLE> tags respectively are: (2011)
(a) SRC and HEIGHT (b) HEIGHT and WIDTH
(c) BORDER and SRC (d) They do not have any common attributes

9. The ______ is used to specify the individual table data in a table. (2011)
(a) <TR> (b) <TD> (c) TH> (d) <TABLE>

10. Which of the following is not an attribute of <A> tag? (2014)
(a) NAME (b) TITLE (c) HREF (d) SRC

11. <ALT> attribute allows: (2016)
(a) addition of an alternative hyperlink.
(b) addition of a border to image.
(c) use of an alternative image in place of the specified image.
(d) addition of alternative text about an image.

12. Which of these belong to <table> tag? (2016)
(a) <thead> <body> <tr> (b) <table> <head> <foot>
(c) <table> <tr> <td> (d) <table> <tr> <tt>

13. Which of the following is not an option for aligning data in a table? (2016)
(a) justify (b) right (c) left (d) center

14. With which code you can make an image work as a link? (2014)
(a) <A href = "URL"> Text </A>
(b) <A href = ABC.Html> <img src = graphic.gif> click here </A>
(c) <A ref = mail to : <img src = graphic.gif> click here </A>
(d) None of the above

15. LINK, ALINK, VLINK are the attributes of (2018C)
(a) <BODY> tag (b) <HEAD> tag (c) <TITLE> tag (d) <A> tag

16. Background is an attribute of (2019)
(a) <BODY> tag (b) <FONT> tag (c) <IMG> tag (d) <A> tag

Answers: **1.** (b) **2.** (a) **3.** (d) **4.** (d) **5.** (a) **6.** (a) **7.** (b) **8.** (b) **9.** (b) **10.** (b) **11.** (d) **12.** (c) **13.** (a) **14.** (b) **15.** (a) **16.** (a)

Fill in the blanks:

1. .... is used to change the colour of a visited link. (2016)
2. .... are used to connect web pages. They are created with <A> tag. (2016)
3. .... attribute is used to give border to an image. (2016)
4. .... tag is used for inserting background image. (2017)
5. <TD> tag can be present only in .... tag. (2016, 2013)
6. .... attribute is used to span two or more columns in a table. (2012)
7. .... tag is used to create inline images. (2013)
8. .... attribute is used to combine columns vertically. (2011)
9. Default colour of hyperlink on the web page is .... (2011)
10. .... tag is used to create a table. (2013)
11. <TR> tag can only be present in .... tag. (2013)

Answers:
1. VLINK
2. Hyperlinks
3. Border
4. <Body Background = " ">
5. <tr> </tr>
6. COLSPAN
7. IMG
8. ROWSPAN
9. Blue
10. <TABLE>
11. <TABLE> </TABLE>

True/False:

1. SRC attribute specifies an alternate text for an image, if the image is not displayed. (2017)
2. A hyperlink can be applied to Text only. (2017)
3. Cell padding attribute is used with <BODY> tag. (2016, 2012)
4. <TD> will make the text bold. (2016)
5. Default alignment of the image is right. (2014)
6. <Title> tag is one of the structural tags of HTML document. (2015)
7. Almost all browsers support HTML. (2013)
8. Alt attribute with <img> tag is used for alternate image. (2014, 2011)
9. It is not possible to create link within current document. (2012)

10. Row span attribute is used to span multiple columns. (2013)
11. Unordered list type creates a numbered list. (2012)
12. Border is an attribute of <A> tag. (2012)
13. Colour of a hyperlink in HTML document cannot be changed. (2011)
14. No value is specified with ALT attribute of <img> tag. (2012)

Answers: 1. False 2. False 3. False 4. False 5. False
6. True 7. True 8. False 9. False 10. False
11. False 12. False 13. False 14. False

II. Short Answer Type Questions

1. Identify which of the following is a tag or an attribute. (2017)
   (i) Img (ii) A

Ans. (i) <IMG> is a tag.
(ii) <A> is a tag.

2. Identify the errors in the following HTML code and write the corrected code with each correction underlined: (2011, 2012)

```
<HTML>
        <TITLE>    IMAGES</HEAD>
<BODY BGCOLOR="PICI. JPG">
        <IMG    HREF="abc.jpg">        HERE IS MY IMAGE FILE
</BGCOLOR>
</HTML>
```

Ans.

```
<HTML>
<HEAD>
<TITLE> IMAGES </TITLE>
</HEAD>
<BODY BACKGROUND = "PICI.JPG">
<IMG SRC = "abc.jpg"> HERE IS MY IMAGE FILE
</BODY>
</HTML>
```

3. Write the HTML code to generate the following table on a web page with the contents and alignment exactly as shown below: (2011)

NAME	CLASS	SECTION
SAHIBA	10	A

Ans.

```
<HTML>
<BODY>
<TABLE BORDER = 2 ALIGN = LEFT>
<TR>
<TD> NAME
<TD> CLASS
<TD> SECTION
<TR>
<TD> SAHIBA
<TD> 10
<TD> A
</TR>
</TABLE>
```

```
</BODY>
</HTML>
```

4. Write the full form of: (2013)

(i) <SUP> (ii) <A> (iii) <IMG> (iv) <P>

Ans. (i) <SUP> – SUPERSCRIPT (ii) <A> – ANCHOR

(iii) <IMG> – IMAGE (iv) <P> – PARAGRAPH

5. Write the HTML code to send an e-mail to abc@xyz.com from your web page. (2013)

Ans.

```
<HTML>
<BODY>
We are there to help you
<A HERF = "mail to : abc@xyz.com"> send an e-mail </A>
</BODY>
</HTML>
```

6. Name the attributes of <A> tag which are used for internal linking in a web page. (2013)

Ans. Attributes of <A> for internal linking

(i) name, *e.g.* <A name = "alpha"> Alpha </A>

(ii) Linking with herf with #

e.g. <A href = "#alpha"> ALPHA </A>

7. Observe the following table and write the HTML code to generate it: (2013)

Period 1	Period 2
Math	Science
English	SSt
Science	SSt

Ans.

```
<HTML>
<BODY>
<TABLE BORDER= 2 ALIGN = LEFT>
<TR>
<TD> Period 1 <TD> Period 2
<TR>
<TD> Maths <TD> Science <TR> <TD> English <TD> SSt
<TR>
<TD> Science <TD> SSt
</TABLE>
</BODY>
</HTML>
```

8. Rachit, a beginner in web designing is not able to understand that how internal linking is different from external linking. Explain him about the same. Additionally tell him about the suitable tag and its attribute(s) for creating internal linking. (2018C)

Ans. LINKS that direct us to different sections of its own document are called internal links. Links that redirect us to sections of any other HTML document are called external links. For internal linking we use <A> tag with name attribute to identify the targeted section, *e.g.* <A name = "section1"> section 1 </A>

Then a link to this named section can be set-up by the following command:

<A href = "# section1"> link to section 1 </A>

9. Priyamvada has just started learning HTML. She has made a list of few HTML tags which she will be using in creating a web page but by mistake she has mentioned wrong attributes in front of the tags. Help her in selecting correct attributes from 'Column B' for the tags given in "Column A'. (2019)

Column A (TAGS)	Column B (ATTRBUTES)
BODY	MAILTO
UL	HEIGHT
A	TYPE
IMG	VLINK

Ans. BODY - VLINK
UL - TYPE
A - MAILTO
IMG - HEIGHT

10. Mention any two attributes of <IMG> tag along with their significance. (2019)

Ans. Any two from the following:

SRC - It is used to give the location of the image.

ALIGN - It is used to set the position of the image.

BORDER - It is used to provide a border around the image.

HEIGHT - It is used to specify the height of the image.

WIDTH - It is used to specify the width of the image.

ALT - It is used to provide alternate text to the image.

Long Answer Questions:

1. Write the HTML code to generate the following output: (2011)

Note the following points while generating the webpage:

(i) Title of the page should be "Dubai Tourism".

(ii) The heading text "WELCOME TO DUBAI" is in Arial font in maroon colour.

(iii) The horizontal lines below the heading are 5 pixels thick and red in colour.

(iv) Image used in the page is burj.jpg.

(v) The bulleted list contains links as specified below:

- The text Morning is a link to the webpage "morning.html".
- The text Evening is a link to the webpage "evening.html".

(vi) Queries can be invited at enquiry@gmail.com

Ans.:

```
<HTML><HEAD>
<TITLE>Dubai Tourism</TITLE>
</HEAD>
<BODY >
<H1 ALIGN= CENTER>
<FONT  FACE=ARIAL  COLOR=MAROON>WELCOME TO DUBAI</FONT>
</H1>
<HR SIZE=5 COLOR= RED  WIDTH= 40%>
<HR SIZE=5 COLOR= RED  WIDTH= 30%>
<IMG SRC="BURG.JPG" ALIGN=RIGHT WIDTH=20%  HEIGHT=30%><BR>
<FONT SIZE=6>
<P> Enjoy the world of pure travel masti</P>
</FONT>
<FONT SIZE=4>FOLLOWING IS A LIST OF MAJOR TOURIST ATTRACTIONS IN DUBAI:
<BR>
<UL>
<LI> <A HREF="MORNING.HTML">MORNING</A> Dolphiranium and Palm Dubai
<LI> <A HREF="EVENING.HTML">EVENING</A> Ski Dubai and Cruise
</UL>
<BR>
</FONT>
<CENTER>
For queries mail us at <a href = "mailto:enquiry@gmail.com>enquiry@gmail.com</a>
</CENTER>
</FONT>
</BODY>
</HTML>
```

2. Carefully study the web page given below. Identify 10 tags (structural(S)/formatting(F) or any other) that have been utilized in creating this web page and write the usage of each of them. (2012)

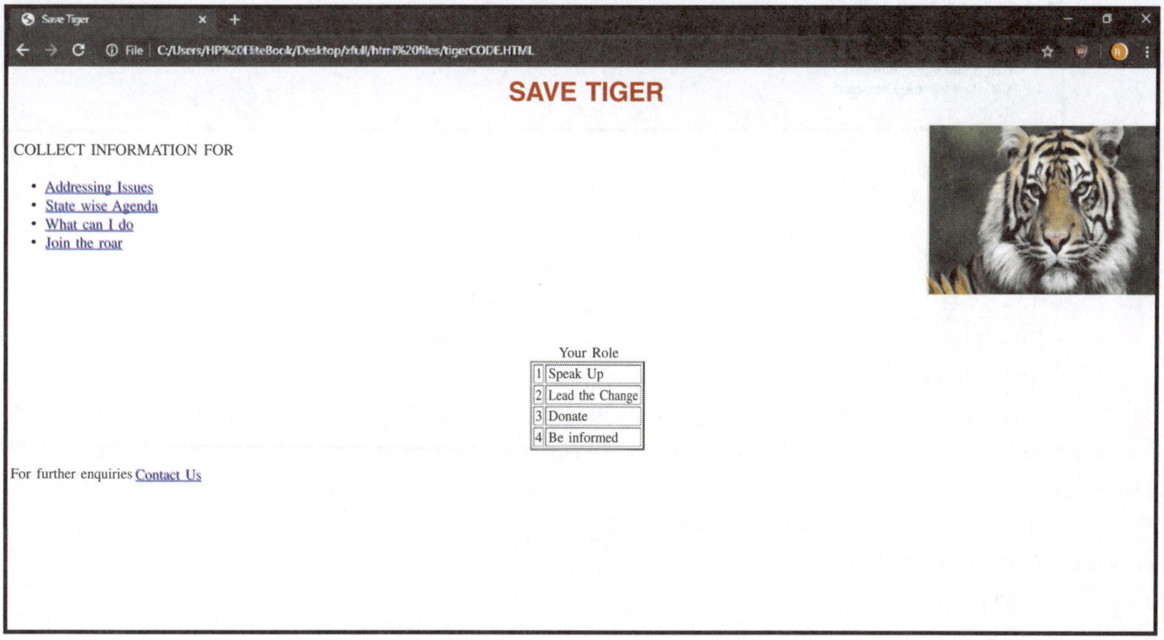

Ans.:

S. No.	Tag	Type of Tag	Use
1.	<HTML>	S	Marks beginning and end of HTML document
2.	<HEAD>	S	Used to begin the head section
3.	<BODY>	S	Used to begin the body section
4.	<H1>	F	Marks the biggest heading
5.	<P>	F	Starts a new paragraph
6.	<CENTER>	F	Displays the element in the center
7.	 	F	Breaks a line
8.	<IMG>	IMAGE	Inserts an image
9.	<TABLE>	TABLE	Creates a table
10.	<FONT>	F	Specifies the attributes of the text
11.	<TR>	TABLE	Creates a row
12.	<TD>	TABLE	Specifies the data in a cell of the table
13.	<LI>	LIST	Defines an element of a list

Q.3 Write the HTML code to generate the following output: (2012)

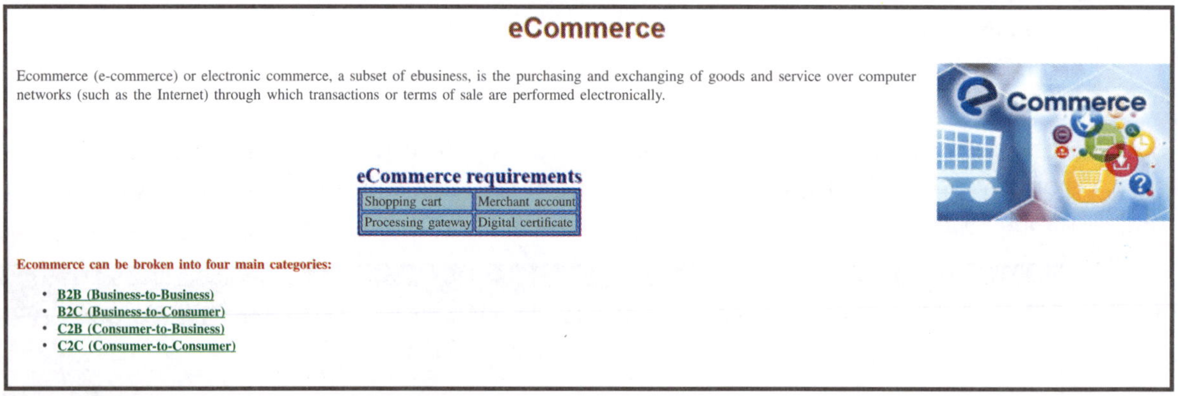

Note the following points while generating the webpage:

(i) Title of the page should be "eCommerce".
(ii) The heading text "eCommerce " is in maroon colour.
(iii) The link colour is green, active link colour is blue and visited link colour is red.
(iv) Image used in the page is ecommerce.jpg
(v) Background of table is cyan
(vi) Table border is blue and of size 2.
(vii) The four links are one.html, two.html, three.html and four.html
(viii) List heading is red.
(ix) Caption of table is blue

Answer:
```
<HTML><HEAD>
<TITLE>eCommerce</TITLE>
</HEAD>
<BODY  LINK=GREEN   ALINK=BLUE   VLINK=RED>
```

```
<H1 ALIGN= CENTER>
<FONT  FACE=ARIAL  COLOR=MAROON>eCommerce</FONT></H1>
<IMG SRC="ecommerce.jpg" ALIGN=RIGHT WIDTH=20%  HEIGHT=30%><BR>
<FONT  SIZE=4>Ecommerce  (e-commerce)  or  electronic  commerce,  a  subset  of
ebusiness, is the purchasing and exchanging of goods and service over computer
networks( such as the Internet) through which transactions or terms of sale are performed
electronically.<BR></FONT>
<CENTER>
<FONT COLOR=BLUE SIZE=5><BR><BR>
<B>eCommerce requirements</B></FONT>
<TABLE  BORDER=2 BGCOLOR=CYAN  BORDERCOLOR=BLUE>
<TR>
<TD>Shopping cart <TD> Merchant account
<TR>
<TD>Processing gateway<TD>Digital certificate
</TABLE>
</CENTER></FONT><BR><BR>
<B> <FONT COLOR=RED>Ecommerce can be broken into four main categories:</
FONT>
<UL>
<LI> <A HREF="ONE.HTML">B2B (Business-to-Business)</A>
<LI> <A HREF="TWO.HTML">B2C (Business-to-Consumer)</A>
<LI> <A HREF="THREE.HTML">C2B (Consumer-to-Business)</A>
<LI> <A HREF="FOUR.HTML">C2C (Consumer-to-Consumer)</A>
</UL>
<BR>
</BODY>
</HTML>
```

4. Carefully study the web page given below. Identify 10 tags (structural(S)/formatting(F) or any other) that have been utilized in creating this web page and write the usage of each of them. (2014)

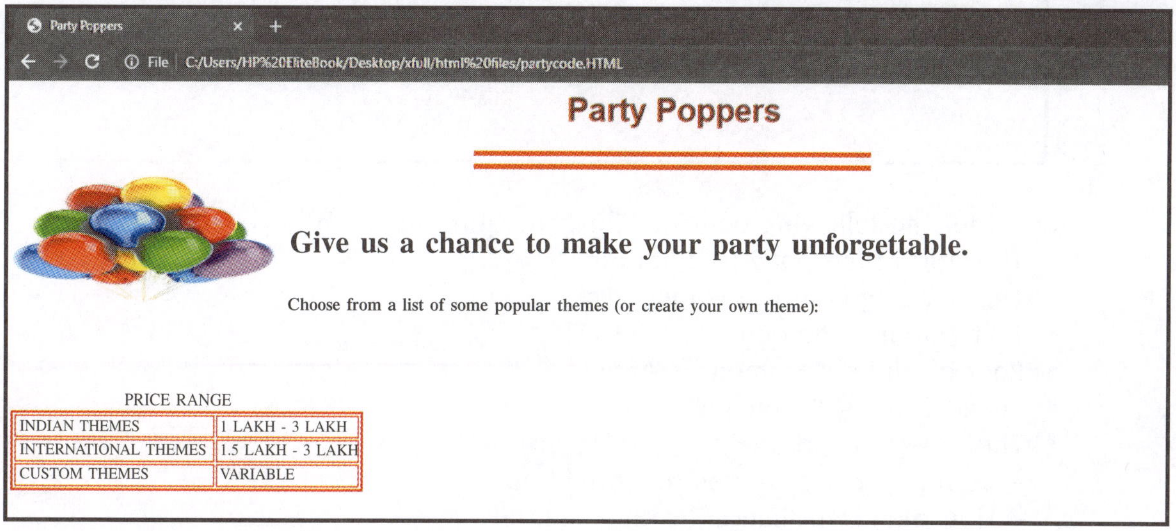

Ans:

S. No.	Tag	Type of Tag	Use
1.	<HTML>	S	Marks beginning and end of HTML document
2.	<HEAD>	S	Used to begin the heading section
3.	<BODY>	S	Used to begin the body section
4.	<H1>	F	Marks the biggest heading
5.	<P>	F	Starts a new paragraph
6.	<CENTER>	F	Displays the element in the center of the webpage
7.	 	F	Breaks a line
8.	<IMG>	IMAGE	Inserts an image
9.	<TABLE>	TABLE	Creates a table
10.	<FONT>	F	Specifies the attributes of the text
11.	<TR>	TABLE	Creates a row
12.	<TD>	TABLE	Specifies the data in a cell of the table

Q.5 Observe the following output and write HTML code to generate it: (2017)

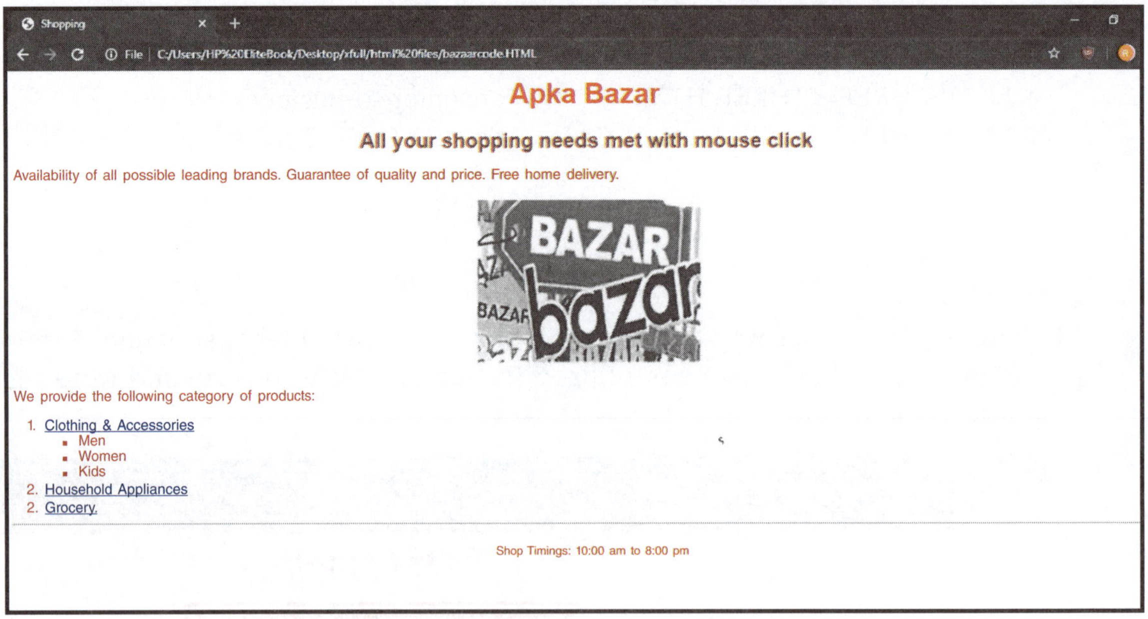

Consider the following points while generating the web page:

- The title of the page is "Shopping".
- The heading is in red colour.
- Text colour is maroon.
- Font of entire document is Arial.
- Image used is "bazar.jpg".
- The pages linked are:
  - Clothing & Accessories to cloth.html
  - Household Appliances to "house.html"
  - Grocery to "grocery.html"
- Bottom message is of size 2.

Ans:

```
<HTML><HEAD>
<TITLE>Shopping</TITLE>
</HEAD>
<BODY  TEXT=MAROON>
<FONT  FACE=ARIAL>
<H1><CENTER><FONT COLOR=RED> Apka Bazar</FONT></CENTER></H1>
 <H2><CENTER>All your shopping needs met with mouse click</CENTER></H2>
<P> Availability of all possible leading brands. Guarantee of quality and price. Free home delivery.
<CENTER>
<IMG SRC="bazar.jpg" WIDTH=20%  HEIGHT=30%><BR></CENTER>
<P> We provide the following category of products:
<OL type=1>
<LI> <A HREF="CLOTH.HTML">Clothing & Accessories</A>
<UL TYPE=SQUARE>
<LI>Men
<LI>Women
<LI>Kids
</UL>
<LI> <A HREF="HOUSE.HTML">Household Appliances</A>
<LI> <A HREF="GROCERY">Grocery</A>
</OL>
<HR>
<P><CENTER>
<FONT  SIZE=2>Shop Timings: 10:00 am to 8:00 pm</FONT>
</P></FONT></CENTER>
</FONT>
</BODY>
</HTML>
```

Q.6 Write the HTML code to generate the following web page with the given below specifications: (2019)

(a) Bordered table should have background colour in pink.

(b) Table's header row with a heading "INCOME TAX SLABS 2017-18" should spread over four cells.

(c) After heading row, first cell of next row should spread over five rows with an image named "it.jpg" stored in d: drive.

(d) Set the space between the cell wall and the cell content to 10 pixels and set the space between the cells to 10 pixels.

(e) At the bottom of the page, a link to next page is there which is linked to another webpage named "next.html".

INCOME TAX SLABS 2017-18			
	S. No.	Income Range	Tax%
	1	0 - 250000	NIL
	2	250001 - 500000	NIL
	3	500000 - 1000000	20%
	4	> 1000000	20%

Ans.:

```
<HTML>
<HEAD><TITLE>Income Tax Slabs 2017- 18</TITLE></HEAD> <BODY>
<TABLE BGCOLOR=PINK  BORDER=1 CELLSPACING=10 CELLPADDING=10 WIDTH =
30>
<TR>
<TH COLSPAN=4>
INCOME TAX SLABS 2017-18
</TH>
</TR>
<TR>
<TD ROWSPAN=5><IMG SRC="D:/IT.JPG" ></TD>
<TD>S.No.</TD>
<TD>Income Range</TD>
<TD>Tax%</TD>
</TR>
<TR>
<TD>1</TD>
<TD>0 - 250000</TD>
<TD>NIL</TD>
</TR>
<TR>
<TD>2</TD>
<TD>250001 - 500000</TD>
<TD>10%</TD>
</TR>
<TR>
<TD>3</TD>
<TD>500001 - 1000000</TD>
<TD>20%</TD>
</TR>
<TR>
<TD>4</TD>
<TD>1000000</TD>
<TD>30%</TD>
</TR>
</TABLE>
<A HREF="NEXT.HTML">Next Page</A>
</BODY>
</HTML>
```

Q.7. Sharda, a beginner in web page designing, is supposed to design a web page to promote yoga among students as shown below: (2019)

Write the HTML code to design the above shown web page considering the specifications as given below:

- Background colour of the page should be yellow and all the hyperlinked text should be red in colour.
- Image named yoga.jpg should be placed in the center of the webpage.
- Heading "The best way to health and fitness" should be first level of the heading and underlined.
- Paragraph should have following formatting styles applicable.
  Colour-Blue, Size-5, Font style-Times New Roman
- At the bottom of the page, "Contact Us" text should be linked with admin@yoga.com e-mail id.

Ans.

```
<HTML>
<BODY BGCOLOR="YELLOW" LINK="RED">
<CENTER><IMG SRC="yoga.jpg"> <BR>
<H1> <U> The best way to health and fitness </U></H1></CENTER>
<P><FONT COLOR="BLUE" SIZE="5" FACE="TIMES NEW ROMAN">
Yoga is a discipline and meditation which needs to be practiced physically, mentally,
and spiritually. It was originated in ancient India. It positively affects you both physically
and mentally and creates perfect harmony among your mind, body and soul.</FONT>
</P>
<BR>
<A HREF="mailto:admin@yoga.com">Contact Us </A>
</BODY>
</HTML>
```

Q.8 Shahnawaz has to create following list through HTML as a part of his social science project. Help him in writing HTML code for the same. (2019)

AFRICAN COUNTRIES AND THEIR CAPITALS

1. EGYPT
   - Cairo
2. ETHOPIA
   - Addis Ababa
3. KENYA
   - Nairobi

Ans.:

```
<HTML>
<BODY>AFRICAN COUNTRIES AND THEIR CAPITALS<BR>
<OL>
<LI> EGYPT
<UL TYPE="circle">
<LI> Cairo
</UL>
<LI>ETHIOPIA
<UL TYPE = "circle">
<LI>Addis Ababa
</UL>
<LI>KENYA
<UL TYPE="circle">
<LI> Nairobi
</UL>
</OL>
</BODY>
</HTML>
```

Q.9 Observe the following table and write the HTML code to generate it: (2017)

<table>
<tr><th>COLUMN 1</th><th>COLUMN 2</th><th>COLUMN 3</th></tr>
<tr><td rowspan="2">ROW 1 CELL 1</td><td>ROW 1 CELL 2</td><td>ROW 1 CELL 3</td></tr>
<tr><td>ROW 2 CELL 2</td><td>ROW 2 CELL 3</td></tr>
<tr><td colspan="3">ROW 3 CELL 1</td></tr>
</table>

Ans.

```
<HTML>
<BODY>
<TABLE   BORDER = 2   ALIGN = CENTER  >
<TR>
<TH> COLUMN 1 <TH> COLUMN 2 <TH> COLUMN 3
<TR>
<TD  ROWSPAN= "2"> ROW 1 CELL 1 <TD> ROW 1 CELL 2 <TD> ROW 1 CELL3
<TR>
<TD> ROW 2 CELL 2 <TD> ROW 2 CELL 3
<TR>
<TD  COLSPAN="3"  > ROW 3 CELL 1
</TABLE>
</BODY>
</HTML>
```

Q.10. Ms. Vani, Head Girl of the school, has to display sequence of events of upcoming school's Annual Day function on the school website. Help her in writing HTML code to create a table in HTML, as shown in the given screenshot. (2019)

ANNUAL DAY FUNCTION - SEQUENCE OF EVENTS		
8:00 AM - 9 : 00 AM	9 : 00 AM - 1 : 00 PM	9 : 00 AM - 1 : 00 PM
OPENING CEREMONY	PRIZE DISTRIBUTION	CULTURAL EVENTS

Ans.:

```
<HTML>
<BODY><TABLE BORDER = "2" >
<TR>
<TH COLSPAN= "3" > ANNUAL DAY FUNCTION - SEQUENCE OF EVENTS</TH>
</TR>
<TR ALIGN="CENTER">
<TD> 8:00 AM - 9:00 AM</TD>
<TD> 9:00 AM - 1:00 PM</TD>
<TD> 1:00 PM - 2:00 PM</TD>
</TR>
<TR ALIGN="CENTER" >
<TD> OPENING CEREMONY</TD>
<TD>PRIZE DISTRIBUTION</TD>
<TD>CULTURAL EVENTS</TD></TR>
</TABLE>
</BODY>
</HTML>
```

7 Cyber Ethics

- Netiquettes.
- Software licenses and the open source software movement.
- Intellectual property rights, plagiarism and digital property rights.
- Freedom of information and the digital divide.
- E-commerce: privacy, fraud, secure data transmission.

Technology has brought a revolution in the field of communication and the Internet has opened the doors to a new virtual world, by providing us with an effective means of communication. The Internet has given speed and volume to the regular means of communication, thereby, slowly replacing the traditional means. In a way, it has improved our social network and the world seems to be a much smaller and compact place now. People are able to connect with others to share their views and chat using audio and video, and to play online games with people, sitting at a distant location.

When a person is online, he/she becomes a citizen of the cyber space. Since, the cyber community is a close-knit virtual community, so an event happening at one place has an immediate repercussion in the whole community. Hence keeping this in mind, one should be very careful while communicating on the internet. In the real world, there is a code of conduct of good behaviour that one is expected to follow. Similarly, in cyber space too, there are some ethics that one must follow and these are called **netiquettes**. There is no rule book for netiquettes but most of the websites have their own rules, which are mentioned on their Terms and Conditions page. The access to any site would depend on the clicking of 'I Agree' or 'Disagree' button.

The basic etiquettes that should be maintained while communicating using the internet, are explained in the beginning of the chapter. Then, the focus is on specifying those contents on the internet, that can be used for free and those that need a permission or license for use. Later on, the chapter discusses some data retrieval and security rights provided to an internet user, and how the data can be securely transmitted while doing online transactions.

7.1 NETIQUETTES

The two words **Net** and **Etiquette** together form the word **Netiquette** which refers to the etiquettes to be followed, while using the internet. Netiquette defines the way communication is conducted, in a positive sense and makes the interaction more pleasant. The communication can be one-to-one like in individual e-mails and messages or can be one-to-many as in chats, web forums, blogs, etc. Following are some **do's and don'ts** to be followed for effective communication on the internet:

E-mails

- Send e-mail to only that person for whom it is meant.
- Do not flood the other person's inbox with spam or forwarded messages.
- Keep the subject line short, simple and focused. It should convey the recipient what the e-mail might contain.
- Quote the e-mail you are replying to, for the recipient's reference.
- Begin your message with a greeting. Words should be carefully chosen and placed.
- Avoid writing an e-mail completely in uppercase letters, as it may appear rude. Mixed case or sentence case is the best option for online communication. Use bold type, instead of all caps, if you need to emphasise some words.
- Check for spelling, grammar, punctuation and clarity of content before sending the e-mail.
- Avoid sending heavy attachments or send them with the recipient's permission.

Social Media, Chats, Blogs and Forums

- Do not post offensive comments, that might hurt the sentiments of any individual or community.
- Respect the views of others and show courtesy while posting your comments.
- Avoid replying in negative to negative comments. Either don't react or reply in a positive note.
- Do not share private information or pictures of others, without their consent.
- Do not post copyrighted material, else you might land up in legal complications.
- Offer help if someone in the group needs help and thank others if they help you.
- Posts are public, so be very careful while posting your message. Read it before posting and analyse the repercussions.
- Check the factuality of the post before hitting the forward button. Forward only meaningful messages which you think people really need to know.
- Don't be a troll online and don't provoke or nag others.
- Cyber bullying and cyber stalking both are crimes.

ADDITIONAL INFO

Trolling is the act of deliberately posting a remark in an online community with the aim of insulting or provoking someone. It is commonly observed in YouTube video comments, Blog comments, Facebook, Instagram, etc.

7.2 SOFTWARE LICENSES

The software license is a legal agreement that lists the conditions under which an individual or an organisation is given the permission to use the software. The license may be free or paid. Some of the different types of licenses are described below:

1. *Single User:* This type of license is issued to a single user and for a single machine. For example, the Microsoft Windows license can work only for a single computer system or PC.
2. *Multi-user:* This license is issued for software, which can be installed on multiple machines and can be used by multiple users but the number of machines will be fixed. For example, a particular software can be installed on the computers of the board members of a company, with access restricted only to them.
3. *Site License:* Many organisations buy license for unlimited access to unlimited users as long as the computers are on a site such as a school or a business house.
4. *Freeware:* Freeware software do not require any fee to be paid to the software developer. These software provide a license for use if the user agrees to abide by the terms and conditions.
5. *Shareware:* The license for a shareware software is issued for a trial period. During the trial period the user can use the software for free, but after the period expires, he/she will no longer be able to access it. To use it, the user will have to pay a certain amount as the shareware fee. Generally, the shareware software contains various adware and certain restrictions on the use, which are removed when the user buys it.
6. *Subscription:* This license is applicable for a fixed interval of time during which the user can enjoy all the upgrades and technical support. After the subscription period expires, the user can either renew the software license or buy the subscription license by paying the fee, else the license is removed.
7. *Creative Commons:* This type of license is given by people, generally artists with their creative work, so that people who appreciate their work can copy, distribute or display it in a non-commercial way. This helps the artists gain popularity and recognition.
8. *Open Source:* Open source licensing provides free access to the software as well as its source code. Anybody can view and modify the source code according to his/her need. It is absolutely free.

7.3 OPEN SOURCE SOFTWARE MOVEMENT

The Open Source Movement is the latest rage in the software market. It is a social movement which aims at providing the users with free software, which they can read, modify and use, according to their requirements. The user can distribute the copies of the original or modified version of the software also. Many software companies have their monopoly over certain software that they sell for very high prices. Their source code is a closed code and the user has to either modify his system of work according to the software or has to shell out extra money to get a tailor-made version of the software. Both these problems are overcome with the open source software as it is free and the source code can be modified.

You have used Scratch software in class IX which is an open source. Likewise, OpenOffice Suit is the open source competitor for MS Office, (a paid software) and Mozilla Firefox is an open source browser. Microsoft has a huge monopoly on the PC operating system, so currently the open source community is working on building an open source OS which can replace it.

7.4 INTELLECTUAL PROPERTY RIGHTS

Intellect of a person means the ability of that person to understand and solve problems. So, all the ideas and inventions, which are a result of that intellect are the intellectual property of that individual. It can be a piece of art, literature, invention, trade secret, etc.

Intellectual Property Rights refer to the legal right of the creator of an intellectual property to be its sole beneficiary. If anyone else uses it without permission or copies and distributes it, intellectual property rights are said to be violated.

Intellectual property Rights can be broadly classified into:

1. ***Patents:*** Patents basically involve the functional features or specifications of a product.
2. ***Trademarks:*** This would refer to a logo or symbol, which represents a company or product.
3. ***Copyright:*** Copyright gives a person, complete rights over his creation (it can be a book, painting, movie, picture or website) and he/she can decide how others will be allowed to use the work.
4. ***Trade Secrets:*** This would refer to the secrets of a particular business or product, which sets it apart from other products.

Different countries have different intellectual property protection laws. Protecting intellectual property rights is important for the following reasons:

1. ***Monetary Benefit:*** The owner of the intellectual property gets a share of the profit as and when, his product is used or bought. He suffers a loss of his profit share if his intellectual property is illegally used by others.
2. ***Economic Growth:*** The economic growth of an organisation depends not only on the profit it makes, by selling its products but also its reputation in the market.
3. ***Compatibility:*** Sometimes, the software which is copied, is not compatible with the software with which it is being used. This creates problems at a later stage.
4. ***Threat to the System:*** Many a times, the pirated software come with certain viruses which are unknown to the user. They may enter the system and may corrupt it.

7.5 PLAGIARISM

Plagiarism refers to copying the contents of someone else's work and reusing it as your own. Very often, the contents of a website are just copied to another website or the work done by a research student is used by some other research student. However, plagiarism is an offence and with information so readily available on the Internet, this offence is becoming very common. Several websites do not allow copying of content and many other give warning messages.

To overcome this issue in academic research works, many universities have introduced stringent measures and punishments. Free online tools are also available, to help identify plagiarism.

7.6 DIGITAL PROPERTY RIGHTS

Digital property includes any data stored in digitised format, which may be in the form of files, e-mails, audio, video, images or even information stored in the internet accounts, like social networking accounts, e-shopping accounts, net banking accounts, etc. The internet service provider has a contract with the internet account holder which assures the privacy of his digital property. So, the rights which an internet user has, over the privacy of his digital property, are called digital property rights.

7.7 FREEDOM OF INFORMATION

An internet user has the right to search and retrieve information of his choice. The user even has the right to express his views and opinions and access the views and ideas of others on the net. This freedom to access information and to express one's views is called the **freedom of information**. This freedom is the right of every internet user and no service provider or content provider can unlawfully apply any restrictions on this freedom.

Restrictions may be applied to some type of contents like hate speeches or views expressed that might incite violence, but then these restrictions have to be applied according to the laws specially designed under the Freedom of Information Act.

A user is allowed to keep his/her identity a secret and not share his/her actual profile on the internet. However, this permission might prove to be malicious also, as the fake profile might be used to harm others. But if such a situation arises, there are several technical ways and agencies like the IT cell, by which the user's true identity can be established.

Many websites and service providers express their terms and conditions, regarding the restrictions which they apply, in case the need arises. The user will have to give his consent and agree to the terms and conditions, in order to gain access to the website. Some social networks also block the account of certain users if they find them violating the rules. But this can also be considered as a restriction to the freedom of information. So, it is the duty of ISP and the content provider to take the responsibility of providing freedom of information and also implement the restrictions expertly and lawfully.

7.8 DIGITAL UNITY

Digital unity basically refers to the Information and Communications Technology (ICT) bringing the world together.

Now the world seems a lot smaller as everyone, everywhere has access to the same information on the Internet. With a digital platform provided by the Internet, distances have vanished and communication has never been this easier or faster.

Meetings are no longer confined to rooms. The whole world seems to be a big conference room where decisions can be taken, after listening to all the members, sitting in different geographical locations.

Students from an underdeveloped country can easily take admission and attain a degree from a reputed institution. Internet has certainly helped bridge the social gap. People located in faraway places can also communicate with people in the other parts of the world. This helps in building up the social gap.

Events taking place in any part of the world can be viewed from various geographical locations. People from various parts of the world can fight for the same cause. So, the digital explosion has in a way, united the whole world, as a single unit. Geographical boundaries hold no meaning and Internet—the networking of computers has given birth to social networking.

7.9 DIGITAL DIVIDE

Digital divide refers to the uneven access to information, between the people who have access to ICT and those who do not have. In a broader perspective, the developed countries have a better access to ICT and are better equipped to exploit the benefits of ICT, especially the Internet.

Developed countries have advanced technology which helps them to use the features of ICT and in turn, further improve their technology. In developing countries and underdeveloped countries, digital gap is obvious due to factors like low speed of Internet, high cost of connections, low technology used in computers, lack of assistance, illiteracy, etc. The gap is quite evident in India itself. While some schools have smart classes with internet connections and students taking laptops and tablets to school, some other schools, in small towns barely have access to the basic infrastructure required like proper classrooms, textbooks, electricity, etc.

So, when these digitally divided students later appear for various exams, on the same platform, they are at disadvantage. Hence, reducing or closing the digital gap is very important.

Several researches are being done to formulate steps for bridging the digital gap. Some of the suggestions have already been implemented while others are in the process.

- One of the ways to shorten the digital gap is to make digital technology **affordable**. The telecom companies should be encouraged to come out with low-priced products like tablets and smartphones which are within the reach of people from low-income group also.
- Another very effective step is to make the digital technology **accessible**. In the cities, most of the people have their private wifi connections. In addition to these, free wifi hotspots are available in public areas like railway stations, amusement parks, etc. In rural and remote area, where private wifi connections are not feasible, public wifi should be provided along with latest technology computers at the community centres and schools. Cyber clubs can also be opened for general public.
- Providing infrastructure is not enough. Bringing **greater awareness** among citizens about the use of digital technology would help in reducing information inequality. The software companies (like Microsoft, Apple) and NGOs are taking initiatives to make the people in rural areas aware about the uses of computers and the internet. To further promote this, the centre and state governments should benefit these companies with some tax exemptions or subsidies.

- More and more services like registration of land, weather alerts, market price of crops for farmers, are being made **available** on mobile devices with the aim that it would force the people to learn to use technology.
- Even if a rural area has the necessary infrastructure, it is worthless if there is no one to utilise it, maintain it and train others to use it. So, **periodic maintenance of the hardware** and **training of the staff** is a must.
- Bringing the awareness about technology and its use should start at the primary level of the schools. The curriculum should imbibe topics related to the digital technology and its applications. Students should be **encouraged to use** the digital platform for collecting information and presenting their project work. This would make the younger generation of every section of the country tech-savvy and thus ready to take on technology in its stride.

7.10 E-COMMERCE

E-commerce is the process of buying and selling goods and services over the Internet. Various online shopping sites like the Amazon, Flipkart, ShopClues, etc. have become very active over the past few years. Apart from making our lives very convenient, e-commerce has also helped various business houses expand their trade, all over the world.

However, there are some drawbacks also to the transactions done online. Where there is money involved, frauds are likely to happen. Since the number of transactions is huge, it is not possible to catch a fraudulent transaction, which causes a loss to the organisation. Many a time, customers also get duped by fraudsters who steal their information or even identity, to commit the financial thefts. Some of the frauds that we generally come across are:

1. ***Phishing:*** The cyber criminals pose as any trusted e-commerce company requesting details of the customer, to carry out a transaction or to do registration or give similar excuses to obtain information and misuse the information of the customer. For example, while making a purchase the customer might share his credit card number and CVV number on the fake site unknowingly and thus become a victim to a financial theft later.
2. ***Third party fraud:*** Once a customer places an order, he/she may be required to share certain details through e-mail. Then in such cases, it might be possible that, a third person intercepts the communication and steals the customer's confidential data.
3. ***Identity Theft:*** Many times, cyber criminals hack mobile phones or our internet accounts and steal our data. Then they use this information to make purchases in our name, using our account details.
4. The most common fraud these days is, making phone calls to innocent people and luring them into sharing their card number, expiry date, CVV number and OTP. Once the criminals have these details, they can then use this information to make purchases using the card details.

How to stay safe

- Never share your card details and CVV number with anyone on the Internet.
- Use a firewall to protect the computer from illegal access.

- Use strong passwords while registering on an e-commerce site.
- Monitor your accounts periodically.
- Keep your software up to date, as the newer versions might have features, to combat new malwares.
- Always prefer the sites that use two tier authentication – password and OTP, on your mobile.
- If using a mobile phone, apply biometric identification features.
- Make sure that the company you are making transaction with, is PCI compliant. PCI (Payment Card Industry) is a security council that ensures that the companies dealing with card transactions maintain a secure environment. Companies like Visa, Mastercard are the members of this council.

Security measures taken by e-commerce companies

- Online shopping sites should assign tracking numbers for every order which would help them locate the position of the order.
- They should train their staff also, to protect the data of their customers.
- These sites should use contact forms, login boxes and search queries to check the authenticity of the customer.
- The order placed by any customer should be cross checked, by sending a confirmation e-mail or by placing a phone call. Even the bank can be contacted for the details of the customer if the amount is substantial and the payment is being made by card.
- Encryption approach should be implemented by converting the original message into an encrypted text which would be difficult for the hacker to decode. This ensures security of the data, during its transmission.
- Secure socket layer should be used which is the most commonly used protocol (set of rules), designed specifically for e-commerce transactions. This protocol encrypts the data, checks the authenticity of client-server information and prevents tampering of data.

KEY TERMS

Netiquettes The basic code of conduct to be followed while using the internet.

Software License A legal agreement that lists the conditions under which an individual or an organisation is given the permission to use the software.

Freeware Freeware software do not require any fee to be paid to the software developer. These software provide a license for use if the user agrees to abide by the terms and conditions.

Shareware The software for which free license is issued for a limited period of time which is called the trial period.

Open Source Software Open source software is freely accessible along with its source code that can even be modified.

Open Source Software Movement A social movement which aims at providing the users with free software which they can read, modify and use according to their requirements.

Intellectual Property Rights They refer to the legal rights of the creator of an intellectual property to be its sole beneficiary.

Plagiarism It refers to copying the contents of someone else's work and presenting it as your own.

Phishing The process of stealing information like passwords, pin numbers, card details etc. and misusing it to harm others.

Digital Property It includes the data stored in digitized format in the form of text, audio, video files e-mails and internet accounts.

Digital Property Rights These are the rights that an internet user has over the privacy of his/her digital property.

E-commerce A business model that allows conducting business and financial transactions on electronic platform which is internet.

POINTS TO REMEMBER

- There is no rule book for netiquettes; most of the websites have their own rules which are mentioned on their Terms and Conditions page.
- While communicating on social media sites, one should not post copyrighted material, personal information and pictures of others without their consent.
- Licenses may be for single user, multiuser, for a specific site, for freeware or shareware software.
- Subscription license expires after the time period of subscription is over but it can be renewed.
- Open source licencing provides free access to the software as well as its source code.
- Various frauds are committed in the e-commerce world by cyber criminals. Phishing, third party fraud, identity theft, unauthorised access to one's bank account are some of the most common frauds.
- One can avoid falling prey to these frauds by being vigilant during online transactions, not sharing confidential information with others and using only reliable sites for carrying out money transactions.
- Online shopping sites or e-commerce sites can also take several measures to prevent cyber thefts, like assigning tracking numbers to every order, keeping a check on the customer's identity, encrypting the customer's information and being PCI compliant.

SOLVED QUESTIONS

Q1. Why is an open source software preferred by people?

Ans. Open source software is free software with an open source code which any user can read, modify and use according to his/her requirement. The user can distribute the copies of the original or modified version of the software also.

Q2. Are netiquettes only confined to communication?

Ans. No, netiquettes cover a wide range of fields in cyber space. Besides promoting a positive and pleasant communication, they also guide a person to refrain oneself from unethical activities like identity theft, phishing, plagiarism, violation digital and intellectual property rights.

Q3. Rajan used his debit card to withdraw money from an ATM at New Delhi Railway station. Later he got an alert on his phone from the bank regarding two more withdrawal transactions which actually he had not carried out? How did this theft of money happen?

Ans. There are many cyber criminals who hack the ATM machines and steal your card information and PIN when you use the machine. Later they use this information to log into your bank account to withdraw money. This type of activity is called Phishing.

Q4. State two unwanted situations that might arise if we use a pirated software. How can these be avoided?

Ans. Using pirated software might infect our computer with a malware or might not be compatible with the other applications which we intend to use at a later stage. To avoid such situations we should always prefer to use either a licensed software or an open source software.

Q5. What are the reasons behind digital divide?

Ans. Lower economic status, illetracy, low speed of internet or no network at all at remote places, primitive technology and lack of assistance are some of the factors responsible for digital divide.

Q6. Does copyright fall under digital property right?

Ans. Digital property right is the right that the creator of the digital property has over its use and distribution. Copyright is the right a person has over an entity so that it cannot be used by anyone else. If the entity is a digital property then copyright becomes digital property right.

Q7. What is encrypted text? How does encryption help reduce e-commerce frauds?

Ans. Converting the text into a code such that only the authorised parties can access it is called encryption of text. E-commerce sites encrypt the confidential data before transmitting, which reduce the chances of data theft by a considerable number.

EXERCISES

I. Very Short Answer Type Questions

Multiple Choice Questions:

1. Which of the following is not a cybercrime?
   (a) Cyber stalking (b) Cyber bullying
   (c) Using shareware (d) Plagiarism
2. Software that provides source code to the users is
   (a) Freeware (b) Open source software
   (c) Shareware (d) Creative commons
3. Which of the following is an open source software?
   (a) MS Windows (b) MS Office (c) Scratch (d) Google Chrome
4. Copying someone else's work and presenting it as one's own is called
   (a) Copyright (b) Identity theft (c) Plagiarism (d) Phishing
5. Which of the following is not a digital property?
   (a) A text file
   (b) An audio file
   (c) A piece of art created on computer using software
   (d) A piece of art created on a canvas
6. Which of the following is not ethical while composing an e-mail?
   (a) Keeping the subject line short
   (b) Not sending heavy attachments
   (c) Checking spellings and grammar
   (d) Writing in uppercase letters
7. While posting a message on social media one should:
   (a) worry about its repurcussions
   (b) bully anyone
   (c) share private information
   (d) post offensive comments
8. A logo or a symbol representing a company or product is
   (a) Patent (b) Trademark (c) Copyright (d) Trade Secret
9. Luring a person to enter his/her confidential information on a fake website to cheat him/her financially is
   (a) Cyber bullying (b) Plagiarism (c) Phishing (d) Piracy
10. Freedom of Information does not include
    (a) right to access information from the web
    (b) right to search information on the web
    (c) right to express views and opinions on the web
    (d) right of ISP to share its customer's information with others

Fill in the blanks:

1. Lower economic status and illiteracy are the reasons behind digital ....
2. Converting text or data into a code before transmitting it on the net is called ....

3. A social movement that aims at providing free software and its source code to the users is known as ....
4. The license given by people for their creative work, to attain recognition is called ....
5. The license obtained by an organisation to allow the unlimited access of software is called ....
6. While composing an e-mail, ... letters should not be used to write text.

II. Short Answer Type Questions

1. What do you understand by netiquettes? Why are they required?
2. How do the websites inform the user about their terms and conditions?
3. Why should we not compose our e-mail message in uppercase letters?
4. What are the two points one should check before forwarding a message?
5. Why is a software license required?
6. What is the difference between multi-user and site license?
7. How is freeware different from open source software?
8. What is the aim of open source software movement?
9. If everyone has the facility to modify open source code, then how can the errors be kept under control?
10. Name two open source software and paid license software each.
11. What are Intellectual Property Rights?
12. Why is it important to protect Intellectual Property Rights?
13. Is Intellectual property different from Digital property? Explain.
14. State any two areas where digital unity has proved helpful to our society.
15. State any two ways by which one can carry out a fraud free transaction on internet.
16. State any two steps an e-commerce organisation should take to keep the data of their customers safe and secure.

III. Long Answer Type Questions

1. List any five ethics to be followed while composing and sending an e-mail.
2. List any five etiquettes one should follow while communicating in a group forum or on social media.
3. What is E-commerce? What are the frauds that we encounter while transacting online?
4. What do you understand by the term Freedom of Information?
5. State any five steps that can help to bridge the digital gap.

8 Scratch

- Revision of the basics of Scratch
- Sprite, tempo, variables and events
- Coordinates and conditionals
- Drawing with iteration
- Update variables repeatedly, iterative development, ask and answer blocks
- Create games, animated images, stories and songs

In class IX you have already learnt to develop simple animations using Scratch 2. In this class you will learn to use many more interesting features of Scratch to improvise your codes and develop complex animations. This chapter uses the latest version of Scratch, i.e., Scratch 3. You will find some changes in the new version such as the placement of elements and their appearance on the home screen and some extended blocks. This chapter first recapitulates the basics of Scratch and then introduces some more coding blocks. The interesting and variety of examples provide you a framework for designing the codes for animated games, quizzes and lot more.

8.1 FEATURES OF SCRATCH

- Scratch is a visual and graphical programming language.
- Commands are prewritten and need to be just dragged and dropped to create a code.
- There is no probability of syntax errors as commands are prewritten.
- Scratch is a very easy and convenient language to develop games and animations using audio and graphics.
- Scratch has an online community which any user can join to share projects with other users.
- It is an open source software and easy to download.

Introduction to Scratch 3

Till now you have been working on Scratch 2. You are already familiar with its interface. It is shown below:

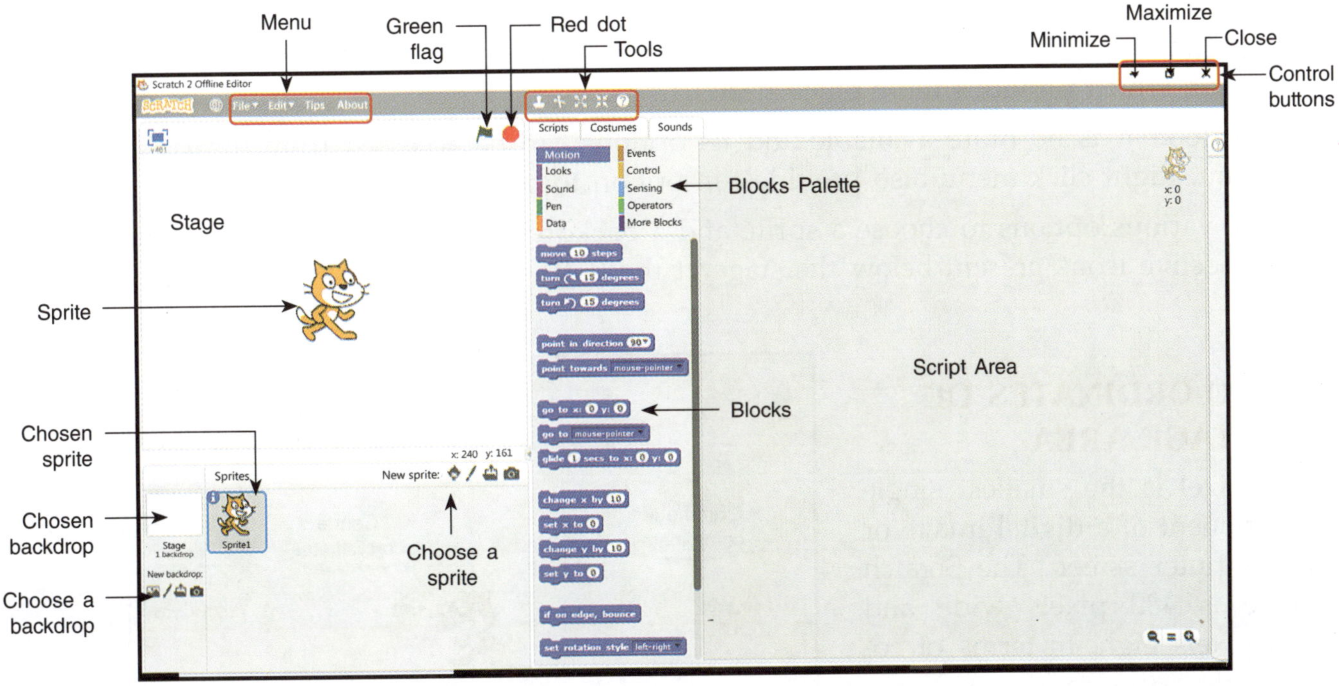

Fig. 8.1: Scratch 2 Window

In Scratch 3, you will find a few differences in the appearance of some of the interface components. The Scratch 3 interface is displayed below:

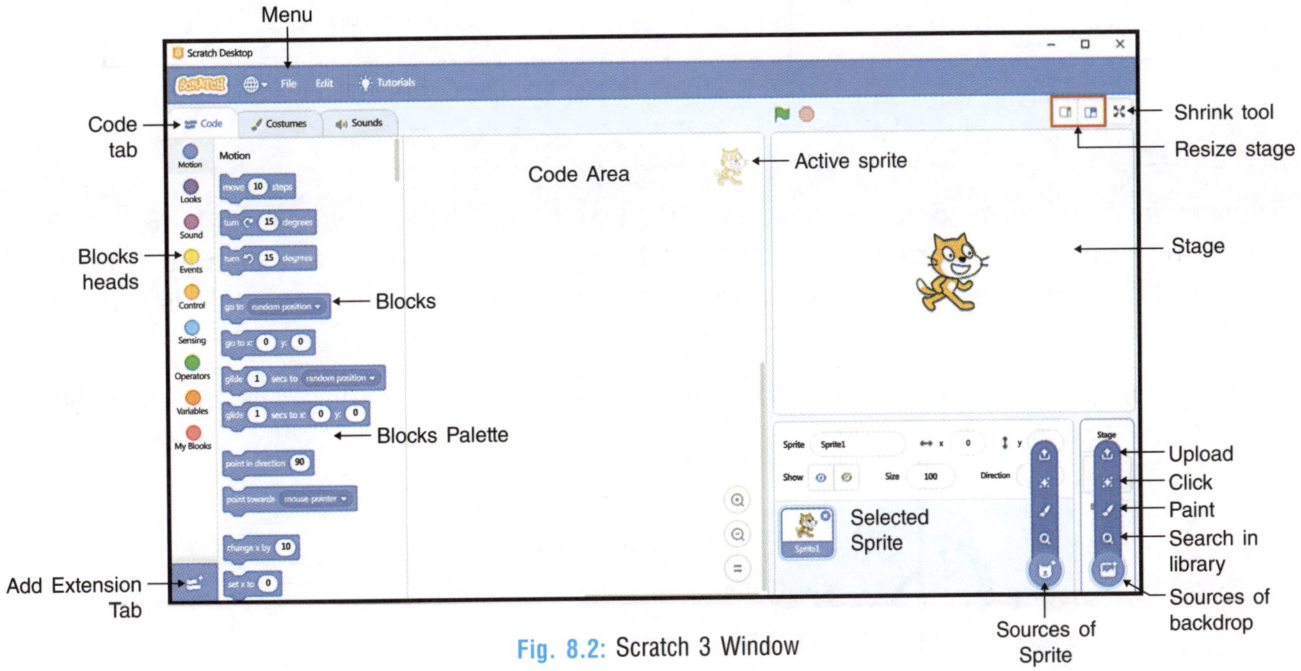

Fig. 8.2: Scratch 3 Window

The differences between Scratch 2 and Scratch 3 interface are:

- It is clearly visible that the Blocks Palette is now on the left, the Script Area is in the centre and the Stage Area is on the right side of the window.

- The Scripts tab has been renamed as **Code** and hence the Script Area is now called as **Code Area**.
- The block heads in the Blocks Palette are now represented by unique **colour coded circles**.
- An additional tab named as **Add Extension** is available at the bottom of the Blocks Palette which provides more block heads.
- The toolbar is no more available and its options can be accessed from the right click menu. Right click menu also provides an option to add **comments**.
- The various options to choose a sprite and a backdrop can now be accessed from their respective icons present below the stage at the bottom.

8.2 CO-ORDINATES OF STAGE AREA

The pixel is the smallest single component of a digital image or a computer screen. The Scratch stage is 480 pixels wide and 360 pixels high. In terms of co-ordinates, the range of Y co-ordinate is –180 to +180 and X co-ordinate is –240 to +240. In Scratch, one unit of X or Y or one step taken by a sprite is equal to one pixel.

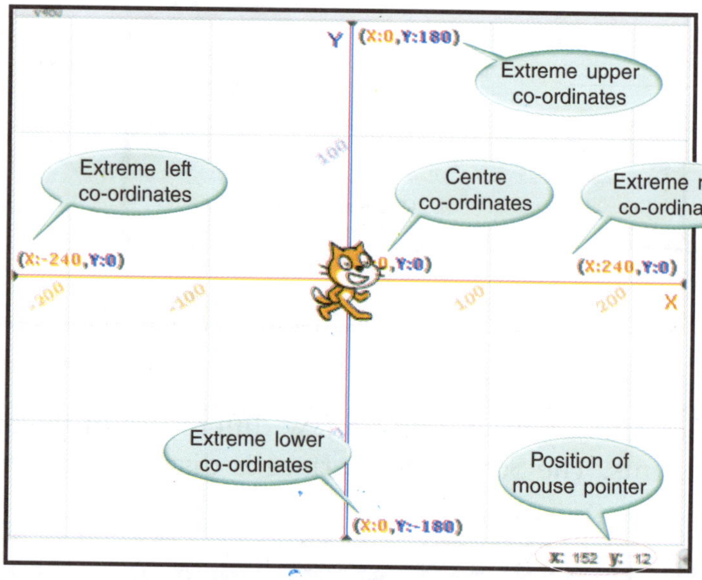

Fig. 9.3: Coordinates of Stage Area

Angle rotation of sprite: Scratch uses an angle measurement that is similar to **degrees**. One degree represents one degree turn clockwise by the sprite. The sprite's default direction value is 90°. Negative degree simply mean rotation anti-clockwise. So –90° is left and –180° is down.

For values greater than 360°, e.g. 450°, the actual value is considered as 450–360=90°.

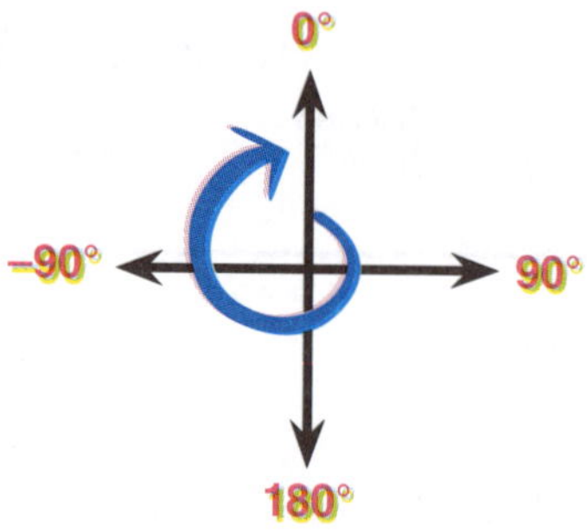

Degrees	Direction
–360, 0, 360	UP
–270, 90	Right
–180, 180	Down
–90, 270	Left

8.3 BLOCK HEADS

You have already worked with blocks under Motion, Looks, Sound, Events and Control heads. Let us now understand three more blocks, viz., Sensing, Operators and Variables.

1. Sensing

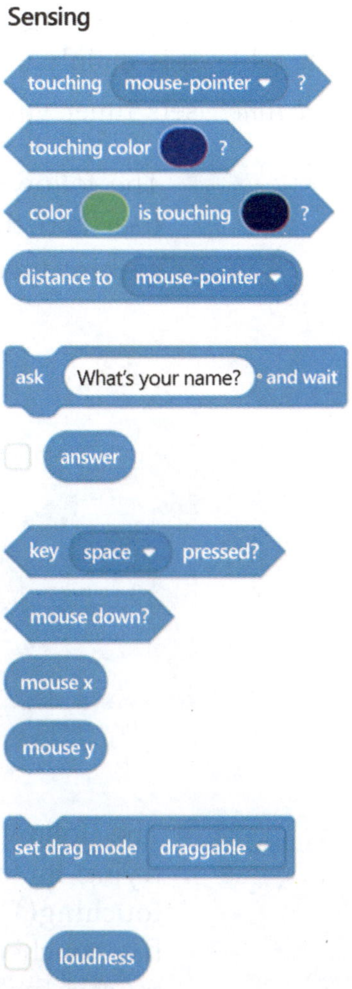

Sensing blocks associate with **sprites and stage detecting conditions** and allow certain actions to be followed accordingly. **A condition may be such as:** when a sprite touches or collides with another sprite or a certain key is pressed or a color touches another color, etc.

The blocks under Sensing block are discussed below:

Boolean blocks:

touching(mouse-pointer/edge)?: checks if the sprite touches the mouse-pointer or edge of the stage or any other sprite and returns True/False accordingly.

touching color()?: checks and returns True when sprite touches the specific colour which can be chosen by clicking on the block's colour swatch and then using the slider.

color() is touching(): checks if the mentioned colour on its sprite touches the other specified colour.

key() pressed?: checks if the specified key is pressed. The available keys are alphabetic, numeric, arrow and space keys. There is an option for **any key** also.

mouse down?: checks if the computer's mouse is being clicked.

Reporter blocks:

distance to(): reports the distance between objects in pixels.

answer: holds the most recent text entered with ask() and wait block.

mouse x: returns the x co-ordinate of the mouse pointer.

mouse y: returns the y co-ordinate of the mouse pointer.

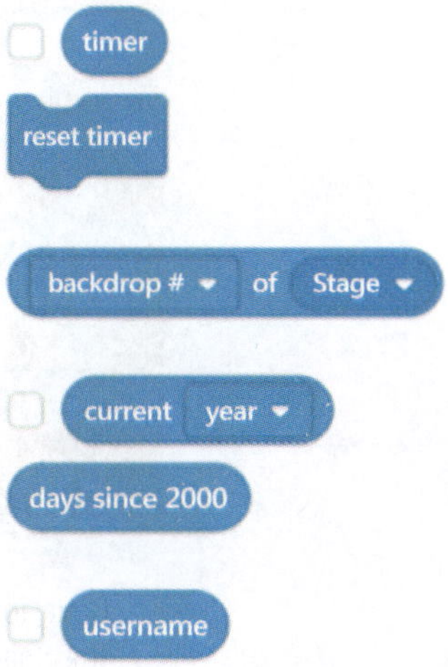

loudness: holds how loud the sound is on the scale of 0–100. If checked ☑, the value of loudness is displayed on the stage.

timer: The timer starts with 0 and increments by 1 every second as a project starts. **Reset timer block should be used at the beginning of a project with this block to get the correct value.**

current(): reports current year/month/date/hour/minute/sec.

days since 2000: reports the number of days and fraction of day since 1 Jan, 2000.

username: reports the current user name if the user has provided any.

(backdrop#) of (Stage): reports the backdrop number of the selected stage.

Stack blocks:

ask( ) and wait: shows an input box at the bottom of the stage in which text can be typed and submitted. The input gets stored in the answer block (ref. Example 1).

set drag mode( ): sets the mode to draggable or non-draggable. It is mainly used in drag and drop games.

reset timer: sets timer value back to 0:0.

> **NOTE**
>
> The reporter blocks with a check box, display their values on the stage in a small box, called the **Stage Monitor**, when the check box is selected (or ticked).

Example 1 The following code uses **ask() and wait** block to ask for the name of the user and then displays a message with the name. The blocks-**reset timer**, **current (year)** and **days since 2000**, are also used.

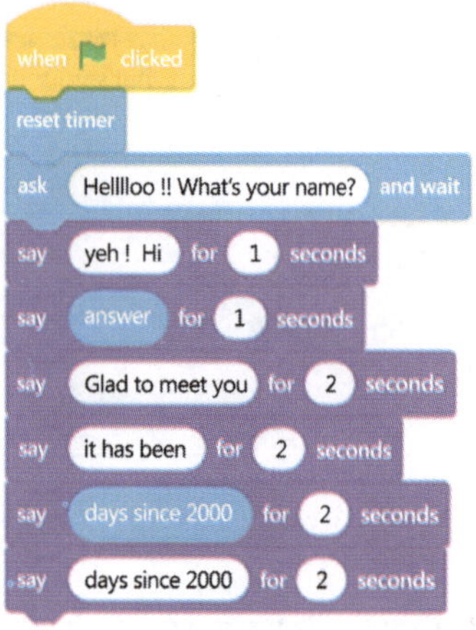

Example 2 The following code shows a snake trying to catch a frog. The code uses **touching()** block to sense if the snake has touched the frog. As soon as it touches the frog a message is displayed.

Code for Frog Sprite

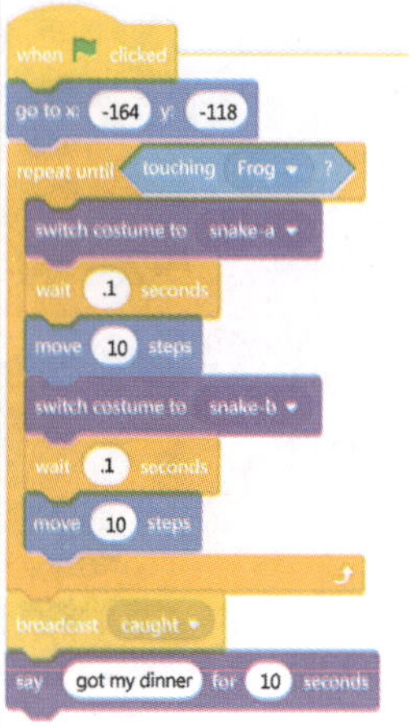

Code for Moving the Snake Sprite

2. Operators

The codes where mathematical expressions and string handling is involved, there operator blocks are used.

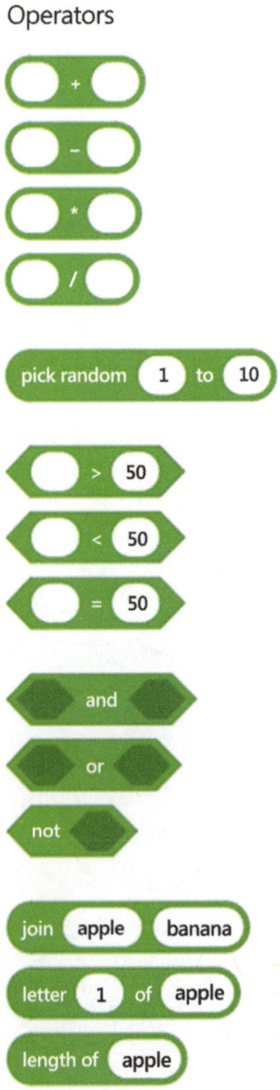

Boolean Blocks:

() > () or () < () or () = (): compare a numeric value with another value. They are also used to compare strings, *e.g.*, a<z returns true. *e.g.* (5) > (6) = False

() and (): compares two conditions; returns True if both conditions are true, *e.g.* (4 < 8) and (5 < 6) = True

() or (): compares two conditions; returns True if any one or both the conditions are true, *e.g.* (1 > 4) or (8 > 4) = True

not(): returns False if the condition is true and returns True if the condition is false. *e.g.* not (TRUE) = FALSE

() contains (): returns True if a string contains the given character. *e.g.* (COLOUR) contains (U) = True

Reporter Blocks:

*() + () or () – () or () * () or ()/():* perform the respective mathematical operation(add, subtract, multiply, divide) on the two given values and stores the result. *e.g.* (5) * (6) = 30

pick random() to (): picks a random number between the two given values, end values included. If both the numbers are integers, result is also an integer. If either of the two values has a decimal, a decimal value is returned, *e.g.* pick random (1.5) to (3) might give 1.9 as result.

join () (): joins the two strings or numbers or a combination of strings and numbers (also known as concatenation). *e.g.* join (GOOD) (LUCK) will give GOODLUCK.

letter () of (): reports the specified character of the given text. Even though the block says "letter", it reports all characters, including letters, numbers, symbols, and even spaces. *e.g.* If answer = $ 450 then letter (1) of (answer) = $

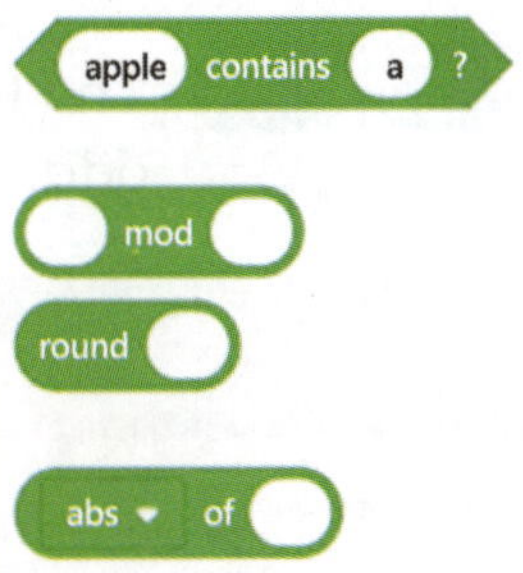

length of (): reports the length of the string, spaces in the string are also counted, *e.g.* If answer is "Good luck" then length of (answer) = 9

() mod (): reports the remainder when the given two values are divided, *e.g.* (5) mod (2) = 1

round(): reports the value after rounding it off to the nearest integer, *e.g.* round (4.4) = 4

() of (): applies the function chosen in the first parentheses to the value written in the second parentheses and reports the result. Some of the functions are abs, sqrt, sin, cos, etc. *e.g.* (Sqrt) of (4) = 2

Example 3 The following code inputs a string, concatenates (joins) it with another string and displays it. (Use of **join** block)

Joins the string 'Hi' with the string stored in answer which is 'HERSCHEL'

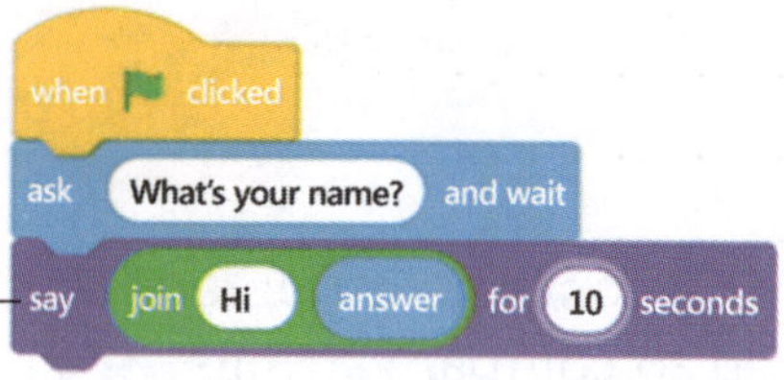

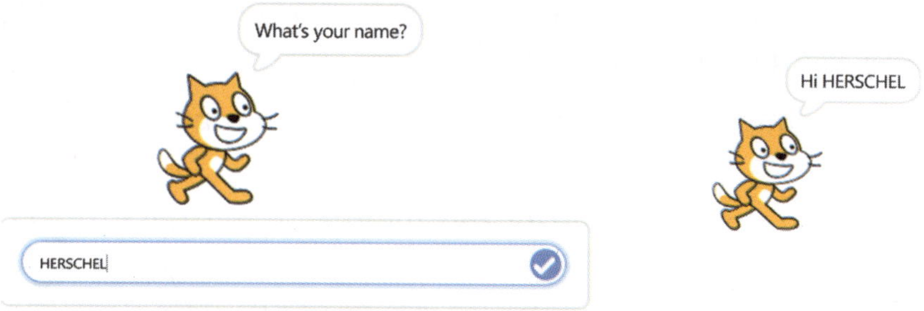

Example 4 The following code inputs the amount in rupees and displays the equivalent number of dollars. (Use of **operators**)

The value of answer is divided with 89 to find the number of dollars 1200/89 = 17

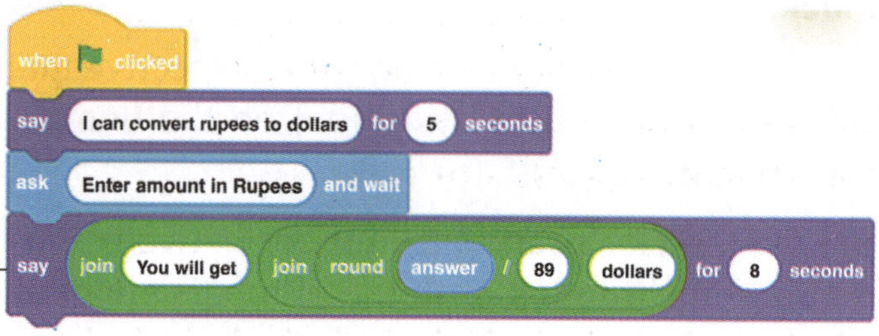

Example 5 The following code asks to enter a number and prints whether it is even or odd. (Use of **conditional** blocks and **operators**)

The number stored in answer is divided by 2 using mod operator. If remainder is 0 then the number given as input is even else it is odd.

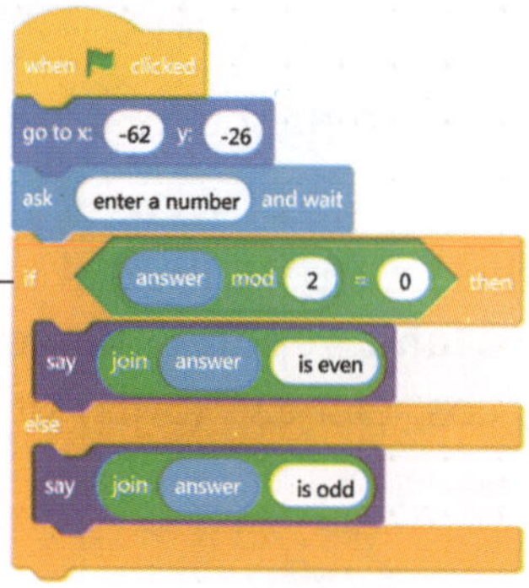

3. Variables

Variable is a location which stores a value and has a name. The value of a variable can be changed. Whenever the value of the variable is required, its name is called. A Scratch variable can have either a number or a string value. Variables find their use extensively in gaming scripts where the score or the number of lives left, is required to be displayed on the screen. Using variables also makes the script short and efficient. There are two types of variables:

(i) **Global or Public variables:** These can be used and changed by any sprite on any stage in a project.

(ii) **Local or Private variables:** These can only be changed by their owner. Stage cannot have local variables.

Creating a variable

Steps to create a variable are:

STEPS

1. Click on **Make a Variable** button under **Variables block** head.
2. The **New Variable** box will appear. Enter the variable name.
3. Select "For all sprites" for creating global variable and "For this sprite only" for creating local variable. Click ok.

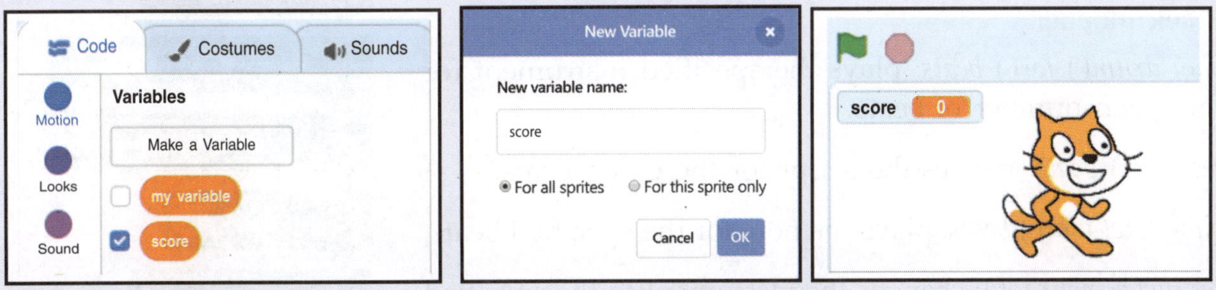

You will see that a reporter block for your variable is created in the variables blocks palette. This block is checked by default and hence it appears on the Stage monitor with a default value 0. Another variable with the name "my variable" is already present under the variables head. The variables can be renamed or deleted by right click options.

Stack Blocks:

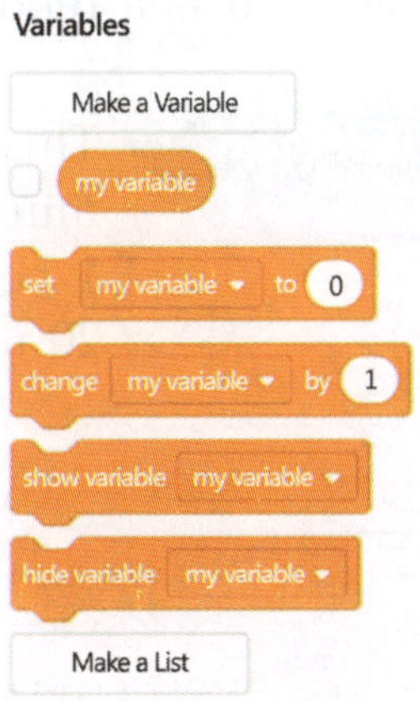

set() to (): assigns a value to the variable, *e.g.* set (score) to (0)

change() by (): changes the value of the variable by the given value, e.g. change (score) by (2)

show variable(): shows the specified variable's Stage monitor at a particular phase of the code execution.

hide variable(): hides the Stage monitor of the variable

Example 6 The following code enters a number and then displays its multiplication table, one value at a time by updating the variable **(count)** repeatedly.

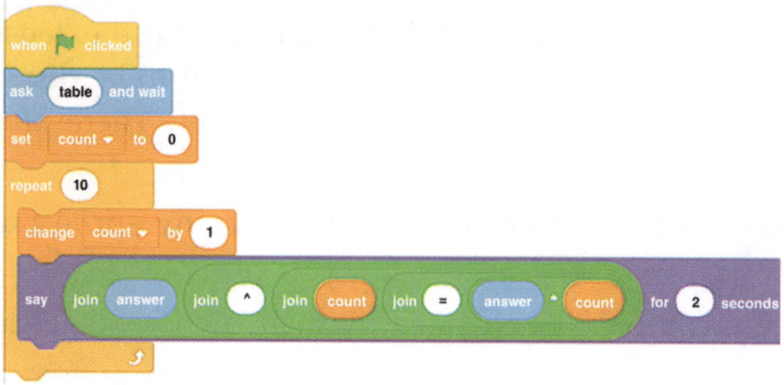

8.4 ADD EXTENSION TAB

Add Extension tab is the special tab added in Scratch 3 at the leftmost bottom. It includes the additional blocks which can be selected in the same way as other blocks. Some of the block heads are discussed below:

1. Music

The Music blocks head is an extension added in Scratch 3.0 which allows you to play music in your script.

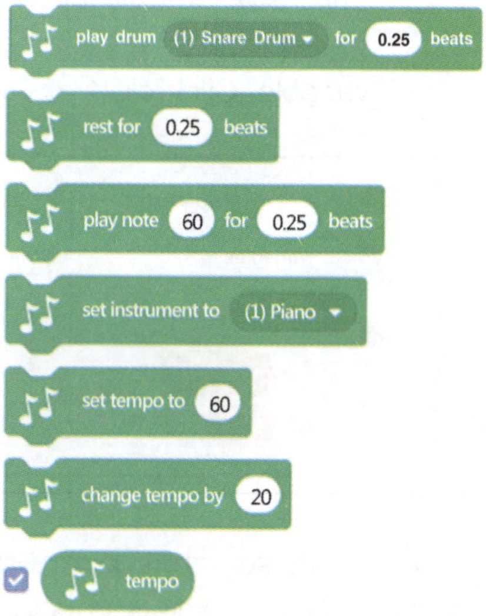

Stack blocks:

play drum() for() beats: plays the specified instrument for the given number of beats.

rest for() beats: pauses the script for the given beats.

play note() for() beats: plays the note for the specified beats.

set instrument to(): changes the instrument to the specified one.

set tempo to(): sets the tempo, i.e., the speed or pace of any piece of music.

Change tempo by(): changes the tempo of music by the specified amount.

Tempo: it is a reporter block and reports the value of the tempo of current instrument.

Example 7 This code sets the tempo to 200 beats per minute. It then plays the Snare Drum for 1 beat 10 times reducing the tempo by 20 in each iteration.

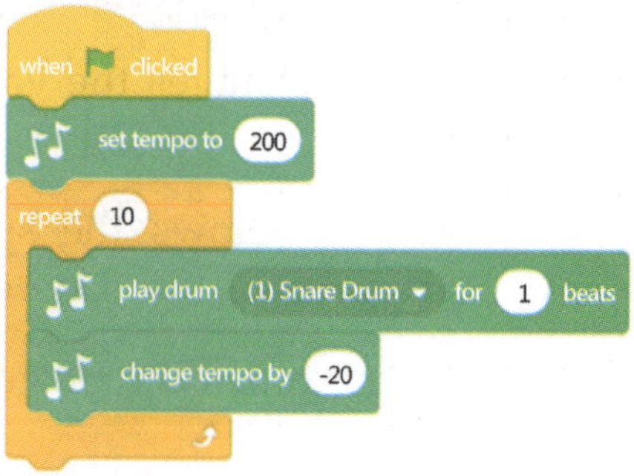

2. Pen

The Pen block head is also an extension to the Block Palette.

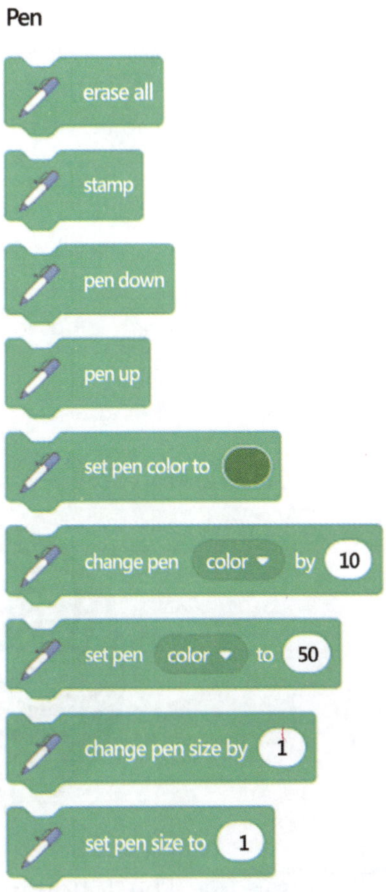

Stack blocks:

erase all: clears the stage area of all the drawings.

stamp: creates sprite's duplicate image on the stage.

pen down: enables the pen to draw.

pen up: disables the pen to draw.

set pen color to(): sets the colour of the pen.

change pen() by(); changes the specified pen colour by specified amount.

set pen() to (): sets the specified colour of pen to specified unit.

change pen size by(): changes the size of the pen by the specified unit.

set pen size to(): sets the pen size to the specified unit.

Example 8 The following code draws 9 squares each time with a new shade of pen turning the Sprite by 40 degrees. (Using **repeated iterations** to draw)

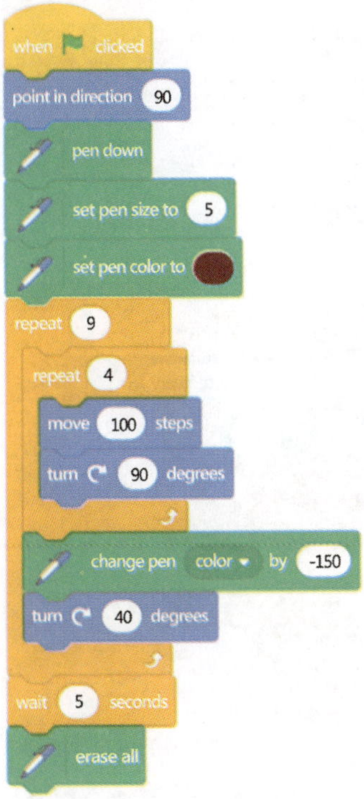

Example 9 The following code draws 24 circles each at 15 degrees with different shade of pen colour each time. (Using **repeated iterations** to draw)

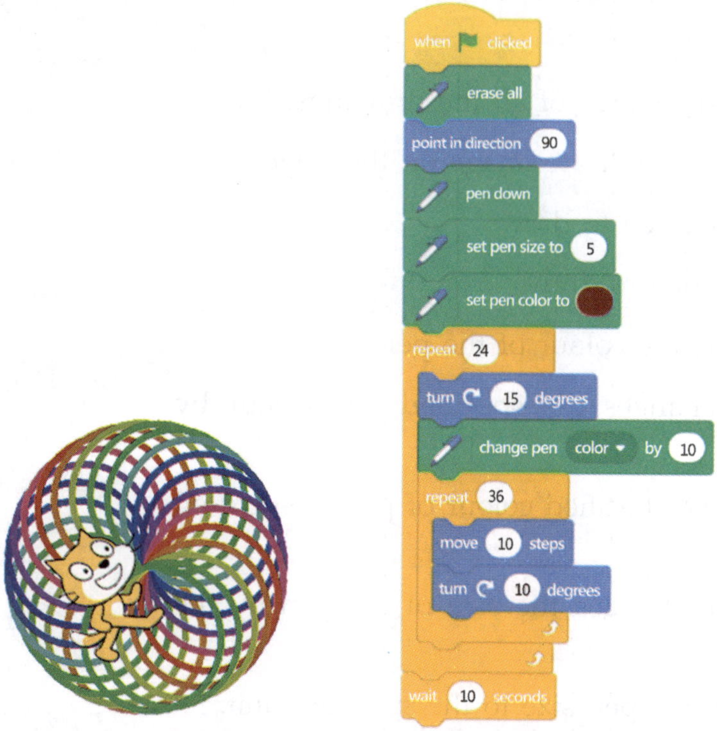

Example 10 The following code is a quiz in which if the user answers correctly, his score of correct answers is incremented by 1 else for a wrong answer, the variable wrong is incremented. Only two questions have been included. You can further add more questions of your choice.
(Incrementing the score in a quiz game)

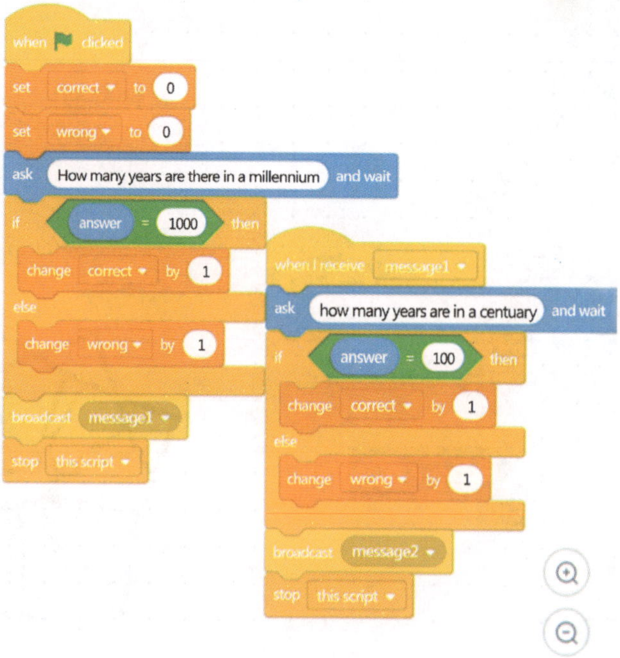

3. Text to Speech

This block head is an extension and contains blocks which speak the dialog instead of displaying it.

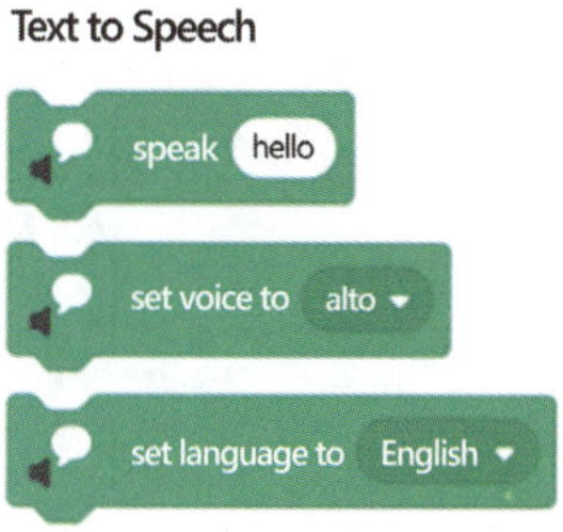

Stack blocks:

speak( ): converts the text message into an audio message.

set voice to( ): allows to choose from a list of voice options.

set language to( ): allows to change the speech to any of the listed languages.

8.5 ANIMATING THE SPRITE

A sprite can be made live on screen by showing its motion, adding speech to it and changing the backdrop. The list of costumes of the selected sprite can be seen under the Costumes tab. A loop can be used to continuously switch to the next costume. If the switching appears too fast, it can be delayed by using delay( ) block or wait( ) block. The following example uses various blocks to make the sprite alive on the screen.

Example 11 The following code shows a sprite (here, parrot) who appears to fly by flapping its wings. It is done by the use of next costume block. As soon as it touches the edge, the backdrop changes and the parrot starts from its original position. Meanwhile it also talks and makes sound.

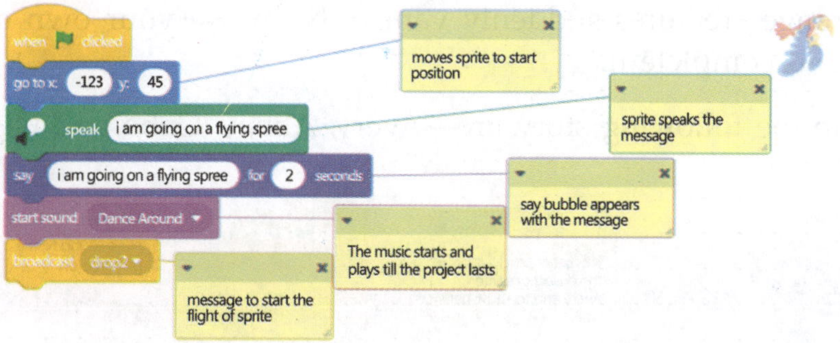

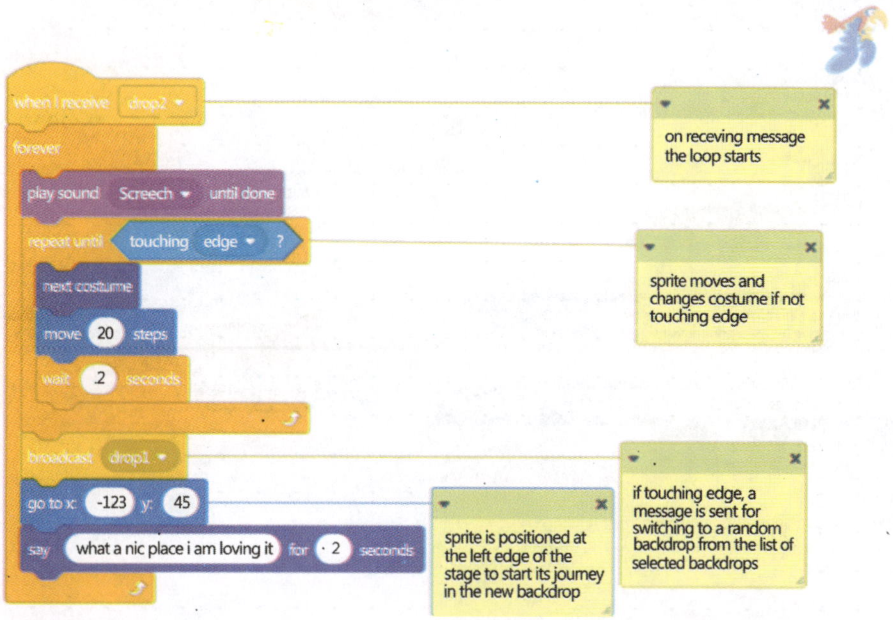

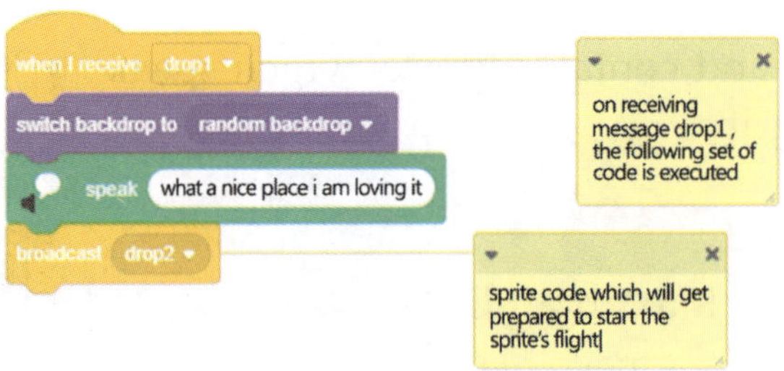

8.6 CREATING A STORY

The following code is a story of two friends in a mountainous area who are thinking of entering the cave. Once they enter, they see a new world and find new creatures who can talk. Then, the strange creatures suddenly vanish. Now use your own creativity to take the story further and complete it.

The sprites used in the following story are—Avery, Abbey, Gobo and Giga.

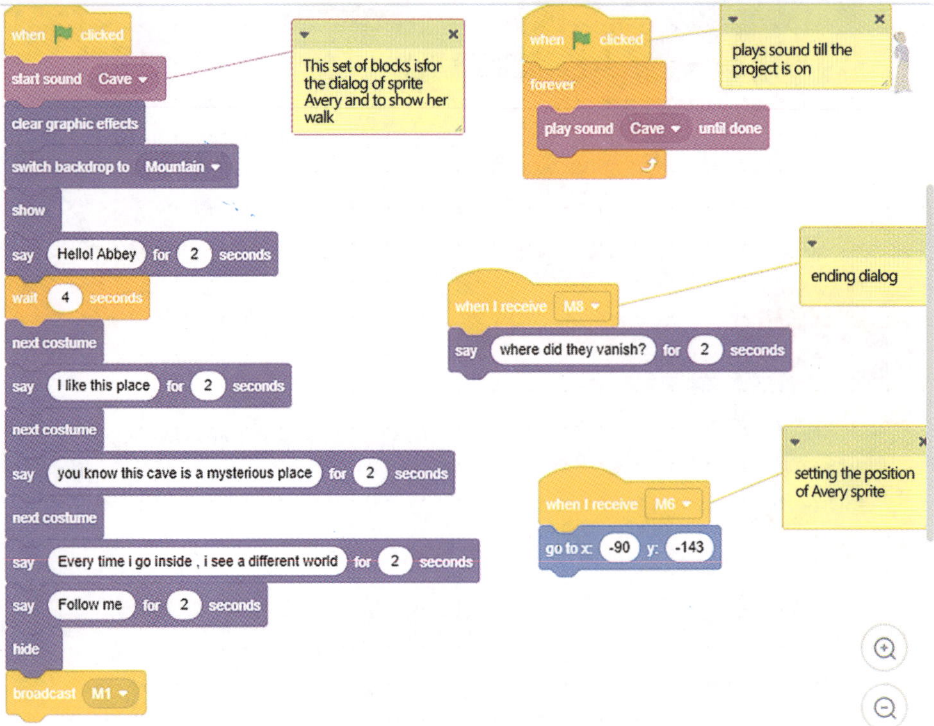

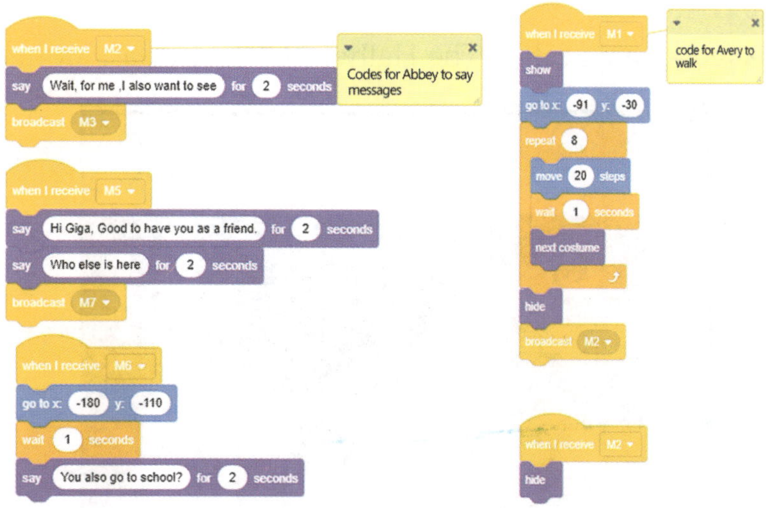
when I receive M2
say Wait, for me ,I also want to see for 2 seconds
broadcast M3
Codes for Abbey to say messages
when I receive M5
say Hi Giga, Good to have you as a friend. for 2 seconds
say Who else is here for 2 seconds
broadcast M7
when I receive M6
go to x: -180 y: -110
wait 1 seconds
say You also go to school? for 2 seconds
when I receive M1
code for Avery to walk
show
go to x: -91 y: -30
repeat 8
move 20 steps
wait 1 seconds
next costume
hide
broadcast M2
when I receive M2
hide

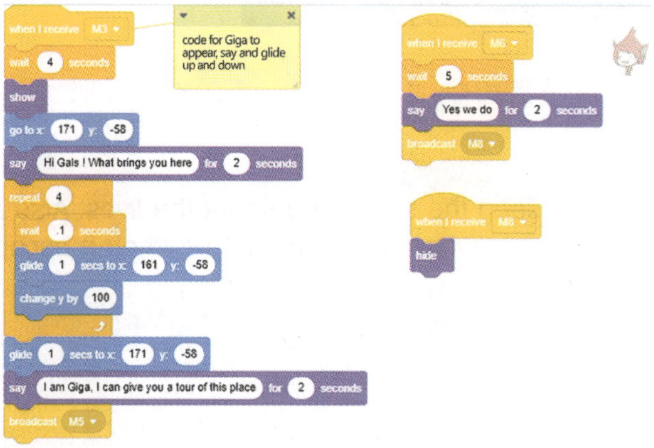
when I receive M3
code for Giga to appear, say and glide up and down
wait 4 seconds
show
go to x: 171 y: -58
say Hi Gals ! What brings you here for 2 seconds
repeat 4
wait .1 seconds
glide 1 secs to x: 161 y: -58
change y by 100
glide 1 secs to x: 171 y: -58
say I am Giga, I can give you a tour of this place for 2 seconds
broadcast M5
when I receive M6
wait 5 seconds
say Yes we do for 2 seconds
broadcast M8
when I receive M8
hide

I like this place

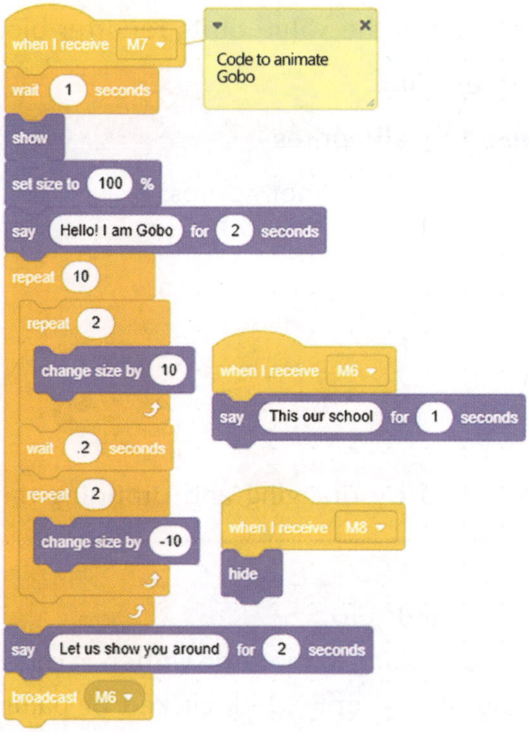
when I receive M7
Code to animate Gobo
wait 1 seconds
show
set size to 100 %
say Hello! I am Gobo for 2 seconds
repeat 10
repeat 2
change size by 10
wait .2 seconds
repeat 2
change size by -10
say Let us show you around for 2 seconds
broadcast M6
when I receive M6
say This our school for 1 seconds
when I receive M8
hide

Hi Gals ! What brings you here

You also go to school?

8.7 CREATING A GAME

We have already created a game called The Hallway Ghost in class IX under Project Work.

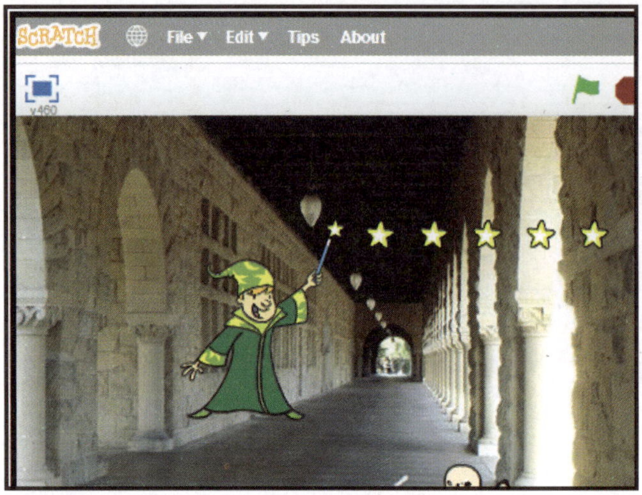

PRACTICE TIME

Now, use the variable blocks learnt in this chapter to keep the score and count the lives. Also add music to the game and include appropriate sound effects when a ghost is hit or when it escapes. Let the wizard and the ghosts have a conversation when they face each other.

KEY TERMS

Stage Monitor A small box on the stage that displays the value of its reporter block.

Variable The name of a location that can store a value.

Global variables They can be used and changed by all sprites.

Local variables They can be used and changed by their owner sprites.

Tempo The speed or pace of a piece of music.

POINTS TO REMEMBER

- Scratch is a visual and graphical language.
- Commands are prewritten and code is developed by dragging and dropping them in the Code Area.
- Scratch is an open source software.
- It is mainly used to develop games, animations and quiz.
- The sprite performs all the actions on stage area according to the code written in code area.
- Sprite and Backdrop can be sourced from the library, uploaded, clicked or painted in paint editor.

- x co-ordinates of Stage range from –240 to +240 and y co-ordinates from –180 to +180.
- By default direction value of sprite is 90°. With every added degree, the sprite turns clockwise by 1°.
- Sensing blocks are used in applications where some action has to be performed when the sprite senses some event like touching a colour of striking a key.
- The codes where mathematical operations and string handling is involved, Operator blocks are used.

SOLVED QUESTIONS

Q1. What is the difference between touching color ( ) and color ( ) is touching ( )?

Ans. touching color ( ) checks if the sprite is touching the specified color.
color ( ) is touching ( ) checks if the color ( ) on the sprite is touching the other specified color ( )

Q2. What is the function of answer block?

Ans. Answer is a reporter block which holds the most recent text entered for ask ( ) and wait block.

Q3. Write the output of the following blocks:

(i) length of (apple)
(ii) (apple) contains (a)?
(iii) round (23.4)
(iv) (26) mod (4)
(v) join (apple) (banana)
(vi) key (a) pressed?
(vii) distance to (mouse pointer)

Ans. (i) Will hold 5 as 'apple' has 5 alphabets
(ii) True as 'a' is there in 'apple'
(iii) 23 as 23.4 < 23.5 so is rounded to the 23
(iv) 2 as remainder of 26/4 is 2
(v) applebanana
(vi) will hold True if Key 'a' is pressed
(vii) will hold the distance between the sprite and mouse pointer in pixels.

Q4. Give the output of the following codes:

(i)

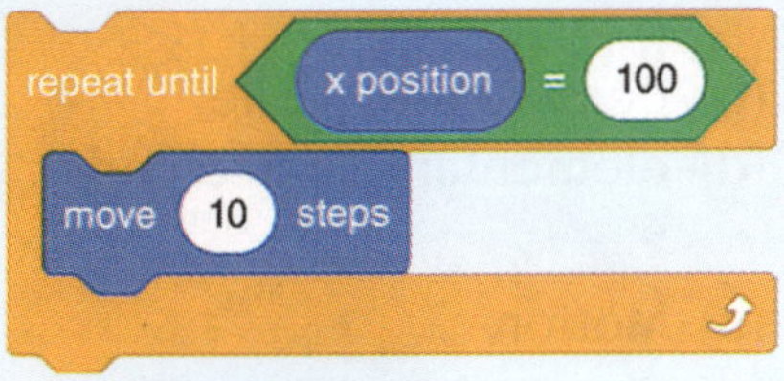

(ii)

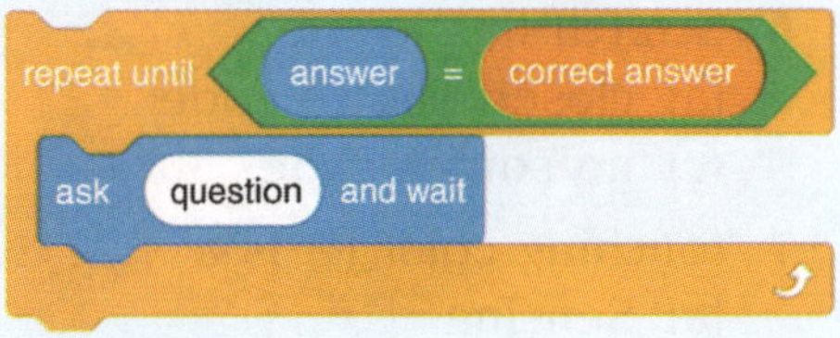

(iii)

Ans. (i) If x position ≠ 100, sprite moves 10 steps. Again x position is checked and sprite moves accordingly. When x position = 100, the loop is terminated.

(ii) This code will keep on asking the question repeatedly until it gets the correct answer.

(iv) The loop will be executed if sprite is not touching the edge. Inside the loop loudness is checked. If it is > 30 a message "No loud noises" is displayed for 2 seconds. If loudness is not > 30 then sprite moves 10 steps.

Again it is checked whether sprite is touching the edge or not.

EXERCISES

I. Very Short Answer Type Questions

Multiple Choice Questions:

1. There is no probability of syntax errors in Scratch because
   (a) There are no commands in Scratch.
   (b) Commands are pre-written in Scratch.
   (c) Errors cannot be deleted.
   (d) Graphical commands do not have any syntax.
2. Range of x co-ordinates of stage are
   (a) –240 to +180 (b) 240 to –180 (c) –180 to +180 (d) –240 to +240
3. Answer block is a
   (a) Stage block (b) Reporter block (c) Hat block (d) C-block
4. Boolean blocks return a value
   (a) True/False (b) Latest value given as input
   (c) Value stored in answer (d) any random number
5. Join ( ) ( ) concatenates
   (a) two numbers (b) A number and a string
   (c) two strings (c) All of the above
6. Scratch has (a/an)
   (a) closed source code (b) open source code
   (c) no source code (d) elementary source code
7. touching color ( ) is a .... block.
   (a) Sensing (b) Motion
   (c) Looks (d) Pen
8. round ( ) block returns
   (a) a circle (b) the nearest integer value
   (c) Sprite to 180° (d) the remainder of division
9. If block pen up is used, then the sprite
   (a) moves upwards (b) draws a line upwards
   (c) does not understand the command (d) does not draw
10. To keep a score in a quiz, we use .... in Scratch code.
    (a) block (b) Pen
    (c) Variable (d) operator

Fill in the blanks:

1. ……………….. block waits for the user to give an input.
2. ………………. block reports distance between objects.
3. If angle of rotation is 380° then the actual value of rotation is ………………… .
4. ………………. Area is where the blocks are dragged and dropped.
5. ………………. is the area where the sprite performs the action.
6. ………………. block is used with timer block to initialize the timer to zero.
7. ( ) mod ( ) block reports ………………. .

II. Short Answer Type Questions

1. State any three features of Scratch.
2. What is a sprite?
3. What is the range of x and y co-ordinates on a Scratch Stage?
4. What is the file extension of a Scratch 3 file?
5. What does a negative sign with rotation degree imply?
6. What is the function of ask ( ) and wait block?
7. What will happen if a reset timer block is not used in a project which uses timer ( ) block?
8. What is a Scratch variable?
9. Differentiate between global and local variables.
10. What should be done to make the stage monitor of a variable appear on the Stage?
11. What do you understand by Tempo?
12. What is the function of stamp block?
13. What is the difference between say ( ) and speak ( ) blocks?
14. Differentiate between the functioning of the following blocks. (You can use an example to explain.)

(i)

(ii)

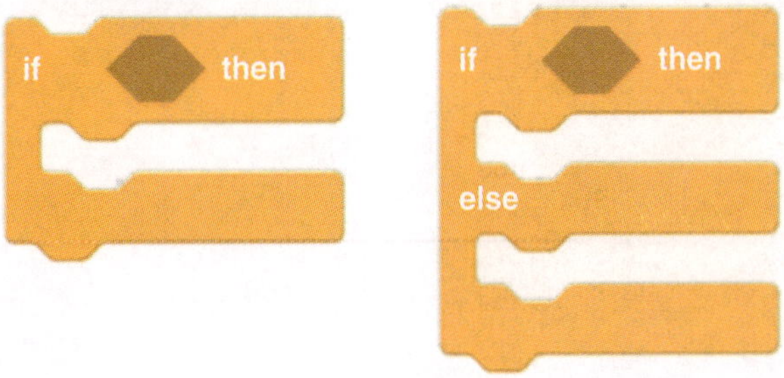

(iii)

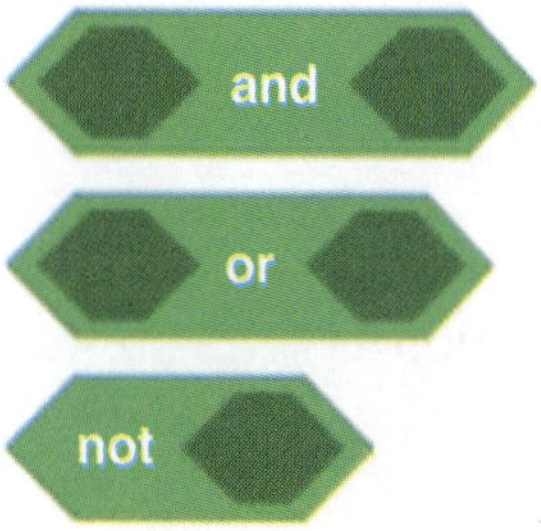

(iv)

(v)

15. Give the output of the following code:

(i)

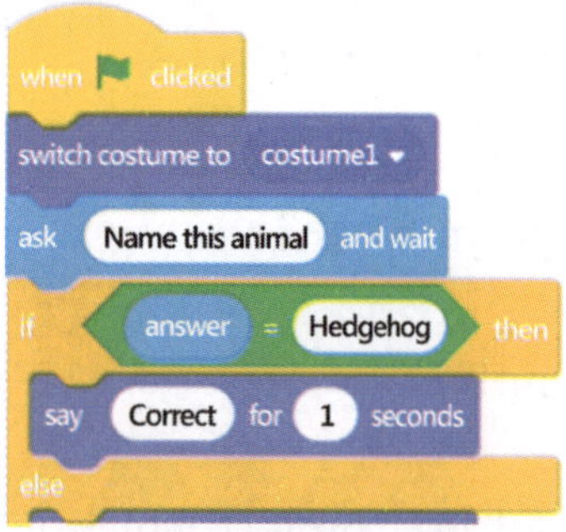

(ii)

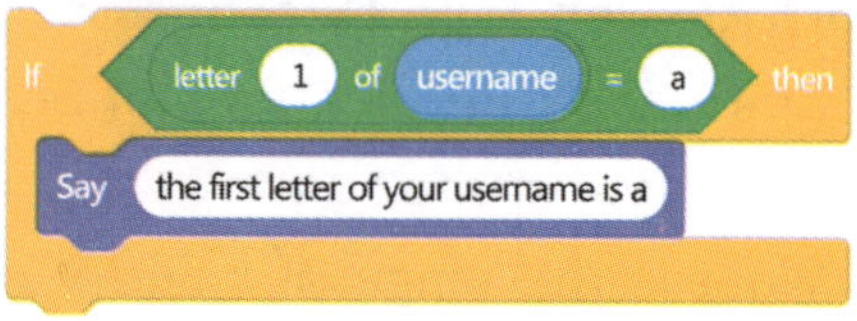

(iii)

(iv)

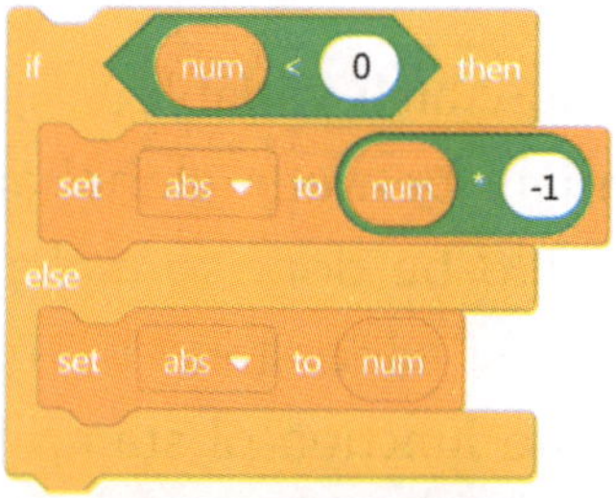

(v)

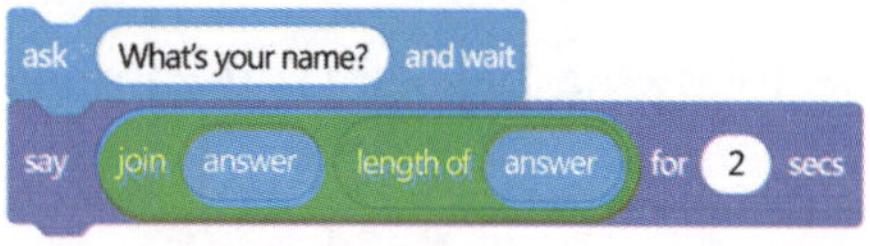

(vi)

16. What is the output of the following code? Rewrite the code using multiple conditioning in a single line.

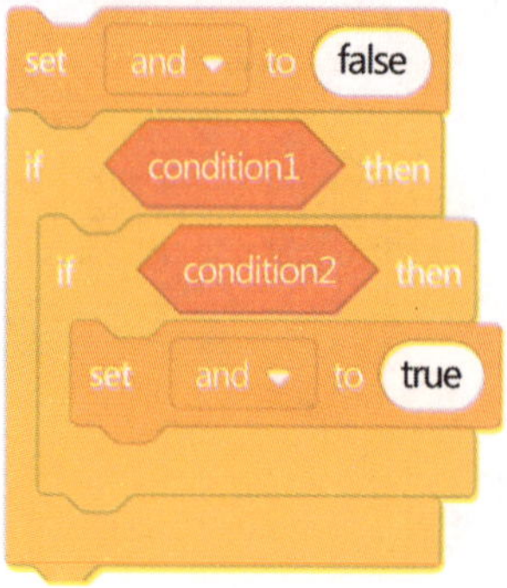

III. Long Answer Type Questions

1. Write a Scratch code to input a number, check if it is even or odd. If it is even, find its square and if the number is odd, make it even.
2. Write a Scratch code to design a test containing at least two multiple choice questions. When the answer entered by the user is correct, the variable score should be incremented by 1 otherwise a suitable message is displayed.
3. Write a Scratch code that shows a conversation between two characters on any topic. Change the backdrop in between the conversation as per the context.

9 Python

- Revision of Python basics
- Conditionals: if, if-else statements
- Loops: for, while (e.g., sum of first 10 natural numbers)
- Practice simple programs

In class IX you have already learnt about the basics of Python programming. In class X you will equip yourselves with the advanced features to develop complex Python code. This chapter first recapitulates the basic python commands and then takes you a step forward in programming by introducing the use of **conditional statements** and **loops**. Till now you have been using the **Command Line Python Interpreter** to execute your codes. In this chapter you will learn to write a code using **IDE** (Integrated Development Environment) named **PyCharm** which is the most commonly used **IDE** developed by JetBrains. The following section will lead you through the steps of downloading and working with PyCharm.

9.1 STARTING WITH IDE

PyCharm Community version is available as an open-source and can be downloaded for free from the web.

STEPS

1. Type **PyCharm** in the search bar of your browser and press enter key.
2. Click on **PyCharm–Official Site** and the Pycharm official site opens up.

   Or

   You can also type https://www.jetbrains.com/pycharm/ in the search bar of your browser. Pressing enter key will take you to the Pycharm official site.
3. Click on **Download** button appearing on the top. Now the screen shows two options– Professional and Community.

4. Click on **Download** under **Community** and make sure the platform **Windows** tab is chosen (Fig. 9.1).

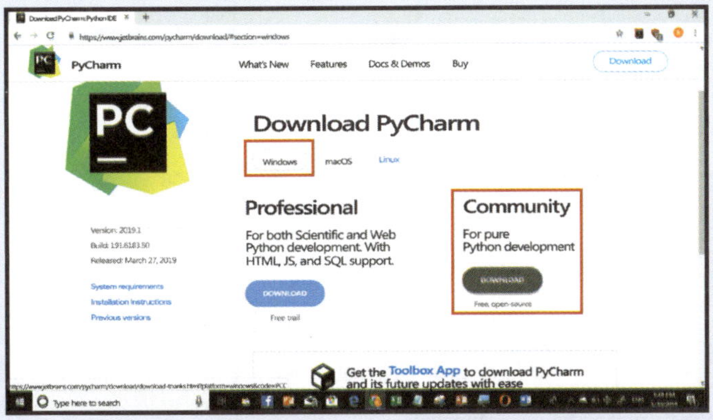

Fig. 9.1: Download PyCharm

5. After the download is complete, run the executable file which has been downloaded. This will start the installation process.

6. Choose the default options as they appear. The installation process will take about a minute.

7. Once the installation is over, PyCharm icon will appear on the desktop. Click the icon to start working in PyCharm IDE. You will be asked to create a project with any name of your choice. Project is actually a folder where your programs will get stored.

8. Once the project is created, it appears on the PyCharm work screen. Right click and choose **New** → **Python File** (Fig. 9.2).

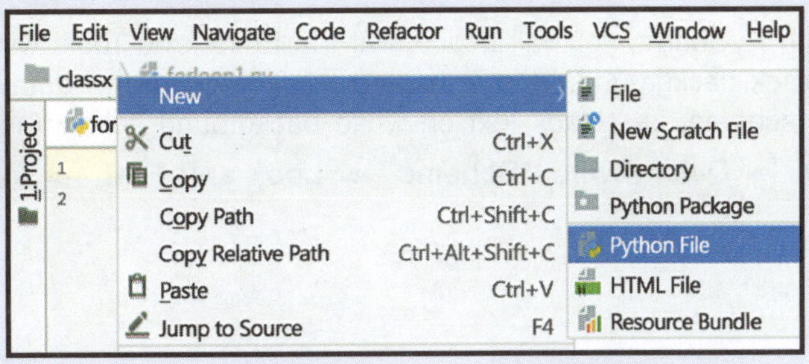

Fig. 9.2: Creating a new python file

9. Give a name to the python file in the dialog box as in Fig. 9.3, and click OK. You will get a work screen where you can type the code in the editor window. To execute the code, right click and choose Run from the menu and get the output in the tools window.

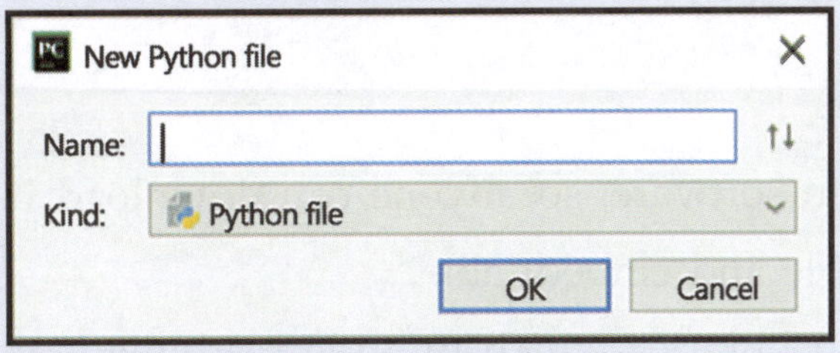

Fig. 9.3: Naming the file

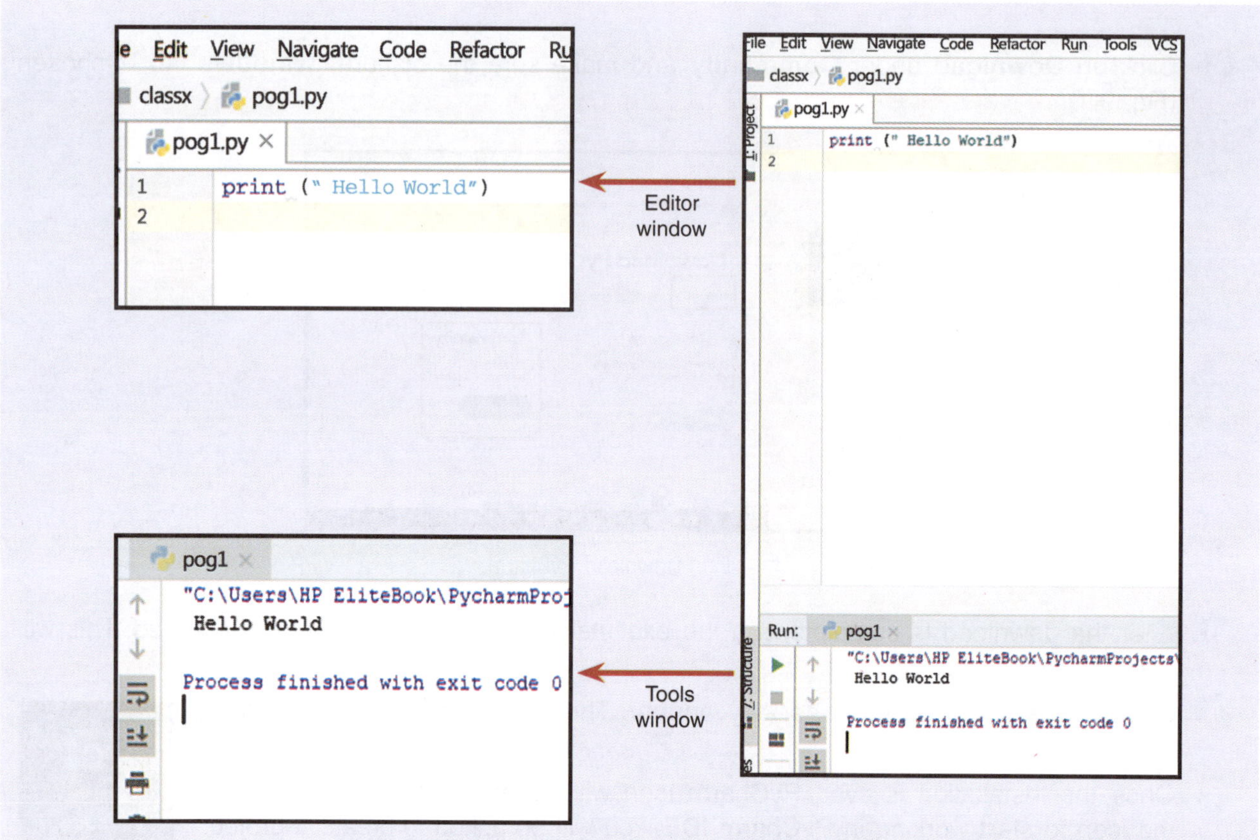

Fig. 9.4: Work screen displaying a code and its output

NOTE

When you start working with PyCharm, you will notice that the Editor and Tools window are in reverse display mode, i.e., white text on black background. This is because in PyCharm the default **Look and Feel** scheme is **Dracula**. To change the scheme, i.e., black text on white background, follow the path mentioned below:

View → Quick Switch Scheme → Look and Feel → IntelliJ

9.2 QUICK RECALL

This section will take you to a quick walkthrough of the basics of Python.

Features of Python

- Python is a simple language so the user can concentrate more on solving the problem than on the syntax.
- Python is case-sensitive.
- Python is free and open software, so anyone can download it and use it.
- It is interpreted, portable and embeddable.
- It has extensive built-in libraries which provide readymade code to the programmers. Unlike compilers, it does not require linking and loading of libraries.

Data Types

There are two types of numeric data – **Integers** and **Floating point**. Another data type which is a sequence of characters is called **String**. The operators used with these data types are:

Operator	Data type of Operands	Data type of Result	Example
NUMERIC DATA TYPE			
Addition +, Subtraction –, Multiplication *	Both operands int	Int	2 + 3 = 5
	Any one or both operands float	Float	2 + 3.5 = 5.5 2.5 + 4.5 = 7.0
Division/	Either one or Both operands int or float	Float	56 / 2 = 28.0
Integer or Floor Division	Both operands int	Int	5 // 2 = 2 (quotient)
	Any one or both operands float	Float	5.0 // 2 = 2.0 (quotient)
Remainder %	Both operands int	Int	5 % 2 = 1 (remainder)
	Any one or both operands float	Float	5.0 % 2.0 = 1.0 (remainder)
Exponentiation **	Both operands int	Int	5 ** 2 = 25
	Any one or both operands float	Float	5.0 ** 2.0 = 25.0
STRING DATA TYPE			
Concatenation +	String	String	"Hello" + "world"= Helloworld
Multiplication *	String	String	"A"* 5 = AAAAA

Variables and Assignment

Variable is the label of the memory location where a value is stored. A variable may be given a value using assignment statement.

Type of Assignment		Result
Single Assignment	A = 20 B = A C = 2*4+A	20 gets stored in A B is given the same value as that of A, i.e., 20 C = 8+A = 28
Multiple Assignment	A, B = 10, 20	A = 10, B = 20
Augmented assignment +=, –=, *=, /=,//=, %=, **=	If A = 10 then A+ = 1 If A = 10 then A* = 2	A+ = 1 → A = A+1 → A = 10+1 = 11 A* = 2 → A = A*2 → A = 10*2 = 20

Functions

Following are the commonly used functions in a Python code:

Function name	Use	Syntax and example
Print()	Prints whatever is enclosed in the parenthesis	Print(numeric constant ,..string,.., variable,.... expression,....) Print("ten + six = ", 10+6) gives **ten + six=16**
Input()	Takes input as string and assigns it to a variable	A = input("enter age") Whatever may be the value given by user, it is assigned to variable A as a string. If 25 is given as input then A gets the value 25 but this value cannot be used with arithmetic operators as it is a string value
Int()	Converts the value to integer	Int(2.4) = 2
Float()	Converts the value to float	Float(2) = 2.0
Eval()	Converts string value to numeric value	a = eval("25") b = 20+a print(b) will print a result 45 as eval( ) will convert string 25 to numeric 25 which then gets added to 20 to give a value 45 to b

Example 1 Write a Python code for entering the amount in rupees and calculating the number of notes of different denominations (10/50/100/200/500/2000) that will make that amount.

Program Code:

```
amount= int(input("Enter the amount in multiple of 10  :  "))
two_thousand= amount//2000
print (" Number of 2000 rupees = ", two_thousand)
amount -= two_thousand*2000
two_hund = amount // 200
print (" Number of 200 rupees = ", two_hund)
amount -= two_hund*200
one_hund = amount // 100
print (" Number of 100 rupees = ", one_hund)
amount -= one_hund*100
fifty = amount // 50
print (" Number of 50 rupees = ", fifty)
amount -=fifty*50
ten= amount//10
print (" Number of 10 rupees = ", ten)
```

OUTPUT:

```
Enter the amount in multiple of 10  :  123450
 Number of 2000 rupees =  61
 Number of 200 rupees =  7
 Number of 100 rupees =  0
 Number of 50 rupees =  1
 Number of 10 rupees =  0
```

9.3 COMPARISON OPERATORS

As the name suggests, comparison operators are used to compare two entities. They give a result of type Boolean which is either of the two values, True or False. The following table shows the result of Print function when comparison operators are used as its arguments.

Command	Output	Reason
print(5>4)	True	5 is **greater than** 4
print (5>=4)	True	5 **is greater than** 4 although 5 is not **equal to** 4
print(5!=4)	True	5 **is not equal to** 4
Print(5==5)	True	5 **is equal to** 5
Print(5<6)	True	5 **is less than** 6
Print(5<=6)	True	5 **is less than** 6 although 5 is **not equal** to 6
Print(5==4)	False	5 **is not equal to** 4
Print(5>=6)	False	5 is **neither equal to** 6 **nor greater than** 6

The comparison operators used in the above table are also called Boolean operators and the expressions that use them are called Boolean expressions or comparison expressions.

9.4 CONDITIONAL STATEMENTS

Let us consider a program which takes age as input and prints the message, "Person is Minor" or "Person is Major" depending on the condition whether age >= 18.

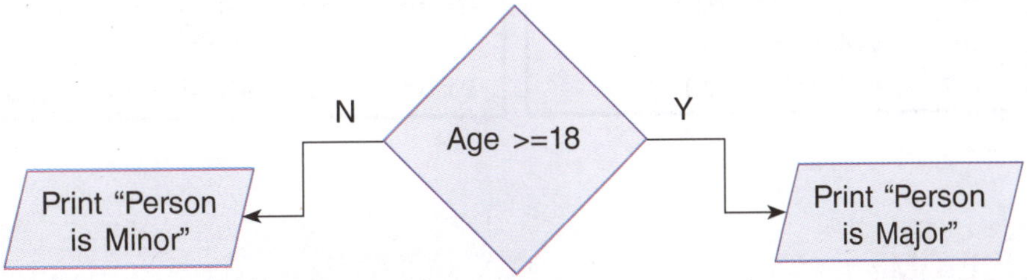

In order to make such decisions, Python provides a **conditional statement** which uses conditions in the form of comparison expressions. These expressions evaluate to the Boolean values True or False.

These conditional statements may be simple if statement, if-else statement, nested conditional statements or multi-way if-elseif-else statement.

if statement

Syntax

if (Condition or Boolean expression):
    Statement 1
    Statement 2
Statement 3
	Note the colon after the condition. This indicates that the indented lines which follow colon form a block which is executed only when the condition is true. Here statements 1 and 2 form such a block.
	
	If condition is true, statements 1, 2 and then 3 are executed.
	
	If condition is false, *block of if statement is not executed and* ***only statement 3 is executed.***
	
	Statement 3 is not indented so it is not a part of if block and is executed regardless of whether the condition is true or false.

Example 2 The following code assigns a value True to a variable raining and prints the messages:

```
raining = True
if (raining):
    print(" carry an umbrella ")
    print(" wear your raincoat ")
print(" Have a good day !")
```

OUTPUT:

```
carry an umbrella
wear your raincoat
Have a good day !

Process finished with exit code 0
```

If the variable raining is assigned the value False, the control will not execute the **if module** and the result will be as follows:

```
raining = False
if (raining):
    print(" carry an umbrella ")
    print(" wear your raincoat ")
print(" Have a good day !")
```

OUTPUT:

```
Have a good day !

Process finished with exit code 0
```

PRACTICE TIME

Write a Python code to enter the radius of a circle. The code should calculate and print the area of the circle only when the radius is greater than zero. A message saying "Circles are Fun" should be printed at the end of the execution.

If-else statement

Simple if statement performs an action only when the boolean expression evaluates to True. It does not perform any action if the boolean expression gives a False result. To perform specific actions when the expression does not hold true, Python provides us **if-else statement**.

Syntax

if (Condition or Boolean expression):
   Statement 1
   Statement 2
:
else:
   Statement 3
Statement 4
	*When condition is **True**, if **module** containing Statements 1 and 2, is executed. The control does not go to the else part but directly executes Statement 4.*
	*When condition is **False**, the control does not go to if module having Statements 1 and 2. It directly jumps to the else part and executes Statement 3, comes out of if-else and executes statement 4.*

Note that indentation plays a vital role in Python coding. Statements with same indent are considered to be in the same block.

Example 3 **(Using Condition)**

Case 1: In the following code, **condition** has been set to **False,** and hence **if module** is not executed and the **control** directly **jumps to the else module** which prints " it's a sunny day". It then comes out of the if-else statement and prints "Have a good day !".

```
raining = False
if (raining):
    print(" carry an umbrella ")
    print(" wear your raincoat ")
else:
    print(" it's a sunny day")
print(" Have a good day !")
```

OUTPUT:

```
it's a sunny day
Have a good day !

Process finished with exit code 0
```

Case 2: When the **condition** is **True,** only if **module will be executed** and else module will be ignored. The last print statement is out of if-else statement so it will be executed in this case also.

```
raining = True
if (raining):
    print(" carry an umbrella ")
    print(" wear your raincoat ")
else:
    print(" it's a sunny day")
print(" Have a good day !")
```

OUTPUT:

```
carry an umbrella
wear your raincoat
Have a good day !

Process finished with exit code 0
```

The condition can also be in the form of a boolean expression which may use comparison operators and give the result either True or False.

Example 4 **(Using boolean expression)**

The following code takes different values for variables a and b as input, compares the two values using a boolean expression (a> b) and prints a message:

```
a=int(input("enter the value of a : "))
b=int(input("enter the value of b : "))
if (a > b) :
    print("a is greater because a = ", a, " and b = ",b)
else:
    print("b is greater because b = ", b, " and a = ", a)
```

OUTPUT:

```
enter the value of a : 78
enter the value of b : 100
b is greater because b =  100 and a =  78

    Process finished with exit code 0
```

PRACTICE TIME

Write a code that asks for the name and age of a person. If age>=18, the code should print a message "<name> is an adult" otherwise the message should be "<name> is a minor"

Nested if-else statement

You can have a if...else statement inside another if...else statement. This is called nested if-else statement. Any number of these statements can be nested inside one another. Indentation is the only way to figure out the level of nesting.

Syntax:

```
if (condition 1):
      Statement 1
else:
      if (condition 2):
            Statement 2
      else:
            Statement 3
Statement 4
```

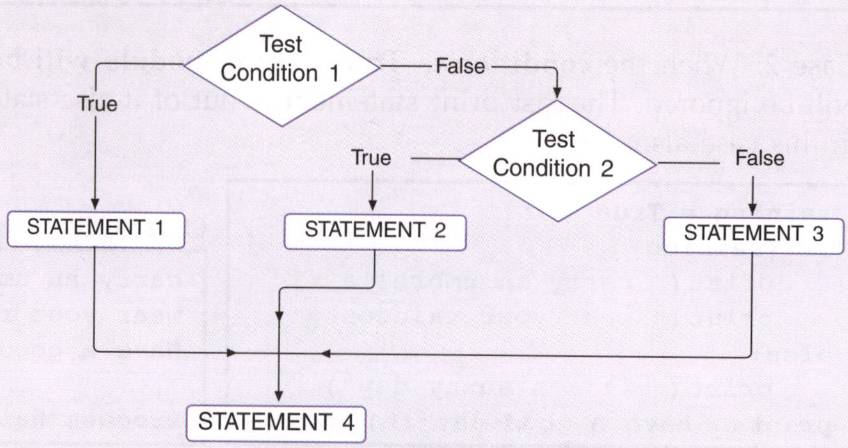

Example 5 The program inputs two numeric values and a character (+ or –). The program then calculates the sum if the character entered is + and the difference if the input character is –.

```
a=int(input("enter the value of a : "))
b=int(input("enter the value of b : "))
opr = input("enter the operator (+,-) : ")
if (opr=="+"):
    print( a, " + ", b , " = ", a+b)
else:
    if (opr=="-"):
        print( a, " - ", b , " = ", a-b)
    else :
        print(" Invalid operator")
```

OUTPUT:

```
enter the value of a : 10
enter the value of b : 20
enter the operator (+,-) : +
10  +  20  =  30
```

```
enter the value of a : 20
enter the value of b : 4
enter the operator (+,-) : #
 Invalid operator
```

PRACTICE TIME

1. Rewrite the code of example 4 to deal with the case when a=b.
2. Write a program to input the marks of a student out of 100 and assign a grade according to the following criterion:

   (>=90 : A), (80-89 : B), (70–79 : C), (60–69 : D), (Below 60 : E)

   The output should display the score and the grade along with proper messages.

Multi-way If-elif-else statement

You must have noticed in the previous example that the use of nested if-else statements leads to deep indentation. To make the program easier to read multi-way if statement can be used.

Syntax:

if (condition1):
    Statement 1
elif (condition2):
    Statement 2
else:
    Statement 3
Statement 4
	*When condition1 is True, Statement 1 is executed, otherwise control goes to else block where another if statement (**else if** written in short as **elif**) checks condition2.*
	When condition2 is True, Statement 2 is executed.
	When condition2 is False, Statement 3 is executed.
	Statement 4 will be executed in all the cases since it is not a part of if-elif-else statement.

NOTE

The if block can have only one else block. But it can have multiple elif blocks.

Example 6 The following is an example of the use of multiple if-else statement to make a simple calculator:

```
a=int(input("enter the value of a : "))
b=int(input("enter the value of b : "))
opr = input("enter the operator (+,-,*,/) : ")
if (opr=="+"):
    print( a, " + ", b , " = ", a+b)
elif (opr=="-"):
    print( a, " - ", b , " = ", a-b)
elif (opr=="*"):
    print( a, " * ", b , " = ", a*b)
elif (opr=="/"):
    print( a, " / ", b , " = ", a/b)
else :
    print(" Invalid operator")
```

```
enter the value of a : 20
enter the value of b : 10
enter the operator (+,-,*,/) : *
20  *  10  =  200
```

```
enter the value of a : 20
enter the value of b : 10
enter the operator (+,-,*,/) : #
 Invalid operator
```

PRACTICE TIME

Write a program to input the marks of a student out of 100 and assign a grade according to the following criterion using multi-way if statement:

(>=90 : A), (80-89 : B), (70-79 : C), (60-69 : D), (Below 60 : E)

The output should display the score and the grade along with proper messages.

9.5 LOOPING

While writing a code, you will come across many situations where a set of instructions has to be repeated n number of times or till the time a certain condition is reached. In computer programming, such a sequence is called a loop. In Python a **loop** can be executed using a **while statement** or a **for statement.**

While Loop

The while loop in Python is used to iterate or repeat a block of code as long as the test expression (condition) is true. We generally use this loop when we don't know beforehand, the number of times to repeat.

Syntax:

while (test expression):

body of loop

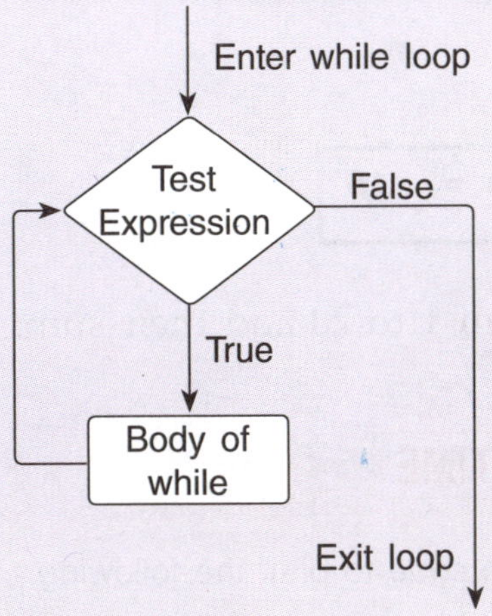

In while loop, test expression is checked first. The body of the loop is entered only if the test_expression evaluates to True. After one iteration, the test expression is checked again. This process continues until the test_expression evaluates to False.

Body starts with indentation and the first un-indented line marks the end of the body.

Example 7 The following code prints "Hello World" 5 times.

```
count = 0
while (count<5):
    print("Hello World")
    count = count+1
```

Example 8 Using while loop calculate the sum of first 10 natural numbers.

```
number = 1
sum = 0
while (number <= 10):
    sum = sum + number
    number = number + 1
print(" the sum of first 10 natural numbers  = ", sum)
```

NOTE

Infinite loops are a common error so make sure that the condition eventually becomes false so that the loop terminates. Another common mistake that you might make is running the loop one time extra or one time less which is referred to as *off-by-one error*. So care must be taken while writing the condition.

Example 9 Infinite loop

```
number = 1
sum = 0
while (number <= 10):
    sum = sum + number
print(" the sum = ", sum)
```

Example 10 off-by-one error—The following code runs one less time so the last number 10 is not added. The result is displayed as 45 instead of 55.

```
number = 1
sum = 0
while (number < 10):
    sum = sum + number
    number = number + 1
print(" the sum = ", sum)
```

OUTPUT

```
the sum =  45
```

Example 11 The following code displays even numbers from 1 to 20 and their sum.

```
number = 1
sum = 0
while (number <= 20):
    if ( number % 2 == 0):
        sum = sum + number
        print(number)
    number = number + 1
print(" the sum = ", sum)
```

PRACTICE TIME

1. Write a Python code to print the following pattern:

```
*****
*****
*****
*****
```

2. Write a Python code to enter a number **a** and the exponent **b** and using while loop calculate $\mathbf{a}^{\mathbf{b}}$.

For Loop

To understand the working of for loop, we must understand the concept of Lists first.

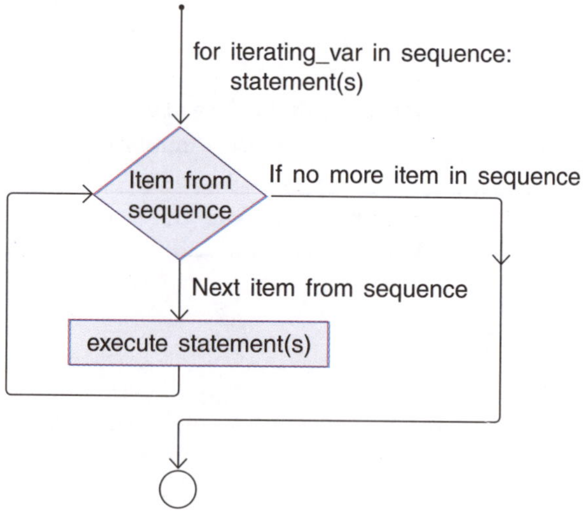

A **list** is a collection of letters, words or numbers which is ordered and changeable. By ordered it is meant that the elements are placed in a sequence and can be accessed using their positions. In Python, lists are written within square brackets.

For example, A = ["red", "blue", "yellow", "green"]

Here, A is a list which has "red" at 0th position, "blue" at 1st position and so on.

```
a=["red", "blue", "yellow", "green"]
print(a[0])
print (a[1])
```

Code

```
red
blue
```

Output

For loop is used for iterating over a sequence which may be a list, a string or a range.

Syntax:

for iterating var **in** sequence:
    statement(s)

NOTE

The sequence may be a string, a list or a range.

Looping through a list:

The following code loops through each element of the list:

```
a=["red", "blue", "yellow", "green"]
for colour in a :
    print(colour)
```

```
red
blue
yellow
green
```

Looping through strings:

The following code loops through the given string thereby displaying each element of the string.

```
a= "SMILE"
for alphabet  in a :
    print(alphabet)
```

```
S
M
I
L
E
```

Looping through a range:

The range( ) function takes 0 as a starting value if starting value is not specified, so range(5) specifies the range of values 0–5 excluding 5.

To specify the starting value it can be written as range(2,5), the values here range from 2 to 5 excluding 5.

To skip values in the range, a step value can also be defined. Range (1,20,3) defines the values 1,4,7,10,13,16,19. By default step value is 1.

Example 12 The following code finds the sum of numbers from 1 to 10:

```
sum=0
for i in range(1,11):
    sum=sum + i
print (" sum of numbers 1 to 10 = ", sum)
```

```
sum of numbers 1 to 10 =  55

Process finished with exit code 0
```

Example 13 The following code prints a pattern as displayed in the output:

```
for i in range(1,6):
    print ("*" * i)
```

```
*
**
***
****
*****
```

Example 14 The following code takes a number as input and prints its multiplication table:

```
num= int(input(" enter a number :"))
for i in range(1,6):
     print (num , " * " , i, " = ", num*i)
```

```
 enter a number :5
5  *  1  =  5
5  *  2  =  10
5  *  3  =  15
5  *  4  =  20
5  *  5  =  25
```

Nested for loop:

A for loop within another for loop is called nested for loop.

Syntax:

```
for iteration variable in (range/string/list):
        for iteration variable in (range/string/list):
                body of inner loop
other statements of outer loop
```

Example 15 The following code and its output will give you a clear view of the values which i and j take with respect to each other in a nested loop:

```
for i in range(1,6):
    for j in range(1,5):
        print("i=",i,"j=",j, end = '    ')
    print()
```

```
i= 1 j= 1    i= 1 j= 2    i= 1 j= 3    i= 1 j= 4
i= 2 j= 1    i= 2 j= 2    i= 2 j= 3    i= 2 j= 4
i= 3 j= 1    i= 3 j= 2    i= 3 j= 3    i= 3 j= 4
i= 4 j= 1    i= 4 j= 2    i= 4 j= 3    i= 4 j= 4
i= 5 j= 1    i= 5 j= 2    i= 5 j= 3    i= 5 j= 4
```

Example 16 The given code prints the first 4 multiples of numbers 1–5:

```
1 2 3 4
2 4 6 8
3 6 9 12
4 8 12 16
5 10 15 20
```

```
for i in range(1,6):
    for j in range(1,5):
        print(i*j, end = ' ')
    print()
```

NOTE

end = ' ' in print statement displays the next number in the same row. To change the row print( ) has been written after we come out of the inner loop.

The outer loop is executed 5 times and for each value of i, the inner loop is executed 4 times so the inner loop is executed 5 x 4 = 20 times

KEY TERMS

Boolean expression The expression that gives a result which is either true or false.

Loop When a set of instructions have to be repeatedly executed n number of times or till the time a certain condition is reached, such a set is called a loop.

Infinite loops The loops that get executed endlessly.

Off-by-one error This error occurs when loop is executed either less or more than the desired number of times.

List A collection which is ordered and changeable.

Nested for loop A loop within another loop.

POINTS TO REMEMBER

- PyCharm is the most commonly used IDE (Integrated Development Environment) developed by JetBrains.
- Python provides a conditional statement which uses conditions in form of comparison expressions. The code decides the path to be followed depending on the result of the comparison expression.
- Conditional expressions evaluate to the Boolean values True or False.
- Conditional statements are in the form of simple if statement, if-else, if-elseif-else (nested conditional statements).
- The if block can have only one else block. But it can have multiple elseif blocks.
- The while loop in Python is used to iterate or repeat a block of code as long as the test expression (condition) is true.
- Infinite loops and off-by-one error are common errors which occur when working with loops.
- A list is a collection which is ordered and changeable.
- For loop is used for iterating over a sequence which may be a list, a string or a range.
- The range(n) function takes 0 as a starting value if starting value is not defined and the last value is n−1.
- For range(m, n, s), starting value is m, the last value is n−1 and the step value is s.
- A for loop within another for loop is called nested for loop.
- end=' ' in print statement displays the next item in the same line.

SOLVED QUESTIONS

Q1. Under what conditions is a for-loop used?

Ans. For loop is generally used when the number of iterations is known.

Q2. Which statement would you prefer—'nested-if' or 'multi-way if-elif-else' and why?

Ans. Use of multi-way if-elif-else is preferred as it reduces the complexity of the code which arises due to deep indentation in nested-if statement.

Q3. What is the difference between a string and a list?

Ans. A string is a list of characters whereas a list is a sequence of objects which may be strings.

Q4. What is the output of the following code if the number is 30?

(i)
```
if (number % 2 = = 0):
    print (number, "is even")
else:
    print (number, "is odd")
```
(ii)
```
if (number % 2 = = 0):
    print (number, " is even)
print (number, " is odd)
```

Ans. (i) 30 is even

(ii) 30 is even
30 is odd

Q5. What will be the output for the following?
```
for i in (4, 20, 4):
    for j in (-4, 10, 4):
        print (i, j, end = ' ')
print ( )
```

Ans.
```
 4  -4        4  10       4   4
20  -4       20  10      20   4
-4  -4       -4  10      -4   4
```

Note: Range is not used

Q6. Give the output of
```
for v in range (5, –20, –4):
    print v
```

Ans. 5
1
–3
–7
–11
–15
–19

Q7. Write the output of the following code:
```
for i in range (1,3):
    for j in range (1,3):
        if (i == j):
            print (i, j, "diagonal element")
```

Ans.
```
1  1  diagonal element
2  2  diagonal element
```

EXERCISES

I. Very Short Answer Type Questions

Multiple Choice Questions

1. The output of the following code is:

```
for i in [2, 3]:
   Print (i)
```

(a) 2
3 (b) error (c) i (d) 5

2. The following code executes the while loop .... times.

```
i = 1
while (i < 4):
         print i
```

(a) 1 (b) 4 (c) 3 (d) infinite

3. What is the output of the following code?

```
x = True
if x:
     print (x)
x = False
```

(a) True (b) False (c) 0 (d) 1

4. In the list A = ["Q", "W", "E", "R", "T"] the position of E is
(a) 3 (b) 2 (c) 5 (d) not-defined

5. The number of iterations in the given loop are:

```
count = 0
while (count < n):
   count + = 1
```

(a) n (b) n − 1 (c) n + 1 (d) infinite

Fill in the blanks:

1. Pycharm is .... (Command Line Interpreter/IDE)
2. A python file is given an extension ....
3. A variable which takes the value either true or false is called a .... variable.
4. .... operators give a result that is either True or False.
5. A simple if statement .... (does/does not) have an else block.
6. For and while statements are used for ....
7. A while loop is used to repeat a block for as long as the condition is ....
8. In a while loop the condition is checked .... (before/after) the loop is executed at least once.
9. Body of a block starts with indentation and the first .... line marks the end of the block.
10. If the range of outer loop is (7) and that of inner loop is (3), the body of the inner loop will be executed .... number of times.

II. Short Answer Type Questions

1. Count the number of iterations in the following loops:

(i)
```
for c in range (5,10):
    print (c)
```

(ii)
```
count = 5
while (count < 20):
    count = count + 5
```

2. Find the error in the following codes:

(i)
```
i = 0
while ( i < 100) :
    print (i)
```

(ii)
```
i = 0
while (i < 100) :
    count + = 1
```

(iii)
```
v = ["a, "e", "i", "o", "u"]
for i in v
    print (v)
```

3. What is the output of the following code?

(i)
```
count = 0
while (count < 100):
    print ("Python is fun")
    count + = 1
```

(ii)
```
for i in (0, 6) :
    for j in (4, 0) :
        print (i, j, end = '  ')
    print ( )
```

4. How is nested if different from multi-way if-elif-else statement?

5. When is a while loop preferred over a for loop?

6. Write the output of the following code:
```
i,j,k=14,6,8
if (i > k):
        if (j > k ):
                print ("i and j are greater than k")
        else:
                print ("j is less than or equal to k")
```

7. Correct the following code:
```
radius = int(input ("Enter radius:"))
if (radius > 0) :
        area = 3.14 * radius * radius
print (area)
```

8. Point out the error in the following code:
```
if (marks > = 60) :
        grade = ' D '
elif (marks > = 70 ):
        grade = ' C '
elif (marks > = 80) :
        grade = ' B '
elif (marks > = 90) :
        grade = ' A '
print(grade)
```

9. What will be the output of the following codes?

(i)
```
i = 0
While (i < 5) :
    print ('2*', i '=', 2*i)
    i +=1
```

(ii)
```
for i in range (1, 5) :
    for j in range (i, 5) :
        print (j, end= '  ')
    print ( )
```

(iii)
```
a, b, c = 10, 20, 30
if (a > b) :
    if (a > c) :
        print (a, 'is the greatest')
    else :
        print (c, 'is the greatest')
else :
    if (b > c) :
        print (b, 'is the greatest')
    else :
        print (c, 'is the greatest')
```

III. Long Answer Type Questions

1. Write a python code to find the product of first 20 odd natural numbers.
2. Write a python code to enter the name of 5 of your friends and then print each name 5 times.
3. Write a code to print the following pattern
   1
   2 2
   3 3 3
   4 4 4
4. Write a code to print the following pattern
   1 2 3 4 5 6
   1 2 3 4 5
   1 2 3 4
   1 2 3
   1 2
   1
5. Write a python code to input the name and score of 5 students and then print the name and score of the student with the highest score.
6. Write a python code to enter a number and find the product of all even numbers till the entered number, e.g., if the number entered is 25, then find the product of $2 \times 4 \times 6 \times .... \times 24$. Print the output with proper message.

10 Lab Exercises

This chapter contains the programming codes for the given list of lab exercises. The designs and contents of the web pages are just a sample for the students. They can further improvise the presentation by using the formatting and styling options of their own choice.

List of Lab Exercises:

- Create static web pages.
- Use style sheets to enforce a format in an HTML page (CSS).
- Embed pictures, audio and videos in an HTML page.
- Add tables and frames in an HTML page.
- Decorate web pages using graphical elements.
- Create a website using several web pages. Students may use any open source or proprietary tool.
- Work with HTML forms: text box, radio buttons, checkbox, password, list, combo box.
- Write a blog using HTML pages discussing viruses, malware, spam and antiviruses.
- Create a web page discussing plagiarism. List some reported cases of plagiarism and the consequent punishment meted out. Explain the nature of the punishment in different countries as per their IP laws.
- Create simple stories with Scratch (involving at least two objects/characters) and iteration OR Write programs for finding the sum/product of first n natural numbers using Python.

Practical 1 : To create a static web page using HTML

Note: The following web page displays the classification of Animal kingdom. Go through the HTML code written for this web page and notice the various formatting tags and attributes used. You can choose a topic of your interest and apply formatting of your choice.

CLASSIFICATION OF ANIMAL KINGDOM

Animal Kingdom is divided into two major categories.

1. INVERTEBRATES - The animals that don't have a backbone
2. VERTEBRATES - The animals that have a backbone

Classification of Invertebrates

1. *Protozoa*
2. *Porifera*
3. *Coelenterates*
4. *Platyhelminthes*
5. *Nemathelminthes*
6. *Annelida*
7. *Arthropoda*
8. *Mollusca*
9. *Echinodermata*

Classification of Vertebrates

1. *Fish*
2. *Amphibians*
3. *Reptiles*
4. *Birds*
5. *Mammals*

HTML Code:

```
<html>
  <head>
  <title>Animal kingdom</title>
  </head>
  <body bgcolor="CYAN"  >
    <U>  <h1   align = "center" > CLASSIFICATION OF ANIMAL KINGDOM</h1>   </U>
    <br><br>
    <font    size = "5"    color = "red"    face = "Arial"  >
            Animal Kingdom is divided into two major categories.   </font>
    <font  color="blue" size="5">
      <ol start="1"  >
        <li> INVERTEBRATES - The animals that don't have a backbone</li>
        <li> VERTEBRATES - The animals that have a backbone</li>
      </ol>   </font>
      <br><br>
      <br><br>
      <u>  <h2  color="green">  Classification of Invertebrates   </h2>  </u>
      <ol>
    <font  face= "MS Sans Serif"  color="purple"><i>
      <li>Protozoa            <li> Porifera           <li>Coelenterates
      <li>Platyhelminthes     <li>Nemathelminthes     <li>Annelida
      <li>Arthropoda          <li>Mollusca            <li>Echinodermata
      </ol>   </i>
      </font>
```

```
        <u>  <h2  color="green">     Classification of Vertebrates </h2>      </u>
        <ol>
        <font    face= "MS Sans Serif"  color="purple">    <i>
        <li>      Fish      <li> Amphibians      <li>Reptiles
        <li>      Birds     <li>Mammals
        </ol>   </i>
        </font>
    </body>
</html>
```

Practical 2A: Use of Internal Styling to enforce a format in HTML page:

Note: The following web page has been designed and formatted using the **internal styling**. **Element selectors** and **#id selectors** have been used.

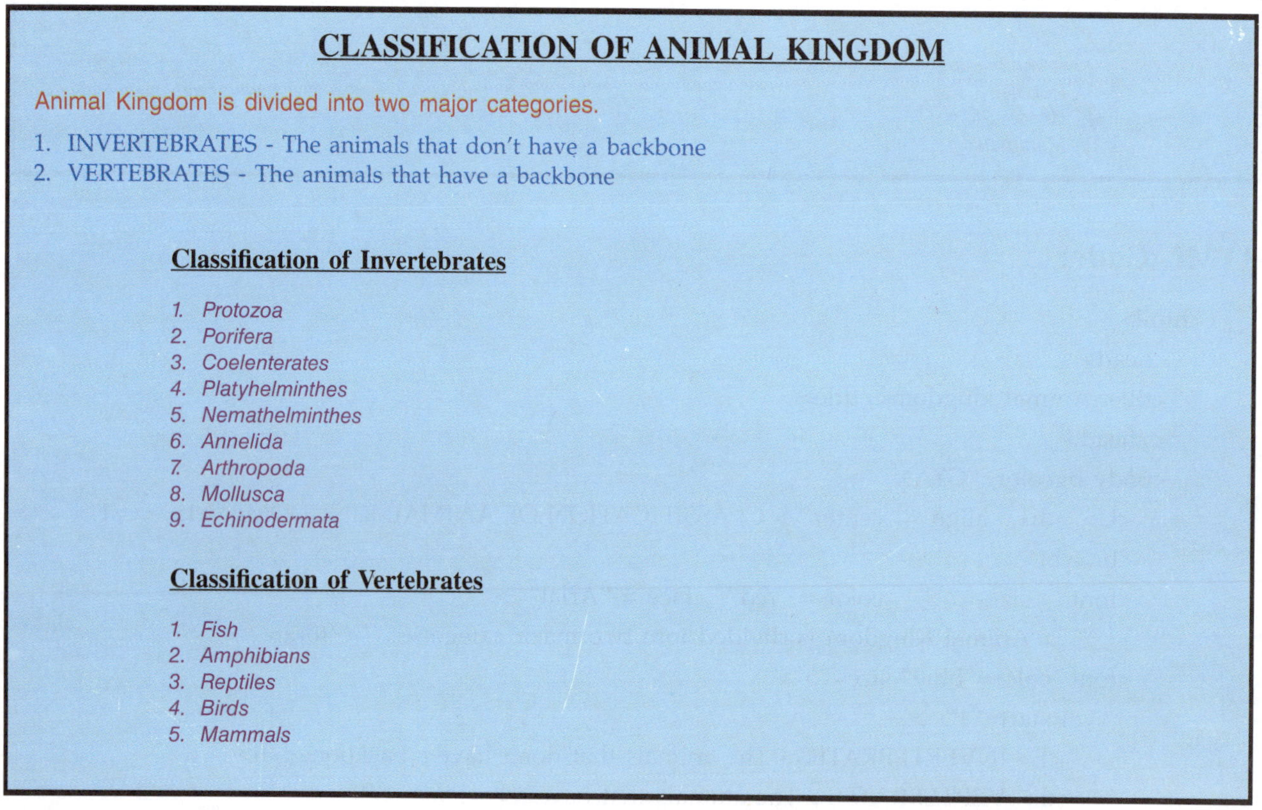

HTML code:

```
<html>
<head>
<title>Animal kingdom</title>
<style>
    body { background-color: CYAN ;}
    h1 { text-align:center;    text-decoration:underline; }
```

```
    #l1 {  font-family: Arial, Helvetica, MS Sans Serif; color: red; font-size: large;}
    #l2 { color: blue; font-size: large;}
    h2 {   text-decoration:underline; color:green; font-size:30px; }
    #l3 { font-family: MS Sans Serif; font-style:italic; color:purple; font-size:20px;}
</style>
</head>
<body>;
 <h1>CLASSIFICATION OF ANIMAL KINGDOM </h1><br>
<br>
<p  id="l1">Animal Kingdom is divided into two major categories.</p>

<ol  id="l2"  start="1"   >
<li> INVERTEBRATES - The animals that don't have a backbone</li>
<li> VERTEBRATES - The animals that  have a backbone</li>
</ol>
<br><br>
<h2> Classification of Invertebrates</h2>
<ol  id="l3">
<li>Protozoa <li> Porifera  <li>Coelenterates
<li>Platyhelminthes  <li>Nemathelminthes  <li>Annelida
<li>Arthropoda  <li>Mollusca  <li>Echinodermata
</ol>
<h2> Classification of Vertebrates</h2>
<ol id="l3">
<li>Fish <li> Amphibians  <li>Reptiles
<li>Birds  <li>Mammals</ol>
</body>
</html>
```

Practical 2B: Use of External Styling to enforce a format in HTML page (CSS):

Note: For **external styling**, a separate CSS file named pract22style.css has been created to format the web page shown in Practical 2A. The updated contents of the head section of the HTML code written for Practical 2A have been given below. The body of the HTML code remains the same. The contents of pract22style.css file are also given.

Head Section of HTML file

```
<html>
<head>
<title>Animal kingdom</title>
<link rel="stylesheet" type="text/css" href="pract22style.css">
</head>
```

Contents of pract22style.css file

```
body { background-color: CYAN ;}
h1 { text-align:center;    text-decoration:underline; }
#l1 {  font-family: Arial, Helvetica, sans-serif; color: red; font-size: large;}
#l2 { color: blue; font-size: x-large;}
h2 {    text-decoration:underline; color:green ; font-size:30px; }
#l3 { font-style:italic; color:purple; font-size:20px;}
```

Practical 3: Embed pictures, audio and video in an HTML page:

Note: The following HTML code has been designed to embed an audio file which plays a song "Save the earth" when Play button is clicked on its Audio Control bar. It also displays a video on the classification of Animal kingdom. A picture displaying the chart of animal kingdom classification is also displayed on the page.

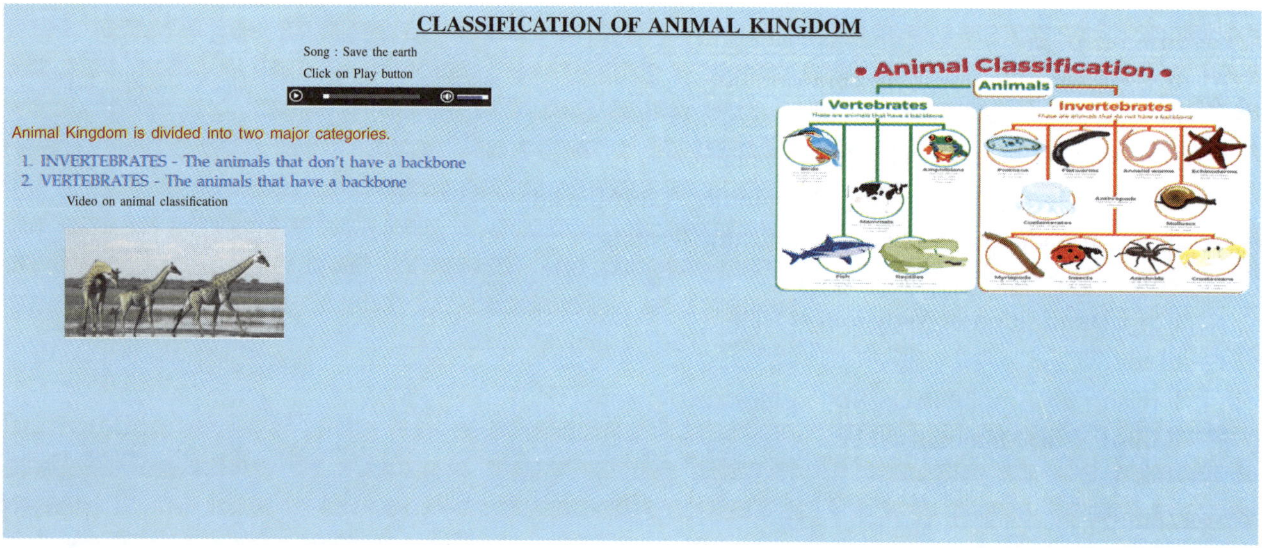

HTML code:

```
<html>
    <head>
        <title>Animal kingdom</title>
    </head>
    <body bgcolor="CYAN"  >
    <U><h1   align = "center" > CLASSIFICATION OF ANIMAL KINGDOM</h1></U><br>
    <img  src="C:\ animalclass.jpg"  align=right   width=700  height=400 >
                <p align=center> Song : Save the earth</p>
                <p align=center> Click on Play button <br>
    <Audio Controls  align=center >
                <source src = "C:\animalsong.mp3" >
    </audio></p>
    <br>
    <font      size = "5"   color = "red"      face = "Arial">Animal Kingdom is divided into
    two major categories.</font>
```

```
    <font color="blue"  size="5">
    <ol start="1">
    <li> INVERTEBRATES - The animals that don't have a backbone</li>
    <li> VERTEBRATES - The animals that  have a backbone</li>
    <ol></font>
            <p  align = left> Video on animal classification  <br>
    <Video Controls  width="320"  height="240" >
    <source src = "C:\classify.mp4" >
    </video>
            </p>
    </body>
</html>
```

Practical 4: Add Tables to the web page:

Note: The following html code has been written to include a table in the web page. Carefully go through the tags used for table creation.

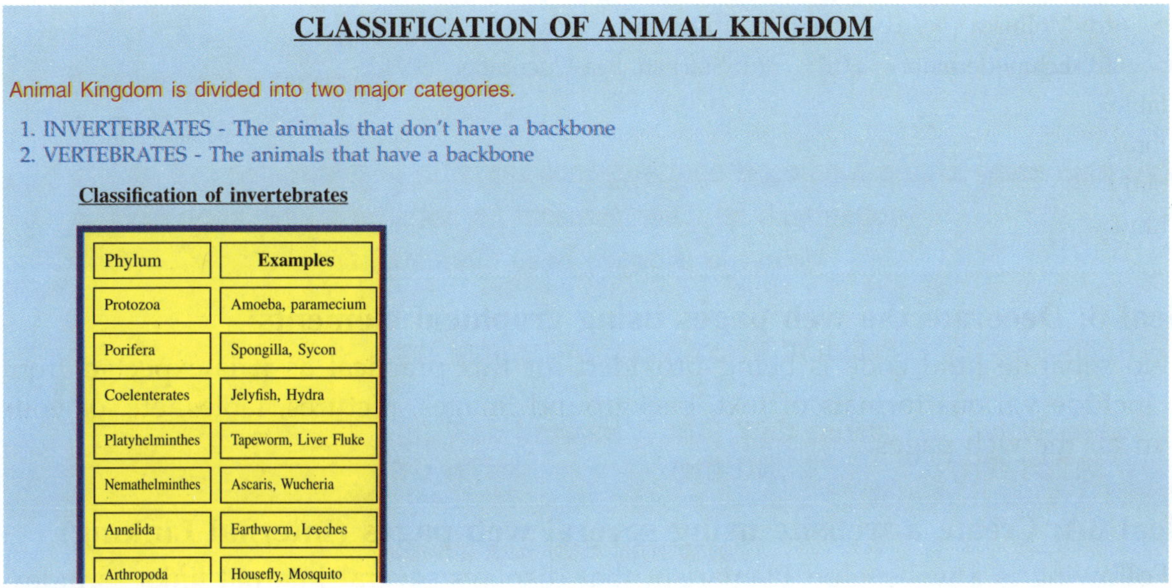
CLASSIFICATION OF ANIMAL KINGDOM

Animal Kingdom is divided into two major categories.

1. INVERTEBRATES - The animals that don't have a backbone
2. VERTEBRATES - The animals that have a backbone

Classification of invertebrates

Phylum	Examples
Protozoa	Amoeba, paramecium
Porifera	Spongilla, Sycon
Coelenterates	Jelyfish, Hydra
Platyhelminthes	Tapeworm, Liver Fluke
Nemathelminthes	Ascaris, Wucheria
Annelida	Earthworm, Leeches
Arthropoda	Housefly, Mosquito

HTML code:

```
<html>
<head>
<title>Animal kingdom</title>
</head>
<body bgcolor="CYAN"  >
<U><h1  align = "center" > CLASSIFICATION OF ANIMAL KINGDOM</h1></U><br>
<br>
<font    size = "5"   color = "red"     face = "Arial">Animal Kingdom is divided into two
major categories.</font>
</font>
```

```
<font color="blue"  size="5"><ol start="1" >
<li> INVERTEBRATES  -  The animals that don't have a backbone</li>
<li> VERTEBRATES    -  The animals that have a backbone</li>
<ol></font>
<u><h2 color=" green"> Classification of invertebrates</h2></u>
<table border=8 bordercolor=blue bgcolor=yellow cellspacing=10 cellpadding=10>
<tr>
<th> Phylum </th>
<th> Examples </th>
</tr>
<tr><td>Protozoa </td><td> Amoeba, paramecium</td>
<tr> <td>Porifera </td><td> Spongilla, Sycon</td>
<tr> <td>Coelenterates </td>  <td>Jelyfish, Hydra  </td>
<tr> <td> Platyhelminthes </td> <td>Tapeworm, Liver Fluke  </td>
<tr> <td>Nemathelminthes </td> <td>Ascaris, Wucheria  </td>
<tr> <td>Annelida </td> <td>Earthworm, Leeches  </td>
<tr> <td>Arthropoda  </td> <td>Housefly, Mosquito  </td>
<tr> <td>Mollusca  </td> <td>Snails, Octopus  </td>
<tr> <td>Echinodermata  </td> <td>Starfish, Sea Cucumber  </td>
</table>
</font>
</body>
</html>
```

Practical 5: Decorate the web pages using graphical elements:

Note: No separate html code is being provided for this practical as it is expected from you to include various formats of text, background images, pictures, tables, etc. of your choice in all the web pages.

Practical 6A: Create a website using several web pages (Internal Linking)

Note: Following is a website on Plagiarism that displays several internal links as index. Clicking on any link will display the respective section of the web page.

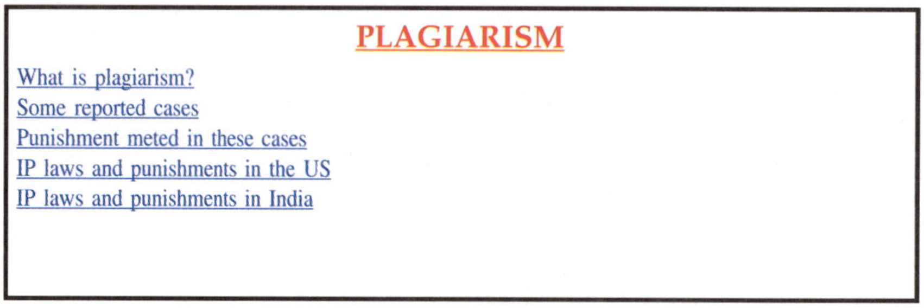

Home page of a website

IP laws and punishments in India

With a view to check plagiarism in higher education, UGC has notified the Promotion of Academic Integrity and prevention of Plagiarism in Higher Educational Institutions Regulations, 2018. "The objective of the regulations is to promote academic research and curb plagiarism by developing systems to detect," The new policy creates four tiers for addressing plagiarism, which is defined by UGC India as "the practice of taking someone else's work or idea and passing them as one's own." The first tier, for what it calls "similarities upto 10%," would carry no penalty. The second tier, in which 10% to 40% of a document is plagiarised, would require students to submit a revised manuscript and force faculty members to withdraw the plagiarised paper. In cases where 40% to 60% of the document is plagiarised, a student would be suspended for a year and the faculty member would forfeit an annual pay raise and be prohibited from supervising students for 2 years. Students who plagiarise more than 60% of their thesis would be kicked out of the program, while the penalties for faculty members would be extended to a loss of 2 years of pay increases and a 3-year ban on supervising students.

Contents of the link – IP laws and punishments in India

HTML code:

```
<HTML>
<BODY>
<font  color="red">
<H1  align = center><U>PLAGIARISM</U></H1></font>
<font size=5>
<a href ="#definition"> What is plagiarism? </a><br>
<a href = "#Reported cases"> Some reported cases </a> <br>
<a href = "#Punishments meted" > Punishment meted in these cases</a> <br>
<a href = "#IP laws and punishments in the US">IP laws and punishments in the US</a> <br>
<a href = "#IP laws and punishments in India">IP laws and punishments in India</a> <br>
</font>
<br><br><br><br><br><br>
<br><br><br><br><br><br><br><br><br><br><br><br><br><br>
<a name = "definition">
<h2>Plagiarism refers:</h2>
        to steal and pass off (the ideas or words of another) as one's own<br>
        to use (another's production) without crediting the source<br>
        to commit literary theft<br>
        to present an idea or product as new and original derived from an existing source<br><br>
In other words, plagiarism is an act of fraud. It involves both stealing someone else's work and
lying about it afterward.
</a>
<br><br><br><br><br><br><br><br><br><br><br><br><br>
<a name ="Reported cases">
<h2>Plagirism reported in India</h2>
The UGC has been informed about three cases have come to notice in last three years against
vice chancellor of Pondicherry University (2015); a reader of Mahatma Gandhi Kashi Vidyapeeth,
Varanasi (2017); and a vice chancellor of Dr APJ Abdul Kalam Technical University, Lucknow
(2018)
```

```
</a>
<br><br><br><br><br><br><br><br><br><br><br><br><br>
<a name = "Punishments meted">
<h2> Punishment meted</h2>
The vice chancellor of Pondicherry University was dismissed from the post in July 2016, and the other two universities have been asked to take action against the two persons
</a>
<br><br><br><br><br><br><br><br><br><br><br><br><br>
<a name = "IP laws and punishments in India"><br>
<h2> IP laws and punishments in India</h2> <br>
With a view to check plagiarism in higher education, UGC has notified the Promotion of Academic Integrity and Prevention of Plagiarism in Higher Educational Institutions Regulations, 2018. "The objective of the regulations is to promote academic research and curb plagiarism by developing systems to detect it."The new policy creates four tiers for addressing plagiarism, which is defined by UGC India as "the practice of taking someone else's work or idea and passing them as one's own." The first tier, for what it calls "similarities up to 10%," would carry no penalty. The second tier, in which 10% to 40% of a document is plagiarised, would require students to submit a revised manuscript and force faculty members to withdraw the plagiarised paper. In cases where 40% to 60% of the document is plagiarised, a student would be suspended for a year and the faculty member would forfeit an annual pay raise and be prohibited from supervising students for 2 years. Students who plagiarise more than 60% of their thesis would be kicked out of the program, while the penalties for faculty members would be extended to a loss of 2 years of pay increases and a 3-year ban on supervising students.
</a>
<br><br><br><br><br><br><br><br><br><br><br><br><br><br><br>
<a name="IP laws and punishments in the US"> <br>
<h2> IP laws and punishments in the US</h2> <br>
Most cases of plagiarism are considered misdemeanours, punishable by fines of anywhere between $100 and $50,000 — and up to one year in jail. Plagiarism can also be considered a felony under certain state and federal laws. For example, if a plagiarist copies and earns more than $2,500 from copyrighted material, he or she may face up to $250,000 in fines and up to ten years in jail.
</a>
</BODY>
</HTML>
```

Practical 6B: Create a website using several web pages (External Linking)

Note: Following is a website on Plagiarism that displays several external links as index. Clicking on any link will open the respective HTML file and display the web page.

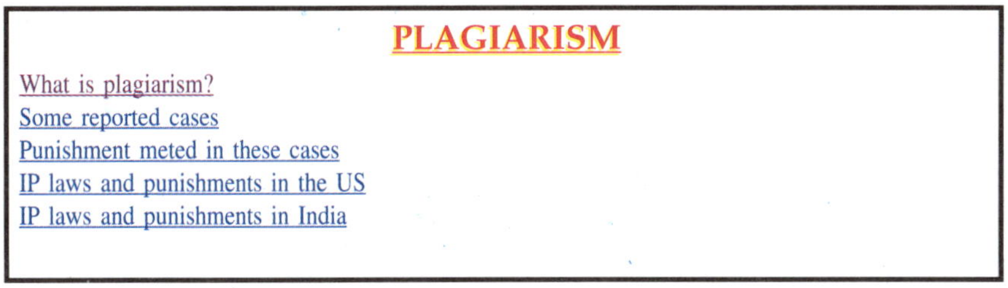

Home Page

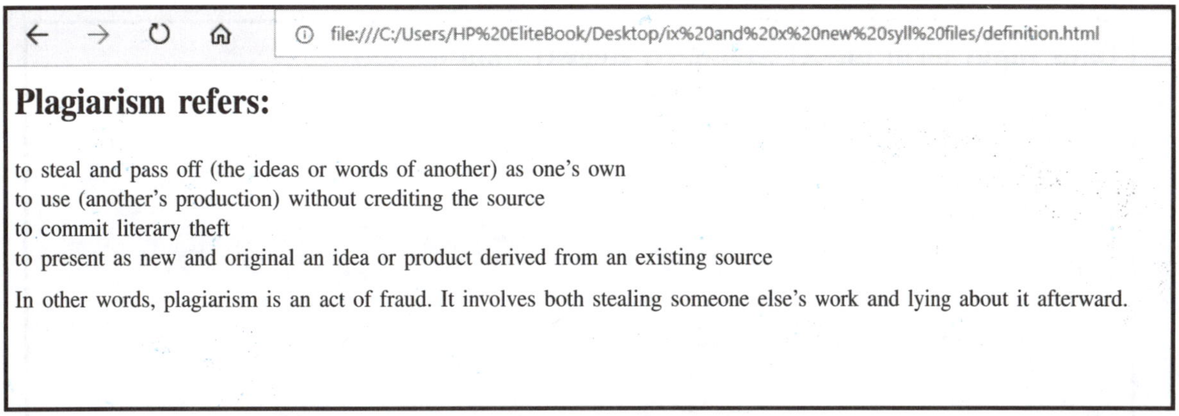

Web page for the clicked link

HTML code for home page:

```
<HTML>
<BODY>
<font  color="red">
<H1  align = center><U>PLAGIARISM</U></H1></font>
<font size=5>
<a href ="definition.html"> What is plagiarism? </a><br>
<a href = "Reportedcases.html"> Some reported cases </a> <br>
<a href = "Punishments.html " > Punishment meted in these cases</a> <br>
<a href = "IPUS.HTML">IP laws and punishments in the US</a> <br>
<a href = "IPINDIA.HTML">IP laws in and punishments in India</a> <br>
</font>
</BODY>
</HTML>
```

HTML code for the file "definition.html"

```
<HTML>
<BODY>
<h2>Plagiarism refers:</h2>
```

```
        to steal and pass off (the ideas or words of another) as one's own<br>
        to use (another's production) without crediting the source<br>
        to commit literary theft<br>
        to present an idea or product as new and original derived from an existing source<br><br>
In other words, plagiarism is an act of fraud. It involves both stealing someone else's work and
lying about it afterward.
</BODY>
</HTML>
```

Practical 7: Design an HTML form using text box, radio button, checkbox, list, combo box, etc.

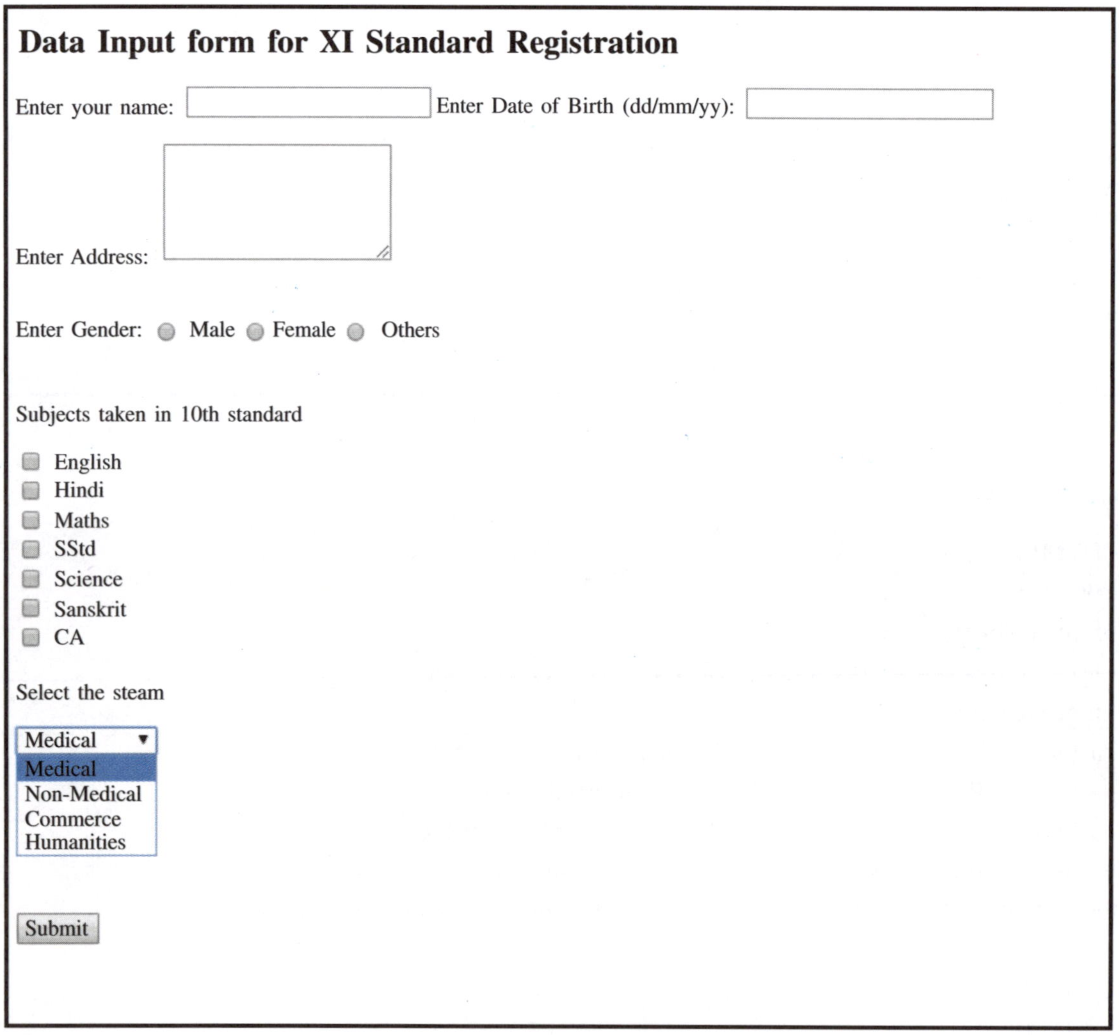

HTML code:

```
<html>
<body>
<h2> Data Input form for XI Standard Registration</h2>
<form>
   Enter your name:
      <input name = "firstname"  type = "text">
   Enter Date of Birth (dd/mm/yy):
      <input name="birth"  type = "text"> <br> <br>

   Enter Address:
      <textarea  name = "Description"  rows="5"  cols="20">
</textarea><br><br><br>
Enter Gender:
<input type ="radio"   name = "gender1"   value = "male"> Male
<input type ="radio"   name = "gender2"   value = "female">Female
<input type ="radio"   name = "gender3"   value = "others"> Others<br><br>
<p> Subjects taken in 10th standard </p>

<input type ="checkbox"   name = "subject1"   value = "English"> English<br>
<input type ="checkbox"   name = "subject2"   value = "Hindi">Hindi <br>
<input type ="checkbox"   name = "subject3"   value = "Maths"> Maths<br>
<input type ="checkbox"   name = "subject4"   value = "SSTD"> SStd<br>
<input type ="checkbox"   name = "subject5"   value = "Science">Science <br>
<input type ="checkbox"   name = "subject6"   value = "Sanskrit"> Sanskrit <br>
<input type ="checkbox"   name = "subject7"   value = "CA"> CA <br>
<p>Select the stream</p>
<select>
<option  value ="Medical" > Medical </option>
<option  value ="Non-Medical" > Non-Medical </option>
<option  value ="Commerce" > Commerce </option>
<option  value ="Humanities" > Humanities </option>
</select>
<br><br><br><br>
<input type ="Submit">
</form>
</body>
</html>
```

Practical 8: Write a blog using HTML pages discussing viruses, malware, spam and anti-virus

Note: The following website displays its web page showing blog post. The HTML code for the web page is also given. CSS is used to create the blog posts which are written as paragraph elements. Two topics have been included for your reference. Including the remaining topics from external links is an exercise for you.

My Blog Post

Malware, or malicious software, is any program or file that is harmful to a computer user. Types of malware can include computer viruses, worms, Trojan horses and spyware. These malicious programs can perform a variety of different functions such as stealing, encrypting or deleting sensitive data, altering or hijacking core computing functions and monitoring users' computer activity without their permission.

Computer virus is a malicious program that self-replicates by copying itself to another program. In other words, the computer virus spreads by itself into other executable code or documents. The purpose of creating a computer virus is to infect vulnerable systems, gain admin control and steal user sensitive data. Hackers design computer viruses with malicious intent and prey on online users by tricking them. One of the ideal methods by which viruses spread is through emails – opening the attachment in the email, visiting an infected website, clicking on an executable file, or viewing an infected advertisement can cause the virus to spread to your system. Besides that, infections also spread while connecting with already infected removable storage devices, such as USB drives.

HTML code for the above web page:

```
<html>
<head>
<link href="blogstyle.css"  rel="stylesheet"  type="text/css"}
</head>
<body>
<h1> My Blog Post </h1><br>
<p>
Malware, or malicious software, is any program or file that is harmful to a computer user.
Types of malware can include computer viruses, worms, Trojan horses and spyware. These
malicious programs can perform a variety of different functions such as stealing, encrypting
or deleting sensitive data, altering or hijacking core computing functions and monitoring
users' computer activity without their permission.</p>
<p> Computer virus is a malicious program that self-replicates by copying itself to another
program. In other words, the computer virus spreads by itself into other executable code or
documents. The purpose of creating a computer virus is to infect vulnerable systems, gain admin
control and steal user sensitive data. Hackers design computer viruses with malicious intent and
prey on online users by tricking them. One of the ideal methods by which viruses spread is
through emails – opening the attachment in the email, visiting an infected website, clicking on
an executable file, or viewing an infected advertisement can cause the virus to spread to your
system. Besides that, infections also spread while connecting with already infected removable
storage devices, such as USB drives.
</p>
</body>
</html>
```

Contents of blogstyle.css file:

```
h1 { background-color: #f0f0f0; margin : auto; width:60%; border: 3px double; text-
     align:center;}

p {margin-top : 20px;margin-left:270px; width:60%; border: 3px double;  font-family:"Times
     New Roman";font-weight:normal; font-size:large;align:center;}
```

Practical 9: Create a web page discussing Plagiarism. List some of the reported cases and the punishment meted out. Explain the nature of punishment in different countries as per their IP laws.

Note: Practical 6A and 6B have been designed on the same guidelines as mentioned for practical 9, so use them as reference.

Practical 10A: The following code is a Scratch game which uses 2 sprites and a backdrop. First sprite is a balloon which has three costumes and the second sprite is a crab. The backdrop has two costumes, one is normal and the other is displayed when the game is over.

The game goes like this: the balloons keep on falling from above and you have to move the crab left or right using arrow keys to burst the balloon. If the crab is not able to burst the balloon, the balloon hits the ground and a life is lost. For every balloon burst, score is incremented by one. Maximum lives are 5.

Code For Balloons

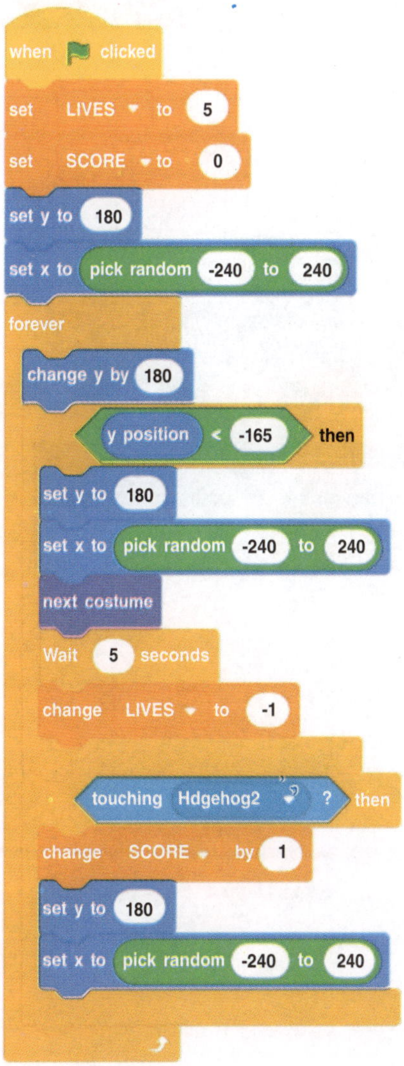

Code For Crab

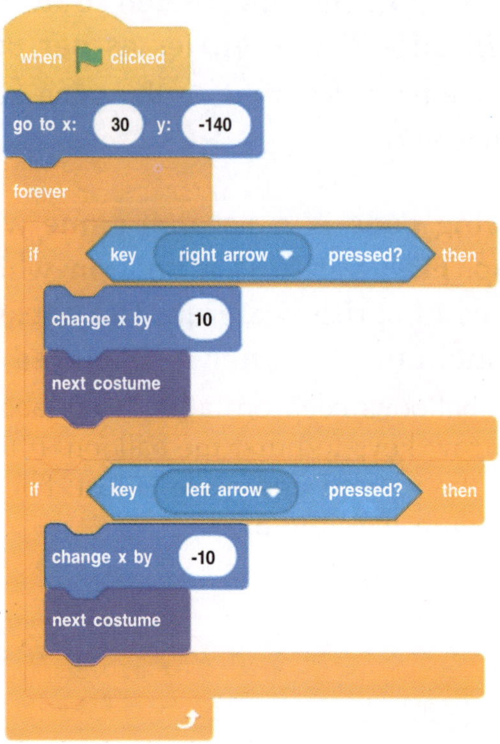

Code For Backdrop

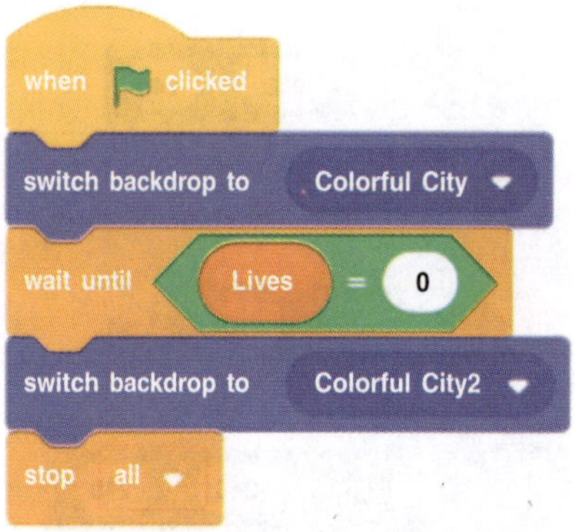

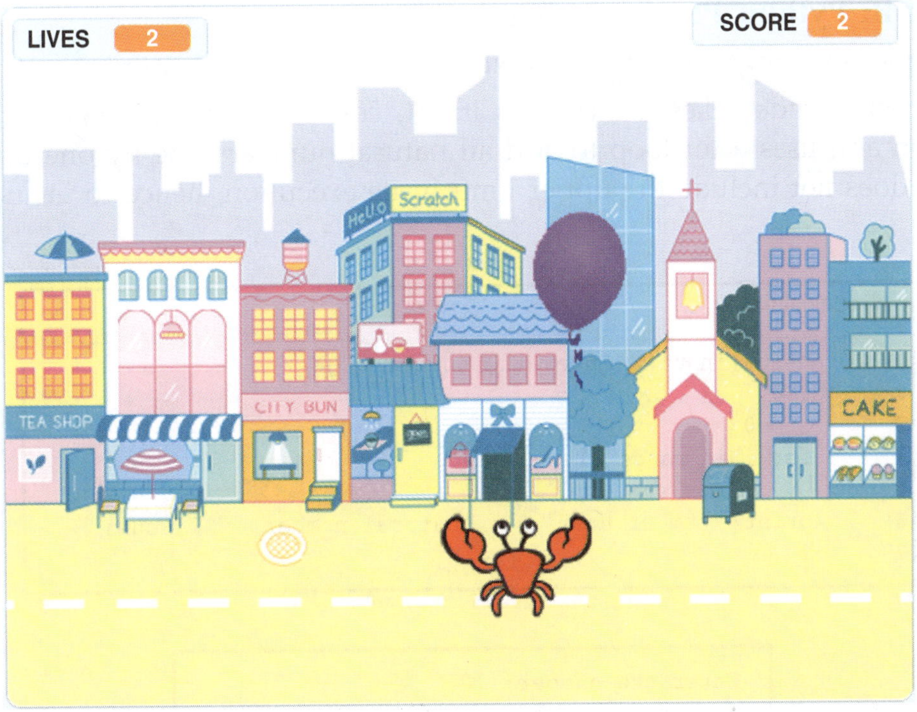

Game screen

Game over screen

Practical 10 B: Python Programming:

1. **Write a python program to find the sum of first n natural numbers.**

   The following code takes a string as input, converts it into integer, stores it in a variable n and uses a for loop to add all natural numbers one by one up to n. Since for loop does not include the upper limit in its execution, hence to include n, n+1 is taken.

sumnatural.py

```
n=int(input(" Enter the number: "))
i=0
sum=0
for i in range (1,n+1):
    sum = sum + i
print("sum of first", n,"natural numbers = ", sum)
```

```
Enter the number: 10
sum of first  10   natural numbers =  55

Process finished with exit code 0
```

2. **Write a python program to find the product of first n natural numbers.**

   The following code takes a string as input, converts it into integer, stores it in a variable n and uses a for loop to multiply all natural numbers up to n one by one. Since for loop does not include the upper limit in its execution, hence to include n, n+1 is taken.

sumnatural.py

```
n=int(input('' Enter the number: ''))
i=0
product=1
for i in range (1,n+1):
    product = product * i
print(''product of first'', n,''natural numbers = '', product)
```

```
Enter the number: 10
product of first  10   natural numbers =  3628800

Process finished with exit code 0
```

CBSE Sample Question Paper 2019-20

Max. Marks: 30 **Duration: 2 hrs.**

General Instructions:

- *The paper contains 4 sections–Section A, Section B and Section C and Section D.*
- *Section A and B has to be attempted by all students.*
- *Students may attempt any one of the two–Section C (Scratch) OR Section D (Python).*

Section – A

1. Expand SMTP. 1
2. Consider the following HTML statement:
   <body bgcolor ="Blue" alink ="red" vlink="yellow">
   In the above statement, what do you mean by 'alink' and 'vlink'? 1
3. Rashmi has to send an e-mail to Raees. She also wants to send the same e-mail to Vandana but does not want Raees to know about it. Which option out of 'cc' or 'bcc' should Rashmi use to enter the e-mail address of Vandana? 1
4. Geetu is an artist. She posts her artwork on the internet. One day she comes to know that Shreyas has downloaded one of the paintings that she had posted without her permission. He had further printed that image on an invitation card.

   Has Shreyas done the right thing? Which right of Geetu has he infringed?

   OR

   Define plagiarism. 1
5. Give one difference between 3G and 4G. 1
6. Define the term Digital Divide. 1
7. Ritwik wants to use a software but does not want to pay for it. Which type of software can he use? 1

Section – B

8. Write any one application each of e-governance and e-commerce. 2
9. Kuhu has just learnt how to do online banking. Name any two precautions that she should take to prevent online fraud. 2
10. Name the following with respect to HTML:
    (i) Attribute for changing bullet type of list tag.
    (ii) Element to create a hyperlink. 2
11. Write HTML code to display the unordered list (with square bullets) of two cities "DELHI" and "MUMBAI". The web page should have a yellow background and the title of the page should be 'My Cities'.

    OR

Write HTML code to display an ordered list (with upper case roman numbers) listing any three subjects being taught in your school. The web page should have a red background and the title of the page should be 'My Subjects'. 2

12. Form a CSS code within the <head>....</head> for the following specifications:
Background colour : blue
For the paragraph,
font family is Dotum and colour of the text is red;
Heading should be in black colour. 2

13. Write the HTML code to do the following:
(i) To display a horizontal line of green colour.
(ii) To create a hyperlink on the word CLICK to an image named testimage.jpeg. 2

14. Write the output of the following HTML code.

```
<html> <head> <title> Table </title> </head>
<body>
<table border="1">
<tr> <td align="center" rowspan="2"> ONE </td> <td> TWO </td> <td>THREE
</td> </tr>
<tr> <td> Rose </td> <td> Lily </td> </tr>
<tr> <td align="center"> Pansy </td> <td align="center" colspan="2"> Dahlia
</td> </tr>
</table> </body> </html>
```

OR

Observe the following table and write the HTML code to generate it: 3

SERIAL NO	CLASS	NUMBER OF STUDENTS		
		ENGLISH	HINDI	REGIONAL
1	XA	35	10	6
2	XB	31	15	4

Section – C (Scratch)

15. Differentiate between 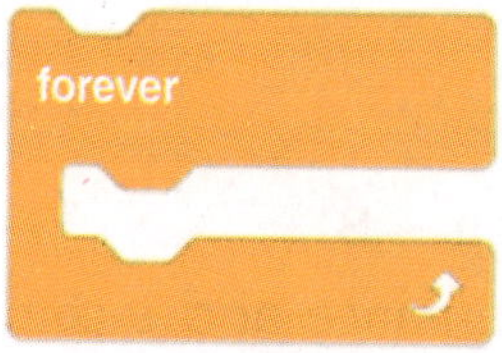

and 

blocks?

OR

Differentiate between 

and 

blocks. 2

16. Study the scripts given below and answer the questions.

(i) What will be the final position of the cat (Scratch mascot) after running the following script? 1

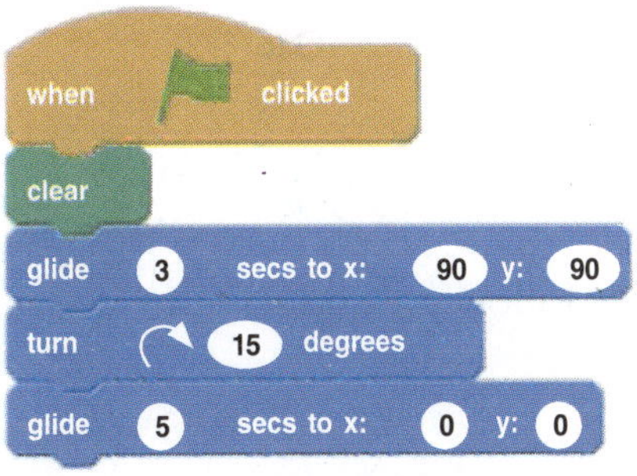

(ii) What happens when the sprite does not touch the edge of the stage? 1

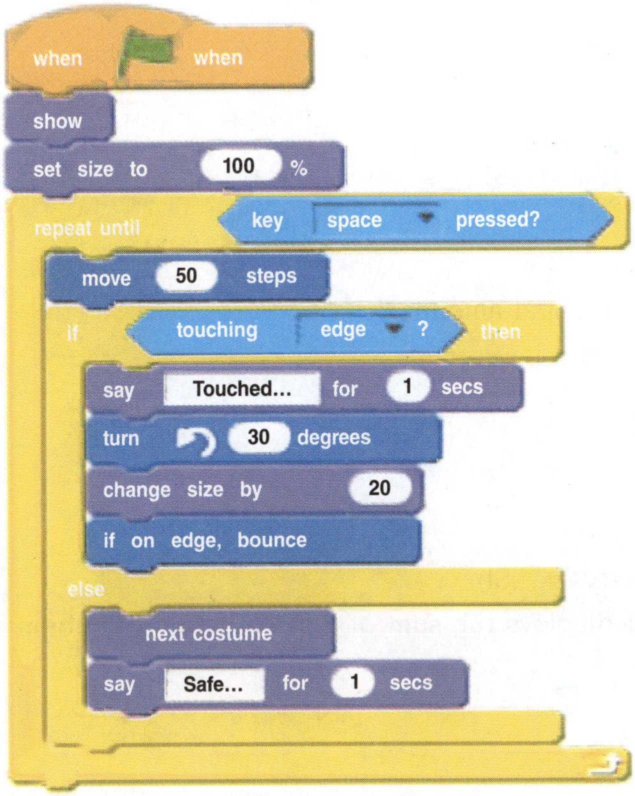

(iii) In question (ii) above, what happens when the sprite touches the edges. 2

17. Name the tab and category of blocks that should be selected to do the following:

(i) Ask the user's name

(ii) Add a variable to store points of the game 2

Section – D (Python)

18. Which of the following are valid variable names in Python?

1plus2 , if, my_book, yes&no, helloworld 1

19. What will be output of the following expressions?

#Considering Python 2.7

```
>>> print ('Test' * 3)
>>> print ('7'+'8')
```

OR

#Considering Python 3.x

```
>>> print ('Test' * 3)
>>> print ('7'+'8')
```

2

20. What will be output of the following code if the user enters Principal amount as 20000 and Time as 10 years.

#Considering Python 2.7

```
P = input("Enter Principal amount:")
T = input("Enter Time:")
if T>10:
    SI = P*T*10/100
else:
    SI = P*T*15/100
print("Simple Interest = ",SI)
```

OR

#Considering Python 3.x

```
P = input("Enter Principal amount:")
T = input("Enter Time:")
if T>10:
    SI = P*T*10/100
else:
    SI = P*T*15/100
print("Simple Interest = ",SI)
```

2

21. Write a code that displays the sum of first 10 natural numbers. 3

Solutions to CBSE Sample Question Paper 2019-20

Section – A

1. Simple Mail Transfer Protocol
2. Alink stands for active link while vlink stands for visited link. When the cursor is positioned on the hyperlinked text, the colour specified in alink attribute (red) is seen. When the link has been clicked once, the colour changes to the one specified in vlink attribute (yellow).
3. bcc (blind carbon copy)
4. No, Intellectual Property Rights

   OR

   When we download someone else's work or ideas and pass them as our own, then this practice is known as plagiarism.
5. • The speed of 4G is about 10 times faster than 3G.
   • We can stream audio and video content using 4G. *(Any one)*
6. The gap between technical knowledge of the people who have access to computers and internet and those who do not have that access.
7. Open Source Software

Section – B

8. **E-governance:**
   • Filing of online application forms for Aadhar card, passport
   • Filing of IT returns online
   • Registering an online complaint for any grievance related to government *(Any one)*

   E-commerce:
   • Able to do online transactions
   • No need to go to bank for updating the passbooks depositing the money
   • Online shopping. *(Any one)*
9. • Do not share user id and password with anyone.
   • Avoid doing transactions from cyber cafe and other public places.
10. (i) type
    (ii) <a>
11.

```
<HTML>
<HEAD>
<TITLE> My Cities</TITLE>
</HEAD>
<BODY bgcolor="yellow">
<UL type="square">
    <LI> DELHI </LI>
    <LI> MUMBAI </LI>
</UL>
```

```
        </BODY>
        </HTML>
```

OR

```
<HTML>
<HEAD>
<TITLE> My Subjects</TITLE>
</HEAD>
<BODY bgcolor="red">
<OL type="I">
        <LI> Science</LI>
        <LI> Maths</LI>
        <LI> Computers</LI>
</OL>
</BODY>
</HTML>
```

12.

```
<head>
<style>
    body { background-color: blue;}
    p {color:red;
    font-family:Dotum;
            }
    h1{ color: black;}
</style>
</head>
```

13. (i) `<hr color="green">`

(ii) `< a href="testimage.jpeg"> CLICK </a>`

14.

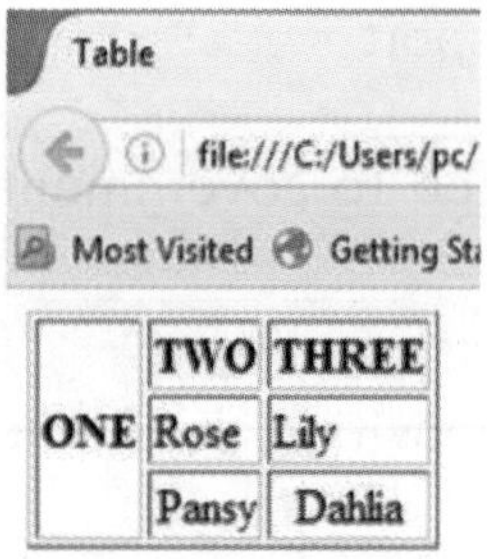

OR

```
<html> <head> <title> Table </title> </head>
<body>
<table border="1">
<tr> <th align="center" ROWSPAN="2"> SERIALNO</th> <td ROWSPAN="2"> CLASS</
th> <th COLSPAN="3">NUMBER OF STUDENTS </th> </tr>
<tr> <td> ENGLISH </td> <td> HINDI </td>
<td>REGIONAL</td></tr>
<tr align="center"> <td align="center"> 1 </td> <td align="center"> X A </td>
<td>35</td><td>10</td><td>6</td></tr>
<tr align="center"> <td align="center"> 2 </td> <td align="center"> X B </td>
<td>31</td><td>15</td><td>4</td></tr>
</table> </body> </html>
```

Section – C (Scratch)

15. The instructions enclosed in the forever block keep on executing till the time the project is running or the Stop button is not pressed. The instructions enclosed in the repeat ( ) block execute for the given number of times.

OR

The instruction blocks enclosed inside the if...block are executed only if the condition is true. Nothing happens if the condition is false.
In case of if..then...else block, the instruction blocks enclosed inside the if are executed if the condition is true. If the condition is false, then the instruction blocks enclosed inside the else part are executed.

16. (i) Centre of the stage

(ii) It changes its costume and displays the caller box with message "Safe" for one second.

(iii)
- Displays the caller box saying "Touched.."
- Turns on the left by 30 degrees
- Increases its size by 20 points
- Bounces back

17. (i) Scripts tab/Sensing category of blocks

(ii) Scripts tab/Data category of blocks

Section – D (Python)

18. My_book and helloworld

19. TestTestTest
78

20. Simple Interest = 30000

21.

```
x=1
sum=0
while(x<=10):
    sum=sum+x
    x=x+1
print (sum)
```

Practice Paper I (with solutions)

Section – A

1. Expand and define SFTP. 1

2. In the following HTML statement what does **ABCD.HTML#E1** refer to?
<A HREF = "ABCD.HTML#E1" >
</A> 1

3. Kusum is able to watch her friend Rekha on her computer screen while she is talking to her. Rekha can also watch Kusum. Are they using Video conferencing or the Chat service of internet? 1

4. Amit got a phone call and the person on the other end introduced himself as the employee of the bank where Amit has an account. He asked Amit to share the details of his debit card which Amit did. Now what possible threat is Amit subjected to?

OR

Define Intellectual Property Rights. 1

5. Give any one advantage of 4G over 3G. 1

6. Rita bought MS Word (word processing package) whereas Komal downloaded OpenWriter software for free for the same purpose. What type of software is Komal using? What are such free software called? 1

7. Ankita studies in a city school which has internet access in all classrooms. The teacher uses a computer and a projector to display videos related to the lecture. Shobha stays in a village and her school barely has the minimum required furniture. The teacher uses only blackboard and chalk to teach. This scenario is referred to as:
(a) Digital Unity (b) Digital Divide
(c) Intellectual Property Rights (d) Open Source Movement 1

Section – B

8. Give an example of facility provided under
(i) E-governance (ii) E-groups 2

9. State any two netiquettes which we should follow while using social networking websites. 2

10. Name the tag that is used in HTML code to
(i) include Submit button in a form.
(ii) write the digits as in the expression $ax^3+ bx^2$. 2

11. Write an HTML code to create a web page with blue background and heading "LANGUAGES OFFERED" in red. The page should display the following list in black with roman numbering:

i. English
ii. Spanish
iii. German

OR

Write an HTML code to create a web page with yellow background and heading "CONSTITUENTS OF A BALANCED DIET" in red. The page should display the following unordered list in black with no bullet:

Carbohydrates
Proteins
Fats
Vitamins and Minerals 2

12. Form a CSS code within the <head> tag for the following specifications:
Background color: Pink
For the paragraph:
Border style – dashed
Border colour – red
Font-family – Times New Roman
Colour of text – Blue 2

13. Write an HTML code to create a form which takes input in checkboxes.

Checkbox Input

Item 1 ☐

Item 2 ☐

Item 3 ☑

[Submit] 2

14. Write an HTML code for the following output:

<table>
<tr><td rowspan="2">DAY/PERIOD</td><td colspan="4">TIME TABLE FOR CLASS X</td></tr>
<tr><td>I</td><td>II</td><td>III</td><td>IV</td></tr>
<tr><td>MONDAY</td><td colspan="2">MATHS</td><td rowspan="2">SCIENCE</td><td rowspan="2">ENGLISH</td></tr>
<tr><td>WEDNESDAY</td><td colspan="2">SOCIAL SCIENCE</td></tr>
</table>

OR

Give the output of the following HTML code:

```
<HTML>
<BODY>
<TABLE border=2 bordercolor=red bgcolor=yellow align=center>
<thead>
<tr>
<td colspan="5" align=center>SPORTS DAY RESULT</td>
</tr>
</thead>
<TR>
<TH> EVENT</TH>
<TH> RED HOUSE</TH>
<TH> BLUE HOUSE</TH>
<TH> GREEN HOUSE</TH>
<TH> YELLOW HOUSE</TH>
```

```
</TR>
<TR>
<TD> BASKETBALL</TD>
<TD> 20</TD>
<TD> 22</TD>
<TD> 18</TD>
<TD> 16</TD>
</TR>
<TR>
<TD> CRICKET</TD>
<TD> 10</TD>
<TD> 12</TD>
<TD> 20</TD>
<TD> 18</TD>
</TR>
</TABLE>
</BODY></HTML>
```

3

Section – C Scratch

15. Explain the use of the following blocks:

(i) Say( ) for ( ) seconds (ii) Ask( ) and wait

OR

Differentiate between the following blocks:
Set size to ( )% and Change size by ( ) 2

16. Study the codes given below and answer the following questions:

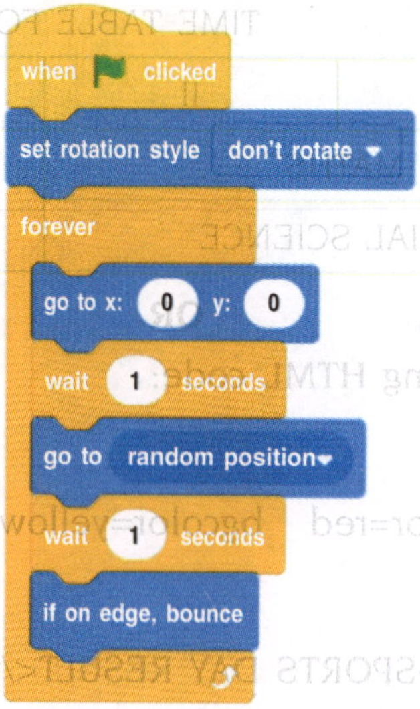

(i) What will happen if the above code is executed?

(ii) How can the execution of the above code be terminated?

(iii) If you want to display the co-ordinates of the sprite on the stage what should you do? 2+1+1

17. Under which block heads do the following blocks belong? 2

(i) 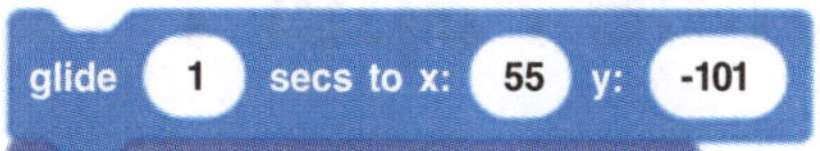

(ii) 

(iii) 

(iv) 

Section – D (Python)

18. What will be the output of the following expressions?

```
a=10
a+=5
print(a)
```
1

19. What will be the output of the following statements?

```
answer=False
a=1
if (answer):
    print("you are telling the truth")
print(a+1)
print("you are not telling the truth")
print(a)
```
2

20. What will be the output of the following program?

```
i=1
p=1
for p in (1,6):
    p=p*i
print(p)
```
2

21. Write a code that displays the sum of numbers from 2 to 20. 3

Solutions to Practice Paper I

1. The Secure File Transfer Protocol or SFTP is a subsystem of the Secure Shell protocol. It is a separate protocol layered over the Secure Shell protocol to handle file transfers.
2. **ABCD.HTML#E1:** ABCD.HTML is the external file name being referred to and E1 is the internal link in the file.
3. Video Conferencing
4. Amit might become a victim of financial theft and lose money from his bank account.

   OR

   Intellectual Property Rights refer to the legal right of the creator of an intellectual property to be its sole beneficiary. If anyone else uses it without permission or copies and distributes it, intellectual property rights are said to be violated. Patents, Copyright, Trademarks, etc. are some examples of Intellectual property.
5. (Any one of the following:)
   - The 4G facilitates IP telephony which uses broadband internet access for transmission of voice. This communication can be between computer-computer, computer-telephone or telephone-computer.
   - 4G has ultra-broadband internet access.
   - Gaming services and High Definition multimedia are easily streamed using 4G.
   - Roaming connectivity without a call drop or signal interference is possible in 4G.
   - No limit on the IP address in 4G whereas 3G had a limited IP address accessibility.
6. Komal is using a free software, which she can read, modify and use, according to her requirement. Such a software is called Open Source Software The user of such a software can distribute the copies of the original or modified version of the software also. More and more software are being developed with the goal of licensing overall community support under open software.
7. Digital Divide
8. (i) **E-governance:** (any one of the following or any other appropriate point)
   - The use of technology has improved the speed of communication which has resulted in quick interaction between various sectors of government. Thus, the process of policy making and implementation has gained speed.
   - Cost of stationery has decreased as the communication and documentation is done using computers.
   - Transparency in the work of government has increased as it allows the public to be informed about what the government is working on as well as the policies they are trying to implement.
   - With transparency comes accountability. The citizens can also question the government, if they find any discrepancy in its working.

   (ii) **E-groups:** (any one of the following or any other appropriate point)
   - E-groups are available on the internet 24X7.
   - People who are shy of speaking, can share their views, as much as they want.

- One can save a group chat and go back to it.
- One can learn from the experiences of other group members and share one's own experiences too.
- Sometimes, the members of the group prove to be a great moral support for others.

9. (Any two of the following or any other appropriate point)

- Do not post offensive comments, which might hurt the sentiments of any individual or community.
- Respect the views of others and show courtesy while posting your comments.
- Avoid replying in negative to negative comments. Either don't react or reply in a positive note.

10. (i) < input type=Submit>

(ii) < sup> </sup>

11.

```
<HTML>
<HEAD>
<TITLE>LANGUAGES OFFERED</TITLE>
</HEAD>
<BODY    BGCOLOR = BLUE>
<FONT COLOR=RED>
<H1>LANGUAGES OFFERED</H1>
</FONT>
<OL TYPE=i>
<li>English
<li>Spanish
<li>German
</OL>
</BODY></HTML>
```

OR

```
<HTML>
<HEAD>
<TITLE> CONSTITUENTS OF A BALANCED DIET</TITLE>
</HEAD>
<BODY    BGCOLOR = YELLOW>
<FONT COLOR=RED>
<H1>CONSTITUENTS OF A BALANCED DIET</H1>
</FONT>
<UL TYPE= NONE>
     <li>Carbohydrates
     <li>Proteins
     <li>Fats
     <li>Vitamins and Minerals
</UL>
</BODY>
</HTML>
```

12.

```
<HEAD>
<STYLE>
BODY{BACKGROUND-COLOR : PINK;}
P{COLOR : BLUE ; FONT-FAMILY: "TIMES NEW ROMAN";
```

```
BORDER-COLOR: RED; BORDER-STYLE: DASHED;}
</STYLE>
</HEAD>
```

13.

```
<HTML>
<BODY>
<FONT FACE=ARIAL>
<H1>Checkbox Input</H1>
</FONT>
<FORM>
Item 1<INPUT TYPE =CHECKBOX    NAME =ITEM1    VALUE= ITEM1><BR>
Item 2<INPUT TYPE =CHECKBOX    NAME =ITEM2    VALUE= ITEM2><BR>
Item 3<INPUT TYPE =CHECKBOX    NAME =ITEM3    VALUE= ITEM3
CHECKED><BR><BR>
<INPUT TYPE=Submit>
</FORM>
</BODY>
</HTML>
```

14.

```
<HTML>
<BODY>
<TABLE  border=1    align=center>
<tr>
<tH ROWSPAN = "2">DAY/PERIOD
<tH colspan="4"> TIME TABLE FOR CLASS X
<TR>
<TH>I
<TH>II
<TH>III
<TH>IV
<TR>
<TD>MONDAY
<TD COLSPAN="2">MATHS
<TD ROWSPAN="2"> SCIENCE
<TD ROWSPAN="2">  ENGLISH
<TR>
<TD> WEDNESDAY
<TD COLSPAN="2"> SOCIAL SCIENCE
</TABLE>
</BODY></HTML>
```

OR

SPORTS DAY RESULT				
EVENT	**RED HOUSE**	**BLUE HOUSE**	**GREEN HOUSE**	**YELLOW HOUSE**
BASKETBALL	20	22	18	16
CRICKET	10	12	20	18

15. (i) **Say ( ) for ( ) seconds**—This block gives its sprite a speech bubble with the specified text. This speech bubble stays on the stage for the specified number of seconds.

(ii) **Ask ( ) and wait**—This block will make an input box at the bottom of the stage area. The user can input the text into the box and submit it. The execution of the code remains halted till the submission of the input.

OR

Set size to ( ) %—This block sets the sprite's size to the specific value. This block is used mainly when the sprite size has to be fixed for some specified range of code.

Change size by ( )—This block changes the sprite's size value. This block is used mostly when the size of the sprite has to be changed on occurrence of an event.

16. (i) The Sprite will wait at the origin for 1 second, then move to a random position and wait there for 1 more second. If it is on the edge, it will bounce without rotating and again go to the origin and will repeat the above activity.

(ii) Execution of the code can be terminated by clicking on the Red (Stop) button present at the top of the Stage Area.

(iii) To display the co-ordinates of the sprite, the x position and the y position blocks have to be selected (checked) from the Motion block.

17. (i) Motion (ii) Looks (iii) Control (iv) Operators

18. 15

19. 2

you are not telling the truth

1

20. 120

21.
```
i = 2
s = 0
for i in (2, 21) :
    s = s + i
print ("sum = ", s)
```

Practice Paper II (with solutions)

SECTION – A

1. Expand SMS and MMS. 1
2. In the following HTML statement what is the linking text?

   <A HREF = mailto:amitkumar@gmail.com ? subject = Feedback & body= This is for the customer>You can click here to mail your comments</A> 1
3. Kusum's e-mail address is kusum1234@gmail.com and her friend Anita's e-mail address is anita1234@hotmail.com. Will Kusum be able to send and receive e-mails from Anita since the domain name of their e-mail address is different? 1
4. ABC Corporation, an international company, has recently noticed their company's logo on the cement bags of a local manufacturer XYZ Cement Ltd. Which right of ABC Corporation is being violated here?

   OR

   Define software license. 1
5. What does G represent in 3G and 4G? 1
6. Why is an Open source software preferred over Closed source software? 1
7. Suggest any one step that will help in narrowing down the digital gap. 1

SECTION – B

8. Give an example of facility provided under
   (i) e-learning (ii) e-reservation 2
9. State any two frauds that one can face while using e-banking service of the internet. 2
10. Name the tag that is used in HTML code to
    (i) give heading to a row in a table.
    (ii) include sound or music in the web page. 2
11. Write an HTML code to create a web page with blue background and heading "LANGUAGES OFFERED" in red. The page should display the following list in black with roman numbering:
    iv. English
    v. Spanish
    vi. German

    OR

    Write an HTML code to create a web page with yellow background and heading "Homophones" in red. The page should display description list in green as follows:

HOMOPHONES:

WAIST:

the part of the human body that's between the upper body and the lower body, e.g., *She got extremely upset when I told her. She was just standing there with her hands on her* **waist** *and didn't say a word.*

WASTE:

when you spend money or time on something you don't really need, it's a waste, e.g., *Let's not* **waste** *more time on this subject. We've said everything that can be be said.* 2

12. Form a CSS code within the <head> tag for the following specifications:
Background color: Blue
Heading – H1 color-red
For the paragraph:
Text: color-yellow, italics, large, font-Times New Roman 2

13. Write an HTML code to create a hyperlink on the image turtle.jpg to an external file named "Reptiles.html". 2

14. Write an HTML code for the following output:

Select Tutorial:

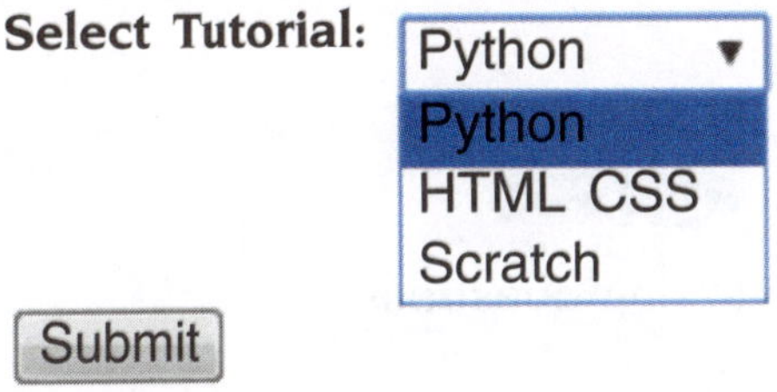

OR

Give the output of the following HTML code:

```
<HTML>
<BODY>
<TABLE border=2   align=center>
<thead>
<tr>
<td colspan=6 align=center >TEACHERS' TIME TABLE</td>
</tr>
</thead>

<TR>
<TH> NAME</TH>
<TH> MONDAY</TH>
<TH> TUESDAY</TH>
<TH> WEDNESDAY</TH>
<TH> THURSDAY</TH>
<TH> FRIDAY</TH>
</TR>

<TR>
<TD>Ms. Shefali</TD>
```

```
<TD  colspan="2">1,3</TD>
<TD> 2,8</TD>
<TD rowspan="2"> 1,8</TD>
<TD> 1,6</TD>
</TR>
<TR>
<TD> Ms. Roshni</TD>
<TD> 1,5</TD>
<TD> 2,6</TD>
<TD> 2,4</TD>
<TD> 1,8</TD>
</TR>
</TABLE>
</BODY></HTML>
```

3

SECTION – C Scratch

15. Explain the use of the following blocks:

(i) 

and

(ii) 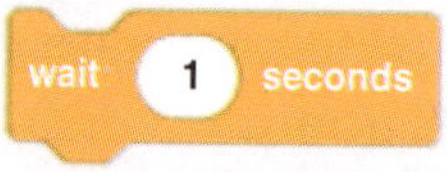

OR

Differentiate between the following blocks:

(i) 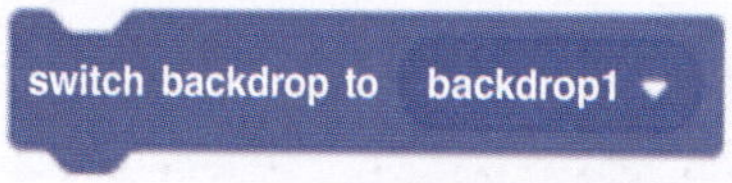

and

(ii) 

2

16. Study the codes given below and answer the following questions:

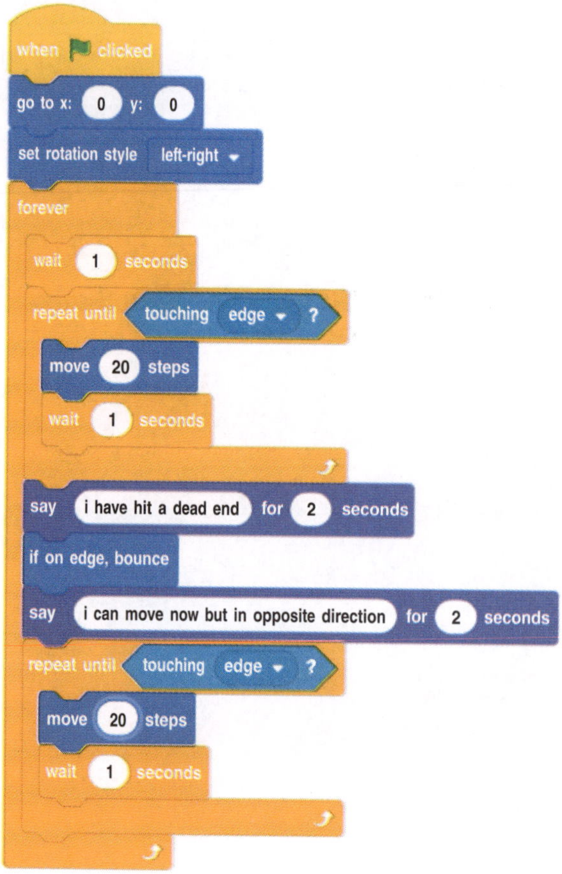

(i) When will the repeat until ( ) loop be terminated?

(ii) When will the message "i can move now but in opposite direction" be executed?

(iii) If you want to count the number of times the sprite has touched the edge, where will you increment the variable in the code? 2+1+1

17. Under which block heads do each of the following blocks belong?

(i) 

(ii) 

(iii) 

(iv) 

2(½+½+½+½)

SECTION – D (Python)

18. What will be the output of the following expressions? 1

```
a= "A"
print(a*5)
```

19. What will be the output of the following statements? 2

```
for i in range (1,3):
    for j in range (1,4):
    print("[", i, j, "]")
```

20. What will be the output of the following program? 2

```
n=1
p=1
while(n<=5):
    p=p*n
    n=n+1
print(p)
```

21. Write a code that displays the product of odd numbers from 1 to 20. 3

Solutions to Practice Paper II

1. SMS – Short Message Service
   MMS – Multimedia Messaging Service
2. You can click here to mail your comments.
3. Yes
4. Intellectual Property Rights is being violated.

   OR

   Software License is a legal agreement that lists the conditions under which an individual or an organisation is given the permission to use the software.
5. G represents the generation of mobile technology.
6. Open source software is free and the source code can be modified by the user whereas one has to buy a closed source software and its code cannot be modified by the user.
7. Making digital technology affordable is one of the ways to reduce the digital gap. (or any other relevant point)
8. (i) **E-learning** – Learner can learn at his/her own pace and also at a time and place convenient to him/her. (or any other relevant point)
   (ii) **E-reservation** – Any reservation be it train, air, hotels, taxi or any other such possible service, it can be done from anywhere, to anywhere and at any time. (or any other relevant point)
9. Cyber criminals use convincing stories to explain why you need to give them money or personal details. Once done they carry out transactions from your account without your knowledge. Fraudsters create a fake website which might look similar to that of an authentic website of a bank. Then, they send an e-mail or SMS requesting that the recipient access the fake website and enter their personal details, including password and username. Since the page looks genuine the user enters the information which is actually being sent to the fraudster. (or any other relevant point)
10. (i) <TH> tag
    (ii) <AUDIO>
11.
```
<HTML>
<HEAD>
<TITLE>LANGUAGES OFFERED</TITLE>
</HEAD>
<BODY
BGCOLOR = BLUE>
<FONT COLOR=RED>
<H1>LANGUAGES OFFERED</H1>
</FONT>
<OL TYPE=i     START=4>
<li>English
```

```
<li>Spanish
<li>German
</OL>
</BODY>          </HTML>
```

OR

```
<HTML>
<HEAD>
<TITLE>HOMOPHONES</TITLE>
</HEAD>
<BODY
BGCOLOR = YELLOW>
<FONT COLOR=RED>
<H1>HOMOPHONES</H1>
</FONT>
<DL>
<DT>WAIST :
    <DD> the part of the human body that's between the
    <DD>upper body and the lower body, e.g., <I> She got
    <DD>extremely upset when I told her. She was just
    <DD>standing there with her hands on her </I> <B> waist </B> <I> and
    <DD>didn't say a word. </I>
<DT>WASTE :
    <DD> when you spend money or time on something you
    <DD>don't really need, it's a waste, e.g., <I> Let's
    <DD> not </I> <B> waste </B> <I> more time on this subject. We've
    <DD> said everything that can be be said. </I>
</BODY></HTML>
```

12.
```
<HEAD>
<STYLE>
BODY{BACKGROUND-COLOR : BLUE;}
H1{COLOR: RED;}
P{COLOR : YELLOW ; FONT-FAMILY: "TIMES NEW ROMAN";
FONT-SIZE: LARGE;   FONT-STYLE: ITALIC;   }
</STYLE>
</HEAD>
```

13.
```
<HTML>
<BODY>
<A HREF=REPTILES.HTML>
<IMG  SRC= "TURTLE.JPG"    HEIGHT=30%   WIDTH=30%>
</A>
</BODY></HTML>
```

14.
```
<html>
<body>
<H3>Select Tutorial:   </H3>
<form>
<select>
<option value = Python> Python</option>
```

```
<option value = HTML CSS> HTML CSS</option>
<option value = Scratch> Scratch</option>
</select>
<br><br>
<input type=Submit>
</form>
</body>
</html>
```

OR

<table>
<tr><th colspan="6">TEACHERS' TIME TABLE</th></tr>
<tr><th>NAME</th><th>MONDAY</th><th>TUESDAY</th><th>WEDNESDAY</th><th>THURSDAY</th><th>FRIDAY</th></tr>
<tr><td>Ms. Shefali</td><td colspan="2">1,3</td><td>2,8</td><td rowspan="2">1,8</td><td>1,6</td></tr>
<tr><td>Ms. Roshni</td><td>1,5</td><td>2,6</td><td>2,4</td><td>1,8</td></tr>
</table>

15. (i) **wait until ( ) block** pauses the script until the given condition is true.
(ii) **wait ( ) second block** pauses the script for the given number of seconds.

OR

(i) **Switch backdrop to (backdrop 1)** will change the current backdrop to the backdrop labelled backdrop1 in the list of the selected backdrops.
(ii) **Next backdrop** switches the backdrops to the backdrop which is next to the active backdrop in the list of the selected backdrops.

16. (i) repeat until ( ) loop will be terminated when the sprite will touch the edge of the stage area.
(ii) The message will be executed when the sprite will touch the edge of the stage area and bounce.
(iii) Variable should be incremented after we exit the repeat until loop ( ).

17. (i) Variable (ii) Sensing (iii) Motion (iv) Event

18. AAAAA

19. [11]
[12]
[13]
[21]
[22]
[23]

20. 120

21.
```
n = 1
p = 1
while (n < = 20):
    p = p * n
    n = n + 2
print (p)
```

APPENDIX

This appendix contains:

- Chapter-wise Assertion and Reasoning Type Questions
- Chapter-wise Case Study Questions

Chapter 1 - Internet

Assertion and Reasoning Type Questions

Following are Questions of Assertion and Reason types. Each question consists of two statements: Assertion (A) and Reason (R). Select the most suitable option considering the Assertion and reason.

(a) Both Assertion (A) and Reason (R) are true and Reason (R) is the correct explanation of Assertion (A).

(b) Both Assertion (A) and Reason (R) are true but Reason (R) is not the correct explanation of Assertion (A).

(c) Assertion (A) is true and Reason (R) is false.

(d) Assertion (A) is false and Reason (R) is true.

1. **Assertion:** To send a file over the network, it has to be uploaded.
   Reason: Uploading means transferring a file from a computer to a network.
2. **Assertion:** WWW is the other name for the internet.
   Reason: WWW is a service provided by the Internet.
3. **Assertion:** Files transferred using FTP can be hacked easily.
   Reason: FTP encrypts the data before transmitting it.
4. **Assertion:** Each data packet should contain its sequence number.
   Reason: The data packets have to be rearranged at the destination address.
5. **Assertion:** HTML allows the insertion of hyperlinks on the webpage.
   Reason: Hyperlinks are the links that allow the user to jump from one website /webpage to another.

Ans. **1.** (a), **2.** (d), **3.** (c), **4.** (a), **5.** (a)

Case Study

1. Naina has just shifted to a new house in India and wants to have an internet connection at her home. She contacts an agency that provides the connection.
   (i) What are such agencies called?
   (ii) Which software should she have on her computer to access the internet after she has got the connection?
   (iii) Which internet service provides access to the immense pool of websites and web pages?
   (iv) Naina wants to open a website. What should she type on the address bar of the browser so that she opens the website directly?
   OR
   Name a language that is used to design the web pages.

Ans. (i) ISP
(ii) Web Browser
(iii) WWW
(iv) URL of the website
OR
HTML

2. Protocols refer to the set of rules which are to be followed while performing a task. TCP/IP is the protocol followed on the internet.
   (i) What does TCP stand for?
   (ii) What is the function of IP?
   (iii) Name any protocol followed while sending/receiving emails.
   (iv) To enter sensitive data or carry out financial transactions, sites using which protocol should be preferred?

   OR

   Which protocol is better http or https? Why?

Ans. (i) Transmission Control Protocol
(ii) IP ensures that the data packets are rearranged in the proper sequence at the receiver's end.
(iii) SMPT or POP3
(iv) https
OR
HTTPS is better as it encrypts the data

Chapter 2 - Services Available on the Internet

Assertion and Reasoning Type Questions

Following are Questions of Assertion and Reason types. Each question consists of two statements: Assertion (A) and Reason (R). Select the most suitable option considering the Assertion and reason.

(a) Both Assertion (A) and Reason (R) are true and Reason (R) is the correct explanation of Assertion (A).
(b) Both Assertion (A) and Reason (R) are true but Reason (R) is not the correct explanation of Assertion (A).
(c) Assertion (A) is true and Reason (R) is false.
(d) Assertion (A) is false and Reason (R) is true.

1. **Assertion:** Web crawlers are very small spider-like machines in our computer and come into action whenever we use the internet.
   Reason: Web crawlers search and collect the relevant web pages as per the user's query or request.
2. **Assertion:** Facebook helps us search for our friends online.
   Reason: Facebook is a search engine.
3. **Assertion:** We can retrieve information from a website by typing the web address of the site.
   Reason: Using a web address is the fastest way of retrieving data from the site.
4. **Assertion:** Google Maps is a service provided by the Google search engine.
   Reason: Google Maps helps in searching for locations.
5. **Assertion:** Cybercrimes occur only on social networking sites.
   Reason: One can create a fake identity on social networking sites.

Ans. **1.** (d), **2.** (c), **3.** (b), **4.** (a), **5.** (d)

Case Study

1. Kaushal had a very close friend, Tushar, in New Delhi during his school time. After finishing school it has been 5 years. Kaushal is settled abroad and Tushar is staying in Mumbai. Kaushal has lost touch with Tushar.

(i) Name a website or application program that Kaushal can use to search for his friend.

(ii) Kaushal types 'Tushar' and searches, he gets a long list of people named Tushar. How can Kaushal limit his search?

(iii) Can he use gmail.com to search for his friend? Give reason.

(iv) What are the crimes that happen through the internet called? Name any one.

OR

Write a precaution one should take while using social media.

Ans. (i) Facebook/Twitter

(ii) He should write 'Tushar' and his last name or 'Tushar Mumbai'

(iii) No, Gmail is used for sending and receiving emails only to those who are in the user's contact list. But Tushar is not on Kaushal's contact list.

(iv) Cybercrimes, e.g., cyberstalking, cyberbullying

OR

We should not share our personal sensitive information which others could misuse.

2. Hansika is surfing the internet and she gets a message "Accept Cookies" on a website. She is unaware of what a cookie is in terms of computer science. She types "cookies" on the address bar of the browser.

(i) What are cookies in terms of computer science?

(ii) What additional and irrelevant information will she get from the browser?

(iii) How can she limit her search?

(iv) Give an example of a web browser.

OR

Do we need an internet connection while working on a browser?

Ans. (i) Cookies are small text files created/updated when visiting a website and are stored on the user's browser.

(ii) Information about cookie biscuits.

(iii) She may type 'cookies in web browser' or cookies on the internet.

(iv) Google Chrome/Microsoft Edge/Mozilla Firefox

OR

Yes

Chapter 3 - Web Services

Assertion and Reasoning Type Questions

Following are Questions of Assertion and Reason types. Each question consists of two statements: Assertion (A) and Reason (R). Select the most suitable option considering the Assertion and reason.

(a) Both Assertion (A) and Reason (R) are true and Reason (R) is the correct explanation of Assertion (A).

(b) Both Assertion (A) and Reason (R) are true but Reason (R) is not the correct explanation of Assertion (A).

(c) Assertion (A) is true and Reason (R) is false.

(d) Assertion (A) is false and Reason (R) is true.

1. **Assertion:** Email can be sent or received only when there is an internet connection.
   Reason: Email is a service provided by the Internet.
2. **Assertion:** A video conference can be used to interview a person sitting several miles away.
   Reason: Dedicated hardware and software are required at both ends to carry out a video conference.
3. **Assertion:** E-banking has become very popular in present times as it lessens the physical effort.
   Reason: E-banking has less risk of online fraud.
4. **Assertion:** E-reservation of hotels always ensures customer satisfaction.
   Reason: The customer can view the room online before making the payment.
5. **Assertion:** E-governance has resulted in efficient governance.
   Reason: E-governance has made timely collection of bills and taxes possible.

Ans. 1. (a), **2.** (b), **3.** (c), **4.** (d), **5.** (a)

Case Study

1. Garima has to buy a hair dryer. She is thinking of going to the market but since it is very hot outside, she is reluctant to go. She then tries buying it online.

   (i) How can Garima be sure of whether the product she is buying is good? Give one option.
   (ii) Name two ways by which she can pay for the product.
   (iii) State one precaution she should take before placing the order.
   (iv) Give one advantage of online shopping.

OR

   Garima just puts the product in the cart and shuts down the computer. The next day she again visits the site and finds the product still in the cart. How has the website still stored the information?

Ans. (i) By looking at the rating or by reading the customer's reviews.
   (ii) Cash on Delivery/Net Banking/Debit or Credit Card/online wallet
   (iii) She should check the reviews, delivery address, whether the product is returnable/refundable.
   (iv) Customer can compare products from different brands and their price, without physically visiting the stores.

OR

   The information has been stored in cookies by the website on the browser.

2. Garima has started teaching online. She is giving the classes using her laptop so that her students can see and hear her.
   (i) What advantage does Garima have, if she is teaching online?
   (ii) What advantage do her students have if they are studying online?
   (iii) How can Garima use the World Wide Web to make her lectures more interesting? Give one application.
   (iv) Name an online platform where she can advertise her classes so that more students can join.

OR

   Give one disadvantage of online teaching/learning.

Ans. (i) She can teach many students simultaneously who may be joining from different and distant locations.

(ii) Students who are not able to attend the classes physically due to long distance or any inability can also learn from the comfort of their home.

(iii) She can insert video clips from the the internet in her lecture to show the activities that are otherwise very difficult to explain e.g. volcano eruption or working of heart.

(iv) Facebook/YouTube

OR

One needs to have a good internet connection otherwise the signal keeps on breaking or the streaming is very slow.

Chapter 4 - Mobile Technologies

Assertion and Reasoning Type Questions

Following are Questions of Assertion and Reason types. Each question consists of two statements: Assertion (A) and Reason (R). Select the most suitable option considering the Assertion and reason.

(a) Both Assertion (A) and Reason (R) are true and Reason (R) is the correct explanation of Assertion (A).

(b) Both Assertion (A) and Reason (R) are true but Reason (R) is not the correct explanation of Assertion (A).

(c) Assertion (A) is true and Reason (R) is false.

(d) Assertion (A) is false and Reason (R) is true.

1. **Assertion:** SMS is a Short Messaging Service.
   Reason: The text message can hold up to 160 alphanumeric characters.
2. **Assertion:** MMS is a wireless communication technology.
   Reason: MMS may include text, audio/video clips and still images.
3. **Assertion:** 4G connectivity is possible only on phone-to-phone communication.
   Reason: Gaming and HD multimedia can be easily streamed using 4G technology.
4. **Assertion:** Google Maps is a location-based service.
   Reason: 2G technology also supports Google Maps.
5. **Assertion:** Almost all E-commerce companies and banks send SMS for every transaction.
   Reason: Such SMS are called bulk SMS.

Ans. **1.** (a), **2.** (b), **3.** (d), **4.** (c), **5.** (c)

Case Study

1. Anjali has received an SMS from Pizza Hut about an offer that could give her a discount of 40% on her order. Choose appropriate words from the ones given below to fill any four blanks:

Bulk	Transactional	SMS	MMS	Promotional

(i) The SMS received from Pizza Hut is ________ SMS.

(ii) All her friends had also received such a message, so it is a _______ SMS.

(iii) She ordered a pizza and paid online. She immediately got an SMS from the bank informing her about her payment. Such an SMS is called ___________ SMS.

(iv) If there were images or videos with the message, it would be a ______(a) and not a ______(b).

Ans. (i) Promotional (ii) Bulk

(iii) Transactional (iv) (a) MMS, (b) SMS

2. Kalpana received this message on her phone.

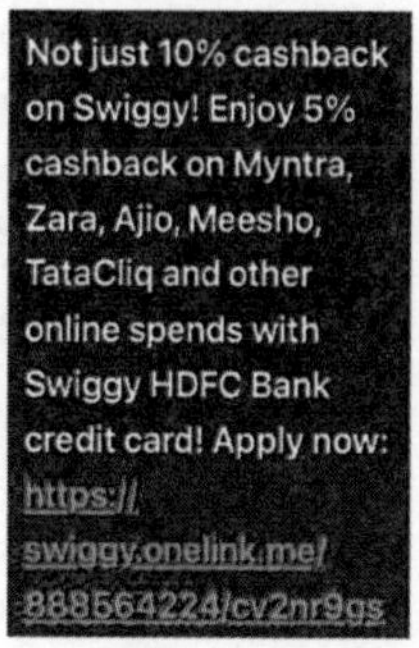

(i) Is it an SMS or MMS?

(ii) What type of message is it? (Transactional/Promotional)

(iii) What is the underlined text called?

(iv) If Kalpana clicks on the underlined text, what will happen?

OR

What precautions should we take while clicking on such text? State any one.

Ans. (i) SMS

(ii) Promotional

(iii) Hyperlink

(iv) The link will open the website which has this link as its address.

OR

She should make sure that the site is an authentic site and she should not share any sensitive information like OTP/CVV/password, etc., if asked for.

Chapter 5 - Hypertext Markup Language and Its Elements

Assertion and Reasoning Type Questions

Following are Questions of Assertion and Reason types. Each question consists of two statements: Assertion (A) and Reason (R). Select the most suitable option considering the Assertion and reason.

(a) Both Assertion (A) and Reason (R) are true and Reason (R) is the correct explanation of Assertion (A).
(b) Both Assertion (A) and Reason (R) are true but Reason (R) is not the correct explanation of Assertion (A).
(c) Assertion (A) is true and Reason (R) is false.
(d) Assertion (A) is false and Reason (R) is true.

1. **Assertion:** HTML is a language that provides a means of organizing and formatting the content on the web page.
   Reason: HTML is a programming language and allows the use of conditional statements.
2. **Assertion:** An HTML file is a text file.
   Reason: We require a text editor to create such a file.
3. **Assertion:** HTML considers "red" differently from "RED".
   Reason: HTML is case insensitive.
4. **Assertion:** While using HTML, text can be aligned using the ALIGN attribute.
   Reason: BY default, text in HTML is left aligned.
5. **Assertion:** An ordered list can be created within an unordered list in HTML.
   Reason: Each item of the ordered list must be enclosed in individual <ol></ol> tags.

Ans. **1.** (c), **2.** (a), **3.** (d), **4.** (a), **5.** (c)

Case Study

1. Rachna has to fill in the blanks in the following code. Help her with the appropriate tags and attributes. The blanks have been numbered on the right side of the code.

```
<HTML>
< ----- >                                                    1a
<Title> "This is a case study"</Title>
< ---- >                                                     1b
<Body>
Following is a rank-wise list of the most loved cartoon characters    4
< ----- >                                                    2a
<li> Mickey mouse
<li> Donald Duck
< --- >                                                      2b
< --- >                                                      3a
< ---- >                                                     3b
```

(i) 1a-------- 1b-------------
(ii) 2a--------- 2b-------------
(iii) 3a--------- 3b-------------
(iv) What changes should be made in the code for the text in the line labelled 4 to appear in red?

OR

What additions should be made in the code so that the output is displayed with yellow background?

Ans. (i) 1a) Head 1b) /Head
(ii) 2a) ol 2b) /ol

(iii) 3a) /Body 3b) /html

(iv) <font color=red>
Following is a rank-wise list of the most loved cartoon characters
</font>

OR

<Body bgcolor=yellow>

2. Smita is the class teacher and has to make several different types of lists. Suggest which type of list should she make in the following scenarios (ordered/unordered/descriptive):

(i) She is making notes where she has to define some terms.

(ii) She is making the roll no. wise list of the students.

(iii) If she wants the list to start numbering from 10 instead of 1 and the numbering to be in Roman numerals, what should she write?

(iv) Which type of list has bullets preceding each of its items? What should Smita write to change the bullet to Disc?

OR

What will be the output of the following code?

```
<dl>
<dt>Milk Shake : </dt>
<dd> Fruit and Ice cream</dd>
<dt>Coffee : </dt>
<dd> Hot or Cold with milk</dd>
</dl>
```

Ans. (i) Descriptive

(ii) Ordered

(iii) <ol start =10 Type='i' >

(iv) Unordered list
<ul type='disc'>

OR

Milk Shake:
  Fruit and Ice cream
Coffee:
  Hot or Cold with milk

Chapter 6 - HTML Continued

Assertion and Reasoning Type Questions

Following are Questions of Assertion and Reason types. Each question consists of two statements: Assertion (A) and Reason (R). Select the most suitable option considering the Assertion and reason.

(a) Both Assertion (A) and Reason (R) are true and Reason (R) is the correct explanation of Assertion (A).

(b) Both Assertion (A) and Reason (R) are true but Reason (R) is not the correct explanation of Assertion (A).

(c) Assertion (A) is true and Reason (R) is false.

(d) Assertion (A) is false and Reason (R) is true.

1. **Assertion:** Hyperlinks are the text that when clicked, display the content related to that link.
   Reason: Internal linking displays the section of the same document and external linking displays another webpage.
2. **Assertion:** CSS can control the layout of multiple web pages, all at once.
   Reason: Internal styling can be used for multiple-page styling.
3. **Assertion:** When from the multiple given options we have to choose only one we use the check box in HTML forms.
   Reason: HTML forms are used to take input from the user and transfer it to the server for processing.
4. **Assertion:** We can send an email directly from a web page.
   Reason: Mozilla Thunderbird, Outlook, Gmail, etc., are some of the common email clients.
5. **Assertion:** A table on a web page may have a cell extended over several rows.
   Reason: It is similar to the merging of cells and can be done using Rowspan.

Ans. 1. (a), **2.** (c), **3.** (d), **4.** (b), **5.** (a)

Case Study

1. Read the following statement carefully:
   <A HREF ="# Birds"> Amazing Birds </A>
   (i) Is this internal linking to the same web page or linking to an external web page?
   (ii) What is the link here that will have to be clicked?
   (iii) What is the default colour of a link on a web page before it is clicked and after it has been visited?
   (iv) Which is a better option – internal or external linking? Give reason.
   OR
   Give one disadvantage of external link.

Ans. (i) Internal
(ii) Amazing Birds
(iii) Blue, Violet
(iv) Using an external link we can get access to another website.
OR
External links are difficult to control. If the linked website gets deleted then we have a hanging link.

2. Mention the HTML form control used for each of the following boxes (any 4):

(i) 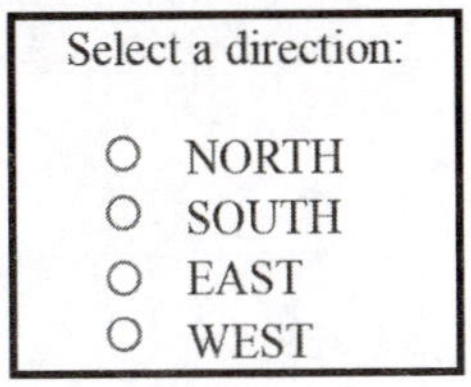

(ii) 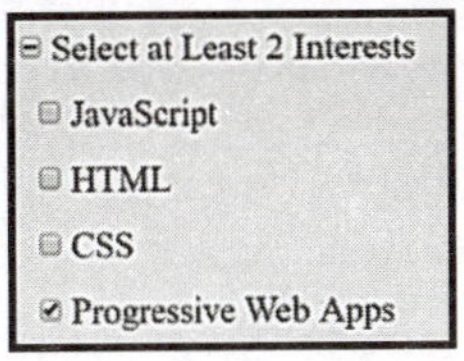

(iii)

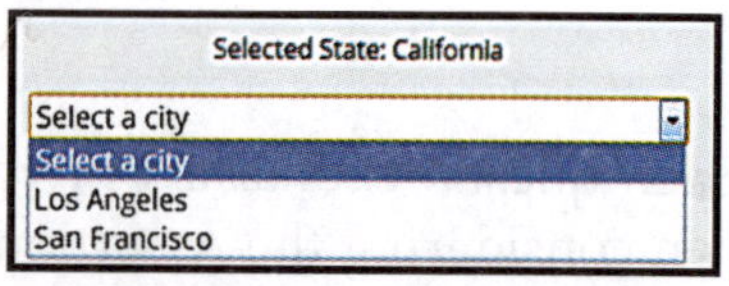

(iv)

(v)

Ans. (i) Radio Button
(ii) Check Box
(iii) Select Box
(iv) Clickable Button

OR

Single-line text input

Chapter 7 - Cyber Ethics

Assertion and Reasoning Type Questions

Following are Questions of Assertion and Reason types. Each question consists of two statements: Assertion (A) and Reason (R). Select the most suitable option considering the Assertion and reason.

(a) Both Assertion (A) and Reason (R) are true and Reason (R) is the correct explanation of Assertion (A).

(b) Both Assertion (A) and Reason (R) are true but Reason (R) is not the correct explanation of Assertion (A).

(c) Assertion (A) is true and Reason (R) is false.

(d) Assertion (A) is false and Reason (R) is true.

1. **Assertion:** Anyone can create a fake profile on social networking sites.
   Reason: The freedom of information gives a right to every internet user to keep his identity secret.
2. **Assertion:** Digital technology should be made accessible to everyone.
   Reason: Everyone has a right to keep one's identity a secret on the internet.
3. **Assertion:** Digital Unity refers to ICT bringing the world together.
   Reason: ICT stands for Internet Connection Technology.
4. **Assertion:** Freeware software requires some fee to be paid to the developer.
   Reason: Open-source software is a free software.
5. **Assertion:** Intellectual Property rights are violated when someone uses a logo of another company even with permission.
   Reason: Violation of Intellectual Property Rights results in monetary loss for the owner.

Ans. **1.** (a), **2.** (b), **3.** (c), **4.** (d), **5.** (d)

Case Study

1. Anjana has to prepare a report for her project so she searches the topic on the internet. She copies the content as it is and pastes it in her report.
   (i) Will this act of Anjana be a cybercrime?
   (ii) What is the specific term given to such an act?
   (iii) What is the ethical way of carrying out such an act?
   (iv) We have come across certain software such as Scratch, OpenOffice, etc., that can be downloaded for free and their code can also be modified. Why is this considered to be legal?

   OR

   What is Phishing?

Ans. (i) Yes

(ii) Plagiarism

(iii) She should cite the source of information and mention it in acknowledgments.

(iv) These software are open source software that are free to download.

OR

Phishing is a form of cybercrime where attackers deceive people into revealing sensitive information or installing malware such as ransomware.

2. Anshika got an email from a popular online shopping site with the subject "Claim your gift". She opened her mail which informed her that she was the lucky 100000th customer so she had won a gift voucher of free shopping worth ₹10,000. All she had to do was to click on the given link and enter some personal details like her name, bank name, account number and an OTP that she would get on her phone. After entering all these details the amount would be credited to her account.

She followed the instructions and after about 10 minutes, instead of receiving ₹10,000 this amount was deducted from her bank account.

(i) Whom was Anshika dealing with?

(ii) Spot two pointers that were referring to the site being a fraud and a fake site.

(iii) State a way this email could have damaged Anshika's computer.

(iv) What is an OTP? Why is it used?

OR

What do you understand by the term Trolling? Is it a type of financial fraud?

Ans. (i) Cybercriminal

(ii) (a) If she is getting vouchers, why is she being asked for the bank details.

(b) If she is being asked to enter the OTP then she should stop immediately.

(iii) By installing malware like ransomware or spyware.

(iv) One-time Password which is generated by the businesses for the customers to log in securely. It is a part of two-factor authentication.

OR

Trolling is when someone deliberately tries to upset others online. It is not a financial fraud.

Chapter 8 - Scratch

Assertion and Reasoning Type Questions

Following are Questions of Assertion and Reason types. Each question consists of two statements: Assertion (A) and Reason (R). Select the most suitable option considering the Assertion and reason.

(a) Both Assertion (A) and Reason (R) are true and Reason (R) is the correct explanation of Assertion (A).

(b) Both Assertion (A) and Reason (R) are true but Reason (R) is not the correct explanation of Assertion (A).

(c) Assertion (A) is true and Reason (R) is false.

(d) Assertion (A) is false and Reason (R) is true.

1. **Assertion:** While using Scratch, whenever the value of a variable is required, it is called by its name.
   Reason: A variable is a location that stores a value and has a name.
2. **Assertion: (23)>(score)**
   If **score** is a variable and stores some value, the above statement will give a numeric result.
   Reason: ' > ' is a Boolean operator.
3. **Assertion:** A game created on scratch can keep the score also.
   Reason: A variable can be created that can store a string or a numeric value.
4. **Assertion:** The forever block in Scratch can be replaced with a repeat block.
   Reason: Both these blocks are Control blocks.
5. **Assertion:** ask() and wait block is used to get input from the user in Scratch.
   Reason: The answer() block is always used with the ask() and wait block.

Ans. **1.** (a), **2.** (d), **3.** (a), **4.** (d), **5.** (a)

Case Study

1.

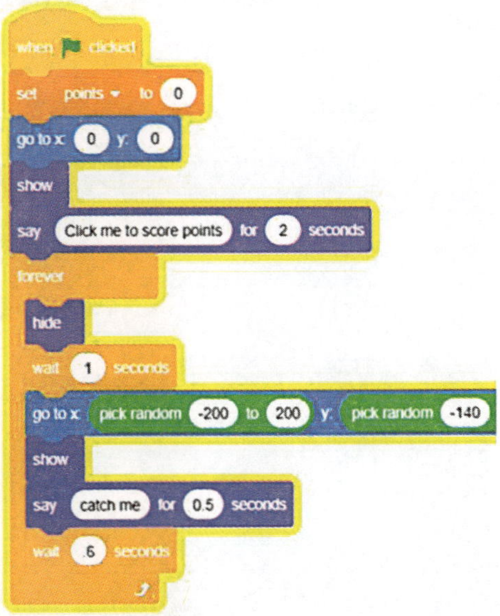

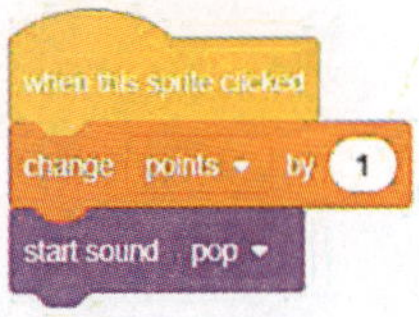

Varun has written the above scratch code. Answer the following questions to prove that you have understood the code:

(i) What does 'points' refer to?

(ii) What is the purpose of the blocks 'show ' and 'hide' in this code?

(iii) When will the pop sound be heard?

(iv) What is the use of 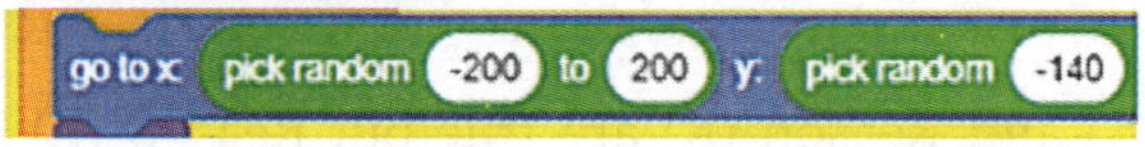

here?

OR

When will this code stop?

Ans. (i) Variable

(ii) Show is making the sprite appear and hide is making the sprite to disappear.

(iii) Pop sound will be heard when the sprite gets hit.

(iv) The code chooses a random position for the sprite to appear.

OR

The code will stop only when we click on the red dot.

2. Reena wants to design a simple animation game. She does not have a very advanced knowledge of programming but is comfortable with the basics of programming.

(i) Will she have to buy the software for Scratch? Give reason.

(ii) If she uses Scratch, will she probably get more syntax errors or logical errors? Give reason.

(iii) Why are the blocks in Scratch colour-coded?

(iv) In the code, Reena wants the sprite to turn when it reaches the end of the screen. Under which blockhead can she find such a block?

OR

Where do variables find their use in Scratch code?

Ans. (i) No because Scratch is a free software.

(ii) Logical errors because the syntax is pre-written.

(iii) Blocks are coloured according to their block heads and indicate their purpose.

(iv) She can find it under Sensing block head.

OR

Variables are generally used to keep scores in games.

Chapter 9 - Python

Assertion and Reasoning Type Questions

Following are Questions of Assertion and Reason types. Each question consists of two statements: Assertion (A) and Reason (R). Select the most suitable option considering the Assertion and reason.

(a) Both Assertion (A) and Reason (R) are true and Reason (R) is the correct explanation of Assertion (A).

(b) Both Assertion (A) and Reason (R) are true but Reason (R) is not the correct explanation of Assertion (A).

(c) Assertion (A) is true and Reason (R) is false.

(d) Assertion (A) is false and Reason (R) is true.

1. **Assertion:** A while loop may not be executed even once.
   Reason: In a while loop the condition is checked at the end of the loop.
2. **Assertion:** The Python statement **print (15 != 28)** would print **True**.
   Reason: != is a Boolean operator.
3. **Assertion:** Python statements starting in the same column are considered to be in the same block.
   Reason: Indentation is used only to improve the clarity of the code.
4. **Assertion:** Indentation is the only way to figure out the level of nesting in a nested **if – else** statement
   Reason: The condition in the **if-else** statement always gives a **Boolean** result.
5. **Assertion: if** statement can have none or at the most one **else** block.
   Reason: A **while loop** can have several **if-else** statements inside it.

Ans. 1. (c), **2.** (a), **3.** (c), **4.** (b), **5.** (b)

Case Study

1. Ramit is writing a Python code for the following:
   Input a number, and print it if it is greater than 200. The program has to stop taking the input if the number is 999 and this number should not be printed.
   The code written by Ramit is as follows:

```
10 num= int(input("enter a number"))
12 while num<>999:
14    if num>=200:
16       print (num)
18    num= int(input("enter a number"))
```

   (i) What will the output of the above code be when the input is
      (a) 100
      (b) 300
   (ii) Why has Ramit not used a for-loop here?
   (iii) Which lines will be executed when the input is 999?
   (iv) What change would you suggest if Ramit wants to count the numbers that were given as input? No need to rewrite the code. Just write the line number and the statement.

   OR

   What change would you suggest if Ramit wants to just count the numbers that were printed? No need to rewrite the code. Just write the line number and the statement.

Ans. (i) (a) nothing will be printed
      (b) 300
   (ii) Since the number of inputs is not known, we can't use a for loop.

(iii) 14, 16, 18, 12

(iv)
```
9   count=1
10  num= int(input("enter a number"))
12  while num<>999:
14      if num>=200 :
16          print (num)
18      num= int(input("enter a number"))
19      count=count+1
```

OR

```
9   count=0
10  num= int(input("enter a number"))
12  while num<>999:
14      if num>=200 :
15          count=count+1
16          print (num)
18      num= int(input("enter a number"))
```

2. Priya and Anna are working on a Python code. Priya has written the following code but it is giving some errors. Anna takes the responsibility of finding the errors and removing them.

```
a= int(input("enter no. 1  "))
b= int(input("enter no. 2  "))
c= input("enter the operation * or /")
if (c=='/'):
    print (a,"/", b, " = ", a*b)
if (c == '*'):
    print(a, "*", b, " = ", a / b)
```

(i) What will happen if she removes int from the first two statements?

(ii) Why has it not been used in the third statement?

(iii) Although this code will not give any syntax errors but still Anna and Priya are not satisfied with the result. Why?

(iv) Which type of error is occurring in the above code? (syntax/ logical/ runtime)

OR

Which type of error will occur if b is input as 0 and c is '/'? Give reason.

Ans. (i) Both the inputs will be treated as strings.

(ii) Here a character has to be given as input and we require it to be treated as a string.

(iii) When * is given as input, the result to be printed should be the product but we are getting the result of division and vice versa.

(iv) Logical error

OR

Run-time error since division by 0 is not defined.